AF540197

Labyrinths of Language

Philosophical and Cultural Investigations

Labyrinths of Language

Philosophical and Cultural Investigations

Franson Manjali

LABYRINTHS OF LANGUAGE:
Philosophical and Cultural Investigations
Franson Manjali

First Published, 2014

ISBN 978-93-5002-276-4 (Hb)

Published by
AAKAR BOOKS
28 E Pocket IV, Mayur Vihar Phase I, Delhi 110 091
Phone : 011 2279 5505 Telefax : 011 2279 5641
info@aakarbooks.com; www.aakarbooks.com

Printed at
Mudrak, 30 A, Patparganj, Delhi 110 091

Contents

Our language can be seen as an ancient city: a maze of little streets and squares, of old and new houses, and of houses with additions from various periods; and this surrounded by a multitude of new boroughs with straight regular streets and uniform houses.

— L. Wittgenstein
Philosophical Investigations (p. 8, § 18)

Language is a labyrinth of paths. You approach from one *side and know your way about; you approach the same place from another side and no longer know your way about.*

— L. Wittgenstein
Philosophical Investigations (p. 82, § 203)

Preface and Acknowledgements

The essays and articles that appear in this book *Labyrinths of Language* have had disparate origins. As the opening lines suggest the title of the book owes itself to the Austrian philosopher Ludwig Wittgenstein, one of the most significant philosophers of the 20th century. However, the reader may be cautioned that not all the chapters deal with either 'labyrinths' or 'language.' They nevertheless are, as the subtitle indicates, the result of philosophical and cultural (including literary) investigations.

Almost all the texts appearing here have been presented as seminar talks or conference papers. Many of the ideas and issues have been constituent parts of the courses I taught at Jawaharlal Nehru University. I am grateful to all my listeners, seminar-participants, and students for their valuable comments and suggestions. All but two of the texts have been published in journals or edited volumes. The following are the previous publication details of the eleven texts in the chronological order of their appearance:

"Between Pragmatics and Deconstruction: Wittgenstein, Bakhtin, and Derrida," in: *Assam University Journal – Humanities and Social Sciences*, vol. 3, no. 1., January 2008, pp. 1-14.

"Culture and Politics in the Novel *On the Banks of the River Mahe*," in: *International Journal of Dravidian Linguistics* vol. 38, June 2009 (155-172). The French version of the paper appeared as: "Résistance de l'oubli et l'écriture de la mémoire dans un roman postcolonial indien: *Sur les rives du fleuve Mahé*" In :

Histoire de l'oubli en contextes post-socialiste et post-colonial. (ed.) P. Vauday et al. Koper: Založba Annales, 2009, pp. 381-93.

"Time, Language and the Destruction of Power," in: *Journal for Cultural Research* 13, Nos. 3-4, pp. 297-307. October 2009. It also appeared in: A. Bradley and P. Fletcher (eds.) *The Messianic Now. Philosophy, Religion and Culture.* London: Routledge, 2011.

"Towards a Philosophy of Image," *in Studies in Humanities and Social Sciences,* Vol. XVI, 1 & 2, 2009 (201-18), Indian Institute of Advanced Study, Shimla.

"The Body of Sense, the Sense of Body," in: *Revista Italiana di Filosofia del Linguaggio* (online Italian Journal of Philosophy of Language–ISSN 2036-6728) Vol. 2, 2010 (Corpo e linguaggio, Body and Language), pp. 95-122.

"On Language and the Assumed Unity of the Human Sciences," in: Dipankar Gupta (ed.) *My Favourite Lévi-Strauss,* New Delhi: Yoda Press, 2010, pp. 101-17.

"Discourse of Death in Philosophy," *Journal of School of Languages,* Autumn, 2010. New Delhi: JNU, pp. 99-107.

"Between the Self and the Other: Language after Levinas," *Journal of Indian Council of Philosophical Research,* Vol. XVIII, No. 4, 2011, pp. 79-100; It also appears in the Proceedings of the National Seminar on *Postmodern Ethical Criticism in the West and the East with Special Reference to Emmanuel Levinas and Mahatma Gandhi.* Department of English, St. Thomas' College, Palai, Kerala, 2012, pp. 7-24.

"Blanchot, Writing and the Politico-Religious," *Journal for Cultural Research,* Vol. 16, No. 4, pp. 344-60, October 2012.

"The 'Social' and the 'Cognitive' in Language: A Reading of Saussure and Beyond," (online) *Texto!* Vol. XVII, No. 3 (2012); Also, appeared in *FMSH Working Papers,* (online); published in *Indian Linguistics,* 2012, pp. 117-127.

"Kafka: Literature, Law and Language," in Sukalpa Bhattacharjee and C. Joshua Thomas (eds.) *Society, Representation and Textuality: The Critical Interface.* New Delhi: Sage, 2013, pp. 121-31.

The remaining two chapters (12 and 13 in this volume) have not appeared as published texts. The author is grateful to the publishers of the journals and books for the courtesy of allowing me to publish the respective texts here, in a slightly modified or unmodified form.

I also acknowledge with gratitude the help and sustenance received from my spouse Manidipa, and friends and colleagues Jean-Luc Nancy, Harjit Singh Gill, Marc Crépon, Rustam Singh, Udaya Kumar, Roy Harris, Jacqueline Léon, Saitya Brata Das, Max Zins, Goutam Biswas, Aïcha Liviana, Arthur Bradley, Soumyabrata Choudhury, Patrice Maniglier, Catherine Malabou, Patrick Vauday, Sukalpa Bhattacharjee, Martin Henson, Manas Ray, Paul Patton, Dipankar Gupta, Sharad Deshpande, Prabesh Jung, Asha Sarangi and many others in the near or distant horizons…

And finally, I would like to thank Prof. S.K. Sopory, the Vice-Chancellor of JNU for allowing me a publication grant from the university.

Introduction

This introduction has the limited purpose of providing brief sketches of the chapters that follow. The first chapter is an exploration in depth of the intertwining of the social and the cognitive aspects of language in Ferdinand de Saussure's classic *Course in General Linguistics.* This text has been put to extensive commentary and a novel interpretation in a recent book by philosopher Patrice Maniglier, *La vie énigmatique des signes*. The key interest of Maniglier is in attempting to revive Saussure's central notion of the 'sign' in the context of AI/ Cognitive Science. The main question here is whether a naturally and mechanically emerging linguistic 'sign' can remain indefinitely open-ended in the sense of the poststructuralists, and whether new cognitive 'cultural milieus' are continuously created on the basis of inter-human contacts. Saussure's 'social' concerns are certainly not averse to such a possibility.

The inter-human, in ethical terms, is essentially a question of the self and the other. Traditionally, the self, rather than being a homogeneous notion, has been treated in many different ways, depending on different cultural situations, and in different historical times and different intellectual discourses. The notion of the 'other' has only been recently brought to the foreground, especially in the phenomenological writings of Husserl, Heidegger, Sartre and Levinas, etc. The second chapter presents a detailed account of how in Levinas's works, language is the very possibility of the mediation between the self and other. Language, rather than coming after the subject, is that which makes both the self and the other appear in their relationship with each other. And moreover, for Levinas, the self is only that which responds to the call of the other, ever and always, in being responsible to the other. This means that there is no autonomous and stable existence of language, but only a continuous reinterpretation in the form of the responsiveness and responsibility of the self to the other.

Evidently, the formalist and structuralist approaches in linguistics had ignored the subjective and inter-subjective dimensions of language. For Lévi-Strauss, linguistics and semiotics were meant to be an effective methodological ground for studying human society and culture, in short, what he called 'social anthropology.' In the third chapter, we focus on the difficulties inherent in such a position which ignores the singularity of language use in any and every human context. Language, rather than being something that binds the human society in a permanent and stable existence, is, from a deconstructive point of view, that which continuously invents and reinvents a given society and culture. We briefly present here the basic argument of Derrida's criticism of structuralism, and of structuralist social anthropology in particular.

In the fourth chapter, we attempt to locate the points of contact and the divergences between the pragmatically-oriented philosophies of Bakhtin and the later Wittgenstein on the one hand and those of the poststructiuralist philosophers, Deleuze and Derrida, on the other. In his critique of formalism and structuralism, Bakhtin (Voloshinov) had asserted the relevance of inter-subjective use of language in understanding the language phenomenon. Meaning for him, was neither out there in language, nor was it in the mind of the language-user. A new meaning is constantly created in response to the language already put to use. Wittgenstein would similarly insist that linguistic meaning lies in the particular uses of words in context. Deleuze and Derrida would go on to extend this critique while arguing for the shaking up and deconstruction of historically and ideologically sedimented structures of meaning.

The fifth chapter is a response to the recent discussions on the notion of the messianic. The philosophical seriousness of the messianic question had opened up for me only after reading Derrida's *Le monolinguisme de l'autre*, a work I then considered as being essentially of linguistic significance. We explore the relevant issues here in relation to Benjamin's early idea of the messianic time. Also attempted is a rapproachment of the messianic idea with that of the notion of the *Avatara* in the Indian context, however feeble the connection may be. Seventh century Indian philosopher of language, Bhartrhari's treatment of time in his *Vakyapadiyam* is discussed in this context.

The link between language, law and literature, with respect to Kafka is the theme of the sixth chapter. Law, for human civilization, is after all a byproduct of language, and it has to employ an imagination that is akin to literary imagination to set itself in place. However, law then acquires its own quasi-autonomy and seeks to govern and control language and literature. Much of Kafka's fiction was an attempt to overcome the raw power of law with the aid of language and literature that the former tries to repress. Kafka's relentless effort was to show that language and literature that pertain to the ordinary world often re-emerge as revolts against the power of law that is employed by the dominant classes of our human society.

The seventh chapter involves a brief study of three essays by Maurice Blanchot that refers to the Indian context. More than the question of Blanchot's critical attitude towards the reception of either Mahatma Gandhi or Indian spirituality in the European intellectual milieu, we attempt to understand the basis of Blanchot's argumentation, especially with reference to the "politico-religious" and "writing". The importance of the notions of the "impossibility of death" and "passivity" which he developed in relation to Levinas's work has been focused on. In spite of his early orientation in the Christian religion, we see that Blanchot who in his later writings emphasizes an 'extreme' literary mode, seems to have striven towards dissolving the opposition between East and West, between theism and atheism, and between religion and literature.

The eighth chapter is a brief intervention in the domain of what may be called the 'discourse of death.' It is philosophically motivated by the writings on death by Heidegger, Levinas, Blanchot, Derrida, Nancy and Agamben. From these philosophers one has learnt that the questions of language and literature cannot be separated from the question of death. Death becomes relevant for these philosophers in their attempts to comprehend the central phenomenon of existence itself. Being can be understood only in relation to death's intimate association with it. At the same time, one cannot but notice the great variation in the philosophical, literary and other discourses on death as it has appeared across different historical periods and geographical regions. Though people everywhere have striven to support and sustain life with varying degrees of intensity and often commemorate death in myriad ways, the phenomenon of death is pervasively varied across cultures and indeed very resistant to yielding itself to a unified description.

The ninth chapter attempts to provide, with reference to Jean-Luc Nancy's work, an account of the two-way relationship between body and meaning. In our world, there have been different traditions of the 'body,' which may be based on religions, old or new, or on national cultures. These various traditions evidently imply different beliefs, attitudes towards, practices involving and treatments of the living or the dead body. These, in turn, may involve personal or social questions of health, hygiene, sacredness, etc., with regard to the body. How one treats one's own body, the other's body, and other living or dead bodies, are often more or less codified in the traditions. This means that bodies are already marked more often than not by a strong cultural meaning. And conversely, meaning itself may or may not be seen as an attribute or extension of the body. For instance, the meaning element may be construed as akin to a seed – implying a certain fertile power of its dissemination or a spurt of meaning. A wide range of philosophical positions on body and meaning, including those of Deleuze and Derrida, have been surveyed in this essay.

A 'philosophy of image' is the topic of the tenth chapter.

'Image' has been submitted to serious philosophical discussion by Bergson, Heidegger, Levinas, Blanchot and Deleuze, and more recently by Nancy and Mondzain. The discussion of the photographic image by Benjamin and Barthes are equally important. The image today is no longer spoken of in terms of the traditional idea of reflection of the thing, but rather in terms of a notion where it deflects the thing, as in resemblance. Heidegger's comparison of the artwork to a 'broken tool' and Blanchot's consideration of the image as a 'corpse' is pertinent here. The essay's main focus is on the relation between image and violence as discussed separately by Nancy and Mondzain. Both take up the question in relation to the even more basic question of truth and discursive language.

In next chapter (11), we discuss a Malayalam novel, *On the Banks of the River Mahe*, as an instance of minor literature, in the sense of Deleuze. The novel, by M. Mukundan, is indeed regarded as a major novel, written in a relatively 'minor' literary language of the world, viz., Malayalam, a language spoken by over 30 million people belonging to or originating from the region of Kerala in the south-west of India. This politically-significant fiction is set in the former French colony of Mahe, and the novel could be considered as a 'minor literature' in Malayalam language itself, since it is written in a non-standard dialect of northern Kerala, and is interspersed with occasional words and sentences in French language. The political and cultural tensions that the literary work present are highlighted here with a perspective that never ignores the corresponding tension at the level of the use of a Gallicized Malayalam language.

The twelfth chapter addresses a currently hot issue: the globalization of English. After providing a brief historical perspective on the colonial imposition of English language and British culture in India, it considers the attendant political and linguistic difficulties of the process. It can be said that the Indian elites, including the political leaders, have always maintained an ambivalent attitude towards English. In the cultural domain, the response has perhaps been more divided. The literary writers and journalists have adopted either bureaucratic English or have attempted to consciously hybridize the English language. This rampant hybridity can now be said to be the norm in India both for the imported language and for the native languages. Outside the realm of political emotions, we can state there is indeed nothing unusual about the emergence of 'mixed languages' as reported by some linguists in contact situations.

In the final chapter, we discuss the emergence, this time, of the field of linguistics itself. It cannot be denied that 'modern linguistics' is intricately and enduringly connected with the history of colonialism. Scholars and philosophers have often struggled to grapple with the nature of the complex relationship between linguistics and (colonial) politics. We make our own modest attempt here to understand the colonial basis of modern disciplines, especially of linguistics, by focusing on the works of the British jurist and linguist Sir William Jones. Our project could be extended further to analyse the works of other linguistically-oriented philosophers like Johann G. Herder, Wilhelm Humboldt and Max Müller, who advanced historical, cultural, civilizational and religious perspectives, on the question of languages, often as a matter of their own political convenience,

1

The 'Social' and the 'Cognitive' in Language: A Reading of Saussure and Beyond[1]

Structuralism, or structural linguistics to be more exact, along with the Paninian grammar are two currents in theoretical linguistics which have appeared and reappeared in modern times in many different *avatars*. It is indeed the hallmark of any profound theoretical work to have a long-lasting impact in its intellectual field. Scholars have noted that the Paninian grammar was reborn in the last 150 years in three distinct and somewhat contrary interpretations. First, with William Dwight Whitney, it was understood as a grammar based on historical principles, then Bloomfield (who described Panini's grammar as 'one of the greatest monuments of human intelligence') viewed it is as a structural-descriptive grammar, and finally with Chomsky and his followers, it was reinterpreted as a generative grammar.[2] Curiously, the fate of structural linguistics does not seem to be anything different. It all began, as we know, with the posthumous publication of the lecture notes (of a series of three courses given during the period 1906-11) from the master of Geneva, Ferdinand de Saussure, *Cours de linguistique générale* (1916), edited and published by his students, Charles Bally and Albert Séchehaye. (We should add here that according to certain accounts, and this is what further confounds matters for any historian of linguistics, Saussure, who was an impeccably qualified Sanskritist, himself was influenced by Panini and by his latter-day follower Bhartrhari). Structural linguistics (especially the version that was established in the United States) is said to have taken a behaviourist turn in the works of Leonard Bloomfield. Saussurean structuralism and the idea of the 'sign' were eventually subjected to diverse treatments under the influence of the Prague school of linguistics with the able and erudite leadership of the Russian linguist Roman Jakobson. It should be remembered that Jakobson was also responsible for bringing to light the Semiotic works of the American mathematician Charles Sanders Peirce. In France, philosophers and philosophically-inclined scholars extended structuralism (in what came to be known as 'generalized structuralism') in diverse directions. Of these, Maurice Merleau-Ponty (philosophy), Claude Lévi-Strauss (anthropology), Jacques Lacan (psychoanalysis) Louis Althusser (political theory), and Roland Barthes (literary and cultural semiology) were the key initial figures. Perhaps, somewhat less significant were the Greimasian school of Semiotics that sought to fulfil the Lévi-Straussian dream of a pure narrative semiotics and Christian Metz's efforts in a semiotics of the cinema.

Certainly, this can still not be an exhaustive account of the flourishing destiny of structuralism, which was only ruptured by the critical trajectories initiated in the 1960s by the poststructuralists Michel Foucault, Gilles Deleuze and Jacques Derrida. Of these well-known philosophers, Foucault in fact maintained an ambivalent and uncertain relationship with structuralism (especially during the phase of his work on 'archaeology'), even if this was only at the beginning of his short but illustrious intellectual career.[3]

More recently, structuralism was submitted to yet another ambitious project of creative transformation in the work of Jean-Petitot who applied René Thom's Catastrophe Theory in the domain of phonology, syntactico-semantics, and Greimasian narrative semiotics, with the goal of developing a topologico-dynamical (morphodynamic) paradigm in the cognitive sciences, and especially for reinterpreting Langacker's and Talmy's space-based cognitive grammars in terms of this paradigm. Petitot's *Morphogenesis of Meaning* (1985/2004 tr.) was intended to open a new domain of cognitive linguistics/ semiotics, owing itself to the catastrophist notions of bifurcation and archetypal morphologies, where Saussure's seminal notion of the 'sign' was all but ignored.

We should imagine that the productivity of an intellectual work (in the present case, structuralism) attests to its depth and richness. It is also to be noted that structuralism as a linguistic movement has perhaps spawned the largest number of histories. I shall not be able to provide a list of all these, but simply refer to the work of one of the better known historians of structuralism, Jean-Claude Milner.[4]

It is in the context of all this and perhaps more that Patrice Maniglier's extraordinarily erudite work *La vie énigmatique des signes* (2008) attracts our attention. Maniglier approaches Saussure as a philosopher, and no other philosopher except Jean-Claude Milner has attempted to touch the heart of the work of this quintessential modern scholar. The thesis that Maniglier defended under the watchful eyes of a jury that consisted of reputed contemporary French philosophers Etienne Balibar, Alain Badiou and Sylvain Auroux, is undoubtedly of exceptional merit, and would invite any philosophically-inclined scholar to a reading or rereading of Saussure's seminal work.

Maniglier's interpretation of Saussure's work, like what was the case of others that preceded him, is indeed a product of his times. Thus, understandably and legitimately, he solicits two contemporary philosophical currents in his support: cognitive science, primarily, and poststructuralism, to a lesser extent. He yields rich dividends from the project. However, even while he contemporizes Saussurean structuralism in terms of the connectionist approaches to cognitive science, and poststructuralism's critique of cultural and linguistic closure, he remains at heart a classicist. This he does by remaining faithful to Saussure's own version of the classical notion of the sign. This lets him explore the most crucial and the least understood aspect of Saussurean linguistics: *the paradoxical nature of the sign.* As Maniglier shows, the nature of the sign is indeed not just paradoxical, that is, not that we can say two contrasting things about it, both of which are correct, but the very existence of the sign presents itself as an enigma, in our not being able to draw a conclusive statement about it: it seems to be present and at the same time not present, dead but at the same time living, fixed and static but at the same time dynamic and mutating (synchronic and diachronic); the signs are formed as if by a predetermined *mechanical* action, but at the same time they seem to have an infinitely open-ended *life* of their own; and they have a reality that is simultaneously 'psychological' (cognitive) and 'social'.

Thus the linguistic sign, and the sign in general, is *enigmatic,* in our not being able to decide as to what it is. And according to Maniglier, following Saussure, it is not as much the sign that is enigmatic, but it is the 'life of signs' (*CGL* 1, p. 15, translation modified; *Cours,* p. 33) that is the enigma. The sign seems to lead two different kinds of lives, one mechanical, more or less following the laws of physics with a predictable outcome, and the other social or cultural, in which the laws can be easily abandoned and where unpredictability reigns. This unpredictability of signs in historical time in Saussure's formulation, Maniglier wants to show, is the site of culture. (That is, even if Saussure does not speak directly of culture: he is more readily concerned with the 'social,' with historical time, and with the 'speaking mass'). In other words, following the position taken by the poststructuralists and those influenced by them, this unpredictability is a defining feature of culture.

Maniglier's project, in the first instance, is to embed structuralism in connectionist cognitive science, and then to understand the incessant learnability that characterizes the connectionist cognitivist enterprise in terms of the open-endedness of culture itself. 'Cultural machines' of connectionism are machines capable of producing open-ended cultural values. They are open-ended not in a solipsistic sense, but rather intersubjectively, involving the endless production of 'sensible milieus' between two or multiple agents. Culture in this perspective is made up of the sensible milieus that exist and evolve between linguistically capable agents.

According to Saussure's well-known formuation, the sign is a two-sided psychological[5] entity consisting of a formal side (signifier) and a meaning side (signified). These are inseparable like the two sides of a sheet of paper. The sign comes to be not by any preexisting necessity that connects the signifier and the signified. Saussure views it as 'a whole that results from the association of a signifier and a signified,' and since "the link between the signifier and the signified is arbitrary" he is led to conclude that "*the linguistic sign is arbitrary.*" (*CGL* 1, p. 67, italics in the original; *Cours*, p. 99-100) In other words, the sign is what emerges in the mind on the basis of a chance bonding between the formal part and the meaning part, without the latter playing any determining role with respect to the former. Before one can have a concept that would determine the shape of the signifier, the linguistic sign has already been formed and is in use by the individual and the social community. (Of course, Saussure does not rule out a period of apprentissage for a child learning the language). The 'conceptual image' that corresponds to the signified of the linguistic sign precedes the formation of any well-formed concept. The individuated signs emerge naturally in one or several human minds, even before man can begin to reflect upon the separate existences of the form and the meaning that constitute the sign. Sign is thus the result of a pre-reflective and individuated[6] psycho-social emergence from or, extension of life, just as a life itself may be regarded as an individuated extension of already existing life or lives (physico-pyscho-social) or of non-biological matter. Furthermore, the signs cannot exist in any single individual, but only in a 'collectivity.' We must assume that in this perspective the bonding of the signifier and the signified in one individual spreads by way of some sort of a communicative contagion to all other members of a community. That is why Saussure insists that the "concrete object of linguistics is the social product deposited in the brain of each individual, i.e. *langue* or linguistic structure." (*CGL* 1, p. 24, translation modified; *Cours*, p. 44) In the course of *time*, this 'social product' of *langue* is deeply implanted in the minds of the individual speakers, and with the aid of which they speak their language, without having to be overtly conscious of it and with mechanical ease. This is also what prevents speakers from being able to introduce their own individual variations in their language. And hence according to Saussure, "the distinguishing characteristic of the sign— but the one that is least apparent at first sight — is that in some way it eludes the individual or social will." (*CGL* 2, p. 17; *Cours* p. 34) Language or *langue*, Saussure notes, cannot be directly derived from speech, nor can the latter be reduced to the former; language is essentially the result of the 'social crystallization' of speech. This last phrase must be taken seriously for, while Saussure agrees with Whitney that language is a social institution, differs from him in saying that it is not like any other socially formed institution, because here participation in it is not voluntary. And perhaps we could add that unlike the family, the social institution of language encompasses all members of a community simultaneously. Language is passively and unconsciously registered (without any premeditation) in the minds of the members of a community. Though it emerges in and is maintained through social interactions, individuals cannot voluntarily create or reject its particular structures.

Saussure himself had pointed to the 'double essence' of signs in proposing a "science that studies the life of signs at the core of social life" (*CGL* 1, p. 15, translation modified; *Cours* p. 33) or semiology. Semiology was meant to be a science that will include primarily the science of language or linguistics, as well as (secondarily) the study of other secondary systems of signs. According to Saussure, "Semiology would show what constitutes signs, what laws govern them." (*CGL* 2, p. 16; *Cours,* p. 33) Since it was meant to be a study of the signs simultaneously present in the minds of socially-related individuals, semiology was expected to be a part of social psychology, which in turn would be a branch of general psychology.

Evidently, Saussure (like many who preceded and followed him) was struggling to identify the proper (scientific) object of linguistic study: "Language is a well-defined object in the heterogeneous mass of speech facts." (*CGL* 2, p. 14; *Cours*, p. 31) It is essentially an object of social psychology. He invites us to picture the nature of this object:

> If we could gather the sum of the linguistic images stored in the minds of all individuals, we could identify the social bond that constitutes language. It is a treasure deposited by the members of a given community through their active use of speaking, a grammatical system that has a potential existence in each brain, or, more specifically, in the brains of a group of individuals. For, the language is never complete in any single individual, but exists perfectly only in the collectivity. (*CGL* 2, p. 13-14; *Cours*, p. 30)

This takes us to Saussure's yet another definition of language:

> It is not to be confused with human speech [*langage*], of which it is only a definite part, though certainly an essential one. It is both a social product of the faculty of speech and a set of necessary conventions that have been adopted by a social body to permit individuals to exercise that faculty. Taken as a whole, speech is many-sided and heterogeneous; straddling several areas simultaneously—physical, physiological, and psychological—it belongs both to the individual and to society; we cannot put it into any category of human facts, for we cannot identify its unity. (*CGL* 2, p. 9, translation modified; *Cours*, p. 25)

And further, the well-defined object of language,

> ...can be localized in a limited segment of the speaking-circuit where an auditory image becomes associated with a concept. It is the social part of speech, outside the individual who can never create nor modify it by himself; it exists only by virtue of a sort of contract accepted by the members of a community. (*CGL* 2, p. 14, translation modified; *Cours*, p. 31)

For Saussure, society is 'inert by nature,' and therefore it is a 'prime conservative force.' (*CGL* 2, p. 74; *Cours*, p. 108) And since 'the life of signs' is at the core of the social life, and since it 'blends with the life of social collectivity,' (*CGL* 2, 74, translation modified; *Cours*, p. 108) language among all social institutions is the least amenable to initiative. Language chooses its own signs, but this is a Hobson's choice, for what it chooses is the only sign that can possibly be chosen. The principle of the 'arbitrariness of the sign' implies that in a language the signifier/signified and their relations are chosen arbitrarily, but the choice that the language makes is mandatory for its speakers. 'Choose,' but 'the freedom of choice is limited to the particular sign that will be chosen.' Or even, 'choose' but 'do not choose.' This is similar to what Derrida calls the 'double bind' in another context: 'Translate, ... but do not translate.' Neither can the individuals alter the choice made by a language, nor has the social body the authority to change even a single word, because it is bound to its language. The contract of conventions and the laws of language are such that they are not freely chosen by a community, but are imposed upon it, unlike in the case of other institutions. Since the conventions and laws of language are inherited by a community from its deep and indefinite past, its origin can never be known, nor can the social body or the individuals ever voluntarily change them.

Since the language that is spoken in any given epoch is the result of what is inherited from a continuous succession of generations, no one can ever know when a contract was at all established. The setting up of the contract can only be imagined and cannot be empirically determined. Signs are deeply rooted in the historical tradition, ensuring their continuity in time.

According to Saussure, the 'social forces' tenaciously conserve the character of the signs arbitrarily formed in language. Therefore there is their unchanging continuity in historical time. The community's insistence on the character of the signs inherited from the past generations ensures their continuity and stability in time. The signs that have been chosen freely and arbitrarily are fixed in a more definitive manner by the passage of time. The transformation of the nature of a sign from its chance origins to its necessary existence in a language is thus a function of the passage of time. Since the sign emerges arbitrarily, it has to depend on the force of tradition which in turn ensures that the sign is enduringly arbitrary.

However, even if the social forces establish and maintain the stability of the arbitrarily formed sign in time, the continuity of the sign leads to its unpredictable mutations with the passage of time. According to Saussure's most astonishing formulation on the relation between the Immutability and the Mutability of the sign, he says:

> In the final analysis, these two facts are intimately connected. The sign is subject to alteration because it continues through time. But what predominates in any alteration is the persistence of the earlier material. Infidelity to the past is only relative. *That is how the principle of alteration is founded on the principle of continuity.* (*CGL* 1, p. 75, translation modified; *Cours*, p. 108-9. Emphasis with italics by the present author).

After providing sufficient examples of alterations in time, Saussure notes that these invariably "result in *a shift in the relationship between the signified and the signifier*" (*CGL* 1, p. 75; *Cours*, p. 109. Emphasis in the original). Such shifts are due to the arbitrary nature of the linguistic sign, since "arbitrariness of the linguistic signs implies theoretically the freedom to establish any connection whatsoever between phonic substance and ideas" (*CGL* 2, p. 76; *Cours*, p. 110). And furthermore, it is because "each of the two elements joined together in the linguistic sign retain its own life to a degree unknown elsewhere" (CGL 2, p. 76, translation modified; *Cours*, pp. 110-11) that the linguistic system consisting of arbitrary signs is "radically powerless to defend itself against forces which constantly tend to shift the relationship between the signified and the signifier" (*CGL* 2, p. 75, translation modified; *Cours*, p. 110). This is why languages everywhere and always alter or evolve "under the influence of all factors that affect either the sounds or the meanings" (*CGL* 2, p. 76, *Cours*, p. 111). This evolution is inevitably and intrinsically part of the semiological life of all languages, from their very beginnings. "The continuity of signs through time, linked to their alteration in time, is a principle of general semiology." (*CGL* 1, p. 76; translation modified; *Cours*, p. 111) However, unlike the continuity of signs in time which are 'in principle available for observation,' their alteration through time cannot be observed as such. Therefore it is better to abandon the attempts to observe precise alterations, and to account for shifts in relations. For, Saussure avers, time changes all things, and language cannot be an exception to this universal law.

Saussure notes that what makes the 'life of language' possible is not just its emergence in the community of speakers (which makes it only 'viable'), but also its development in historical time. Certainly, viewing language in time but without taking into account the speaking mass or the community, its elements cannot be seen to change. It is the social forces plus the development of language in time that bring about linguistic alterations. Time and social forces work together, to induce the alterations. Saussure goes on to show with the aid of a schema that

> Language is no longer free, because the passage of time allows social forces at work on it to carry out their effects on it, and what we arrive at is a principle of continuity that cancels freedom. But continuity necessarily implies alteration, more or less considerable shift in relations. (*CGL* 2, p. 78; *Cours*, p. 113)

Perhaps, what Saussure envisages is the necessary continuity of the arbitrarily formed signs of language in historical time, where alterations, theoretically inevitable owing to the mutual independence of the signified and the signifier, are wrought by the more or less blind social forces. Language is 'constrained' to continue in its historical path and to undergo alterations. Be it in continuity or in change, freedom is denied to languages. And moreover, even when there are alterations in the structure of a language, from a diachronic point of view what precedes and what follows are not two entirely differently languages. For, Saussure notes: "the river of language flows incessantly." (*CGL*, p. 139, translation modified ; '... le fleuve de la langue coule sans interruption...' *Cours*, p. 193.)

We must account for two more fundamental aspects of Saussure's theory of the sign which may appear contrary to the preceding descriptions. The first of these is the division of signs into categories that are *absolutely* and *relatively* arbitrary. This is where, as it has been noted, Saussure's semiotic theory begins to approximate to that of C.S. Peirce's division of signs into *icons, indices* and *symbols*. Saussure maintains that not all signs are arbitrary to the same degree; he redefines them in terms of their degrees of motivation, that is, the natural connection between the signified and the signifier. He admits that only a small set of signs consisting mainly of the individualized lexemes, is really absolutely arbitrary or immotivated. And no sign is absolutely motivated. The majority of the signs are intermediate between absolute and relative arbitrariness, or which is the same thing, between immotivation and motivation. As per Saussure's famous example, "the French word *vingt* ('twenty') is unmotivated [therefore arbitrary], but *dix-neuf* ('nineteen') is not unmotivated to the same degree because it evokes the terms with which it is composed and others to which it is associated, for example, *dix, neuf, vingt-neuf, dix-huit, soixante-dix*, etc..." (*CGL* 1, p. 130; translation modified; *Cours*, p. 181) Saussure's emphasis here, as distinct from the instances of motivation such as onomatopoeia or phonaesthetics discussed in the main section on the arbitrariness of the sign, is on morphological and syntactic iconicity on the basis of which languages can vary along an axis indicating those with maximum arbitrariness or 'immotivation' (the 'lexicological' ones) at one end, and those with minimum arbitrariness or high level of motivation (the 'grammatical' ones) at the other. In this context, Saussure observes that

> ...the entire system of language is based on the irrational principle of arbitrariness of the sign which if applied unrestrictively greatly complicates matters; but the mind has succeeded in introducing a principle of order in certain parts of the mass of signs, and it is here that the relatively motivated has its role. If the mechanism of language were entirely rational, we could study it as such; but as it is only a partial correction of a naturally chaotic system, we accept the point of view imposed by the very nature of language, by studying this mechanism as that which limits arbitrariness. (*CGL* 2, p. 133, translation modified; *Cours*, pp. 182-83)

What is interesting here is that Saussure is correcting a view that he elsewhere introduces as a 'principle of primordial importance' (*CGL* 2, p. 68, *Cours*, p. 100): *arbitrariness of the sign*. Arbitrariness is an irrational principle of irregularity that governs most of the linguistic signs, but the human mind has invented a rational principle of motivation or regularity based on iconicity (where like meanings have like forms) for the purpose of ordering a naturally chaotic system. In Saussure's classification, the classical languages like Sanskrit and Latin are ultra-grammatical, that is less arbitrary, and more motivated, while English and French (as compared to German) are highly immotivated or more arbitrary. In its historical movement, French has abandoned the highly motivated and 'grammatical' character of Latin and adopted its own highly lexicological character, e.g. Latin *inimicus* (more iconic and more motivated: *in* + *amicus*) became French *ennemi* (less iconic and less motivated). In other words, the French language, shunned the internal order and regularity that it should have inherited from Latin, and abandoned itself, like English, to embrace what would be a relatively 'chaotic system' marked by a high degree of arbitrariness, whose extreme example, in fact, would be the Chinese language. (See *CGL* 2, pp. 133-34, *Cours*, pp. 183-84)

Significantly, Saussure's text does not say if the induction of order and regularity in language by means of motivated signs is a case of language change due to active human intervention involving the speaking agents. If that is the case, then his strict distinction between *parole* and *langue* cannot be maintained, and motivation can be understood as a function of conscious human agency, even if the temporal process of change is of considerably long duration. However, he prefers to view it merely as something wrought by the human 'mind.'

But elsewhere, in his discussion of linguistic evolution due to analogy or analogical innovation, Saussure explicitly accepts at least a partial role of the speaking subject. He says:

> Nothing enters the language before having been tried out in speaking. All evolutionary phenomena have their origin in the sphere of the individual. This principle particularly applies to analogical innovations. Before Latin *honor* becomes a competitor capable of replacing *honôs*, a subject must improvise it and the others imitate and repeat it, until it becomes obligatory in usage. (*CGL* 2, p. 168, translation modified; *Cours*, p. 231)

Analogical variations always take place in language and often in large numbers. But most of them are not successful in effecting a change in the structure of a language. Analogical change is based on the imitation of a real or assumed regularity. Since new forms are attempted to be created on the basis of existing elements and old regularities, these analogical changes do not amount to linguistic renovation. Thus, their effect in real linguistic evolution is indeed minimal. Saussure provides us with a most apt imagery to understand this renovative and simultaneously conservative process of language evolution: "A language is a dress covered with patchworks made with its own material." (*CGL*, p. 171; translation slightly modified, *Cours*, p. 235)[7] In the particular kind of life that language is supposed to be, it revives itself constantly by transforming itself with pieces of its own material, each time used differently. Its parts degenerate and disappear only to regenerate and reappear in another form, without there ever being distinct phases of life, growth and death.

Maniglier has correctly focused on the significance of this position. Referring to Saussure's concept of 'life,' he points out that:

> The system has its own virtue, a kind of intrinsic reality that resembles more the activity of an anthill than an organism's. It is their capacity to regenerate themselves from their own refuse that gives systems a life, not their capacity to reproduce.... Saussure compares language to an "anthill where if one plants a stick and it would be instantly repaired from its breaks."[8]

While discussing the geographical aspects of language change, Saussure also accounts for the propagation or dissemination of features from other languages and cultures. Here, he disavows any specificity for the linguistic phenomenon. The intercultural changes are "subject to the same laws as any other habit, such as fashion." (*CGL* 2, p. 205; *Cours*, p. 281) One can observe in any community two opposing forces either favouring the changes or opposing them: parochialism and the force of social intercourse. If languages submit themselves to only parochial forces that want to remain faithful to its own core traditions, then it can lead to an infinite variety of linguistic particularities. But it is countered by forces of intercourse that obliges people to communicate with each other. Saussure notes: "Intercourse brings to a village visitors from other localities, displaces a part of the population on the occasion of a festival or fair, unites people from different provinces under one flag. In short, it is a unifying principle which counters the disuniting attitude of parochialism." (*CGL* 2, p. 206, translation modified; *Cours*, pp. 281-82) Intercourse aids in the 'extension' (by accepting and propagating innovations) and the 'cohesion' (by preventing dialectal fragmentation and suppressing innovations as and when they arise) of a language. Here again, Saussure seems to be accepting the role of the social speaking agents.

Maniglier's admirable attempt summarized in his recent article on "Processing Cultures: Structuralism in the History of Artificial Intelligence" (Maniglier 2011) is to bring some of the central tenets of Saussure's work in contact with some of the recent, interesting trends in Cognitive Science. The notion of structure is inevitable for AI. What Maniglier proposes to draw from structuralism is the notion of mind as collective (social and cultural) and as historical. How can we theoretically proceed from the sign as a social-psychological and historical object to machines that are both cognitive and historical? How can cognition/intelligence be conceived of as a socio-cultural and historical emergent property that is amenable to processing by machines?

The first step is to define culture as a sensible milieu. Such a model of 'cultural emergence' has been suggested in the AI model of Luc Steels (discussed in Maniglier 2011, p. 160). From the continuous production of sensible data in two or more different agents, there can be random emergence of sensible milieus on the basis of an internal/objective 'feeling of agreement' between the agents. From differences in the sensible data one is led to their unpredictable felt sameness. This would be the basis of an artificial 'common mind'[9] or intelligence as a collective phenomenon. Now, Maniglier attempts to show that this process has already been described in Saussurean structuralism.

For Saussure, as we have already tended to see, from the perspective of linguistic study, the mind is something like an 'empty'[10] mechanism with a social axis as well as a historical axis. It is empty because the linguistic sign, the semiological entity, is pre-reflective and preconceptual. But the sign with an empty cognitive content has a reality only as part of a collectivity ('*Masse*') and as something always liable to change in time. This is also why, as Maniglier notes, this complex system made up of potentially empty signs can never be mastered by any single individual. And moreover, whether the social body wishes to conserve or change its linguistic structure by means of different mechanisms, the force of time, in due course, can change almost everything in language. As we have seen, the arbitrariness of the sign (and the concomitant instability of the relation between the signified and the signifier), the force of time and the uncertain activity of the social body, all these together, ensure that languages are in a state of permanent variation.

The fundamental point that Maniglier makes is that for Saussure the linguistic changes that constantly take place are not changes at the physical or the psychological level of the signifier or the signified respectively, but changes are at the level of the linguistic structure; they are semiological changes. The empty and incorporeal character of the sign implies that each time a word is uttered, its material manifestation bears a different relationship with the entity of the linguistic sign. In this sense, speech or language-use consists of only variable entities. This is what leads Maniglier to claim that "the domain of semiology is characterized by this peculiar form of object with *variable entities*." And further, "semiology is the science that studies how signs never cease to change as long as they are used and are 'circulating.'"[11] The point is that linguistic variation is not just a matter of socio-linguistic or dialectal variation, or even individual stylistic variations, but rather that variation in time is constitutive of the basic structural element of language, that is, the sign.

Of course, there is still the unresolved question of the relationship between the psychological part of the linguistic sign and conceptual thought. According to Maniglier's interpretation of Saussure, as the mental structural element of language changes, thought also undergoes a change. In his view, derived from Saussure: "Language is certainly made up of signs, but signs are themselves parts of *thought*—not just a material carrier used to express it. More surprisingly, thought exists only in time and it never stops changing. It is as if what allows us to think would also lead us to think something else without us even noticing it...."[12]

The question of the relation between the 'mental' that is exclusively part of language, and the mental that is more generally associated with thought or intelligence is theoretically indeed the most difficult question to solve. Maniglier invites us to observe here two 'conflicting' modalities of the emergence of signs and their series, first in terms of the appearance of 'terms' or the sign-units by way of a 'play of *differences*' (for, as Saussure puts it *"in language there are only differences"* (*CGL* 2, p. 120; Cours, p. 166. Emphasis in the original) and then by way of the appearance of 'values' by way of a 'play of *oppositions*.' The 'terms' emerge as a function of the pure differences between sensible qualities, while the 'values' are a function of the positional appearances of terms in a closed system that language is at any given point of time. Qualitative differences are embedded in a system of oppositions, rendering the language to be a mere 'form' without there being any substance or any 'positive terms.'

What is significant about the second system of oppositions is that it is highly language-specific. 'Values' emerge relative to a series of terms within a particular system. There is a dynamic and evolutionary relation between the differentially produced qualitative entities or terms, and the oppostionally produced serial and systemic values. According to Maniglier, this is where the essential instability or the variability of the systems and its elements are to be located:

> The serial organization of the "terms" (the post-processing) is carried out on the basis of the concrete qualitative differences that constitute them. These differences can be altered—for a number of stylistic, physiological, sociological, etc. reasons—without changing the structure of the oppositions. That is why the overall equilibrium is *susceptible* to change, but *only in as much as a new interpretation intervenes, only inasmuch as someone will create*—on

> the basis of new differential terms—a previously non-existent series of oppositions that will modify the possible analysis of linguistic performances.[13]

Thus, the definition of language that Maniglier derives from Saussure is that of an infinitely differentiating and varying complex system consisting of incorporeal or mental elements that are organized as states of qualitative and serial variations. The variations of the complex system, as in the connectionist AI, are a response to its exposure to the outside world, that is, *the sensible social/cultural milieus.* But as far as the system is concerned, the variational ordering processes are involuntary, and from a Saussurean point of view, they "are rigorously *mechanical: they are based on an innate faculty... a non-specific faculty, namely the semiological faculty.*" And further... : "*Languages are involuntary by-products* of the linguistic faculty's exercise."[14]

Thus, signs as *terms* are the products of the differentiating mechanisms of the individual humans' innate cognitive faculty, and they emerge only in sensible (cultural) milieus, but their values are in continuous oppositional and serial variation, which negates the possibility of any teleological social-cultural stabilization. In other words, owing to the potential differentiability and the variability of the signs, our thoughts which are part of the sensible cultural milieu cannot be fixed and stabilized, and conversely, since our cultural cognitive milieus are exposed to ever new contexts, alterations in terms of qualitative differentiations and serial variations happen incessantly. According to Maniglier, Saussure's position "straddles between individualizing cognitivism and the holism of the objective spirit."[15] (*Ibid*. p. 169)

What all this portends is the indefinite and infinite cultural, cognitive and linguistic variability of human social life, even when the rigorous mechanical laws and their unpredictable internal evolution are common to both humans and machines. Maniglier suggests that the pool of variable intelligences of the future, could consist, not only of what can be derived from a multiplicity of human cultural contexts, and from the evolving intelligent machines, but also from cultural milieus emerging from man-machine cognitive and social interactions. I think, perhaps the picture will be more perfect if we can expand it to triangular cultural milieus that include the lived world of the animals too. We should look forward to a not-so-foreseeable future, where animals, humans, and machines can converge in contingently evolving cultural milieus where everyone can live happily thereafter.

NOTES

1. This is the text of a talk at the Department of Philosophy, University of Essex, UK, held on April 28, 2011. It was written in New Delhi and Paris, and completed in Wivenhoe village, Essex, UK.
2. See what the late linguist P.B. Pandit had commented in his review of a book of selected papers of J.R. Firth: "Reading contemporary notions into earlier writers, though currently fashionable, is a hazardous occupation. Panini has undergone three American avatars: the historical avatar with Whitney, the descriptive avatar with Bloomfield and now the generative avatar!" (Pandit, 1970: 283) Evidently, he was referring to Chomsky's attempt at connecting up with (if not appropriating) the work of Panini: "... it seems that even Panini's grammar can be interpreted as a fragment of such a "generative grammar" in essentially contemporary sense of this term." (Chomsky, N., 1965, p. v).
3. Foucault, F.: "What I have tried to do, is to introduce the analyses of a structuralist style into those areas where they haven't penetrated until now, that is to say into the domain of the history of ideas, the history of knowledge systems, the history of theory. In this way, I have undertaken to analyse the birth of structuralism in terms of structuralism itself" (Translated by Stuart Elden from *Dits et écrits I*: 583).
4. Milner, J.-C., *Le périple structural, figures et paradigme*, Seuil, Paris, 2002.
5. It is useful to note that Saussure uses the term 'psychological' in the traditional sense to refer to the state or activity of the mind. It is what comes to be or stored in the mind, or performed by it. It does not refer to the process of knowing, cognition, or its result.
6. I use this term in the sense of Gilbert Simondon in his work on 'Ontogenesis'. According to Simondon: "The individual would ... be grasped as a relative reality, a certain phase of being that

supposes a preindividual reality, and that, even after individuation, does not exist on its own, because individuation does not exhaust with one stroke the potentials of preindividual reality. Moreover, that which the individuation makes appear is not only the individual, but also the pair individual-environment." (Simondon, G., 2009: 5)

7. Consider a comparable analogy on language in L. Wittgenstein: "Our language can be seen as an ancient city: a maze of little streets and squares, of old and new houses, and of houses with additions from various periods; and this surrounded by a multitude of new boroughs with straight regular streets and uniform houses." (*Philosophical Investigations*, p. 8)
8. Maniglier, P., 2011, p. 170; the inset quote is from Saussure 2002, p. 266.
9. I am referring to a notion suggested by Phillip Petit. According to Petit, 'common mind' can be understood in the material and everyday sense, and as 'shared or social mind,' 'not insulated or solipsistic', that 'emerges on the basis of interaction and community between them... so that the fact that one individual is minded entails that others are minded too.' (Petit, 1993: 342)
10. As Maniglier informs us Saussure states this problem slightly differently. "Linguistic phenomena can never be reduced to specific saptio-temporal phenomena like the individual articulatory gestures ... linguistic events are *incorporeal*." (Maniglier, 2011: 164). Saussure had noted that even "the linguistic signifier in its essence is nothing phonic, it is incorporeal, constituted, not by its material substance, but uniquely by the differences that distinguish its sound image from all others." (*CGL 2*, pp. 118-19, translation modified; *Cours*, p. 164) Later, Maniglier further clarifies: "Linguistic entities are *unobservable* realities in the precise sense of being unmeasurable." (Maniglier, op. cit., 164)
11. Maniglier, 2011, p. 165.
12. Ibid., p. 165.
13. Maniglier, 2011, op cit., p. 167.
14. Ibid., p. 168.
15. Ibid., p. 169.

2

Between the Self and the Other: Language after Levinas

The first thing that comes to one's mind while beginning to speak of the notion of the 'self'' is that it cannot be covered by one homogeneous notion. There have been different notions of the self in different traditions and cultural contexts, in different historical times and in different intellectual discourses. It may indeed be difficult to provide a comprehensive and exhaustive account of all these notions in the space of this essay and on the basis of my rather limited knowledge. However, one may attempt a quick scan of some of the notions. The current English language may itself attest to the following notions of self or related notions: *first person, individual, ego, soul, I, subject, identity*, etc. To this one may add other familiar terms that come from other languages: *âtman, aham, swa* from Sanskrit; *soi* and *âme* from French, and *selbst* from German. What is interesting about these notions, even if we limit our consideration to the English language, is that they belong to diverse registers and have their provenance in different historical and linguistic-cultural contexts. For instance, 'ego' is a Latin word for 'I' and is often currently used in the English language registers of psychology and psychoanalysis. Similarly, 'soul,' '*âtman*' and '*âme*' are more likely to be used in philosophico-religious discourses; 'subject' and 'identity' in philosophical, legal and political discourses; and 'person' in linguistic as well as philosophical registers.

The word 'other' may at the first impression seem to be devoid of any such difficulties arising from related terms and words. But this is not exactly the case. The English word 'other' has a clear phonological relationship with the words, *mother* and *brother*, and perhaps less so with *father*. Further, it seems to bears a semantic proximity with words like *alien* (etymologically, the 'non-linked'), *stranger*, *foreigner* (both words suggest a provenance from the outside) and *outsider* itself. This seminar is purportedly concerned with the 'self and the other,' but I presume more strictly with (redefining) our understanding of the relationship between the self and the other.

I think it is possible to say that the 'self' was projected onto the foreground in our human history with the advent of the modern age that privileged the rational or the thinking subject (i.e. the Cartesian *cogito*). Since then, we have believed that the control the priestly or the feudal order exercised over the individual subject could be thwarted and rejected by the human reason with which everyone was genetically endowed. This belief or idea, as we know, eventually led to revolutions in the social and intellectual domains everywhere, especially in the Western world. Kant had characterized this enlightened emergence of man and the advent of modernity in history as his irrevocable coming to maturity. The thinking/rational man could effectively pose himself if not in opposition to, then on par with, God and the Lord. By thinking, he could understand the order of the world, organize his affairs according to this order, and if needed supplement and augment this order. The intellectual power and expression of a certain bourgeois class which had broken off and emerged from the feudal yoke, accumulated wealth through its own novel enterprises, and which had established its own domination over those who were outside that class economically and culturally, was being projected as a property that was at least potentially available universally, that is, for all humans. The modernist universalism thus had a geographically limited and historical starting point. Henceforth, that is from the point of the emergence of human reason, we have the power to transform ourselves and our world, which could be the model not only for perpetuating our own notion of historical progress in the world, but also for those whom we have, before our emergence as the dominant class, excluded from our world, and those who are any way outsiders. (It is to be noted here that both Kant and Hegel had assigned a role for the 'other' in man's thinking. For Kant, the subject had to test out with the other the validity of his own thinking. And for Hegel, the universal progress of rational thought is mediated by a continuous process of mutual recognition and negotiation of power between a subject and his other which results in man's self-consciousness.) Effectively, the Western bourgeois subject was deemed as the rational and enlightened subject, the model of a universal subject, as well as the paradigm for the historical progress of other humans, i.e. those who were excluded and were outside. Prejudiced scholarly descriptions were made and remade of those other humans (like the 'orientals,' as Said has endeavoured to show in his *Orientalism*) who could not be described in terms of the standards assumed for itself by the enlightened Western subject. Orientalist accounts by Western scholars signify the most trenchant example of how an economic and intellectual consolidation of a describing self, can create and reinforce distorted and reified images of the 'other.' (Said's analysis in *Orientalism* helps us to perceive this particularly in regard to the European scholarship on the oriental Arab world.)

The European self-image, however, was grossly shaken by the works of at least two great philosophers of modern times, i.e. Marx and Nietzsche. Both Marx and Nietzsche sowed the seeds of an immanent conflict between a dominant self and the oppressed other within the European context itself. Marx understood clearly that all intellectual creations are the ideological byproducts of a dominant class position. In the place of discourses charged with the ideologies of the bourgeois class, Marx and Engels, stressed the advance of the ideology of the working class, in polemical opposition to the former. This dialectical overcoming of the power and ideology of the bourgeoisie by those of the proletariat, we know, was the central maxim for the Marxists. Nietzsche, on the other hand, moved along a slightly different trajectory, claiming that Western (Socratic, Christian and the modern scientific) notions of ontological essence, piety, morality and truth are all mere outmoded functions of sterile and fossilized languages, which had lost all their 'sensuous force.' Unlike Marx's economic stress on a socio-economic emancipation of man, Nietzsche campaigned for a continuous artistic-linguistic enhancement of the European man. Both Marx and Nietzsche were utterly skeptical of all that made up the self-assurance of European modernity, and therefore sought to restore the dignity of the 'other' man that lay submerged in its soil, or the man that was yet to emerge. In other words, these philosophers tried to lift the veil with which the dominant European self had managed to keep its own other, in different ways, economically, politically, culturally and aesthetically repressed.

A similar intellectual project is implicit in Freud's work, but it concerned a yet different realm of repression: that of sexual pleasure. The main goal of Freudian psychoanalysis was to show that certain neurotic/psychological illnesses or disturbances had their origin in human society's attempt to repress the developmental infantile sexual pleasure for the sake of the anthropological-cultural order of the family and society. But this repression remained unsuccessful, and therefore the pleasure that was attempted to be repressed kept returning as the effect of an indelible unconscious mark that disturbs, when we least expect, in our supposedly conscious states. Freud's work showed how the consciousness of the self is always and already affected by the mark of the repression of the desire for the body of the maternal other (primarily) as a source of pleasure, in our unconscious. As the French psychoanalyst Lacan has tried to show, Freudian psychoanalysis consisted in relating, along metaphoric and metonymic trajectories, much of what goes on in our unconscious actions, dreams or discourses, including the slips of the tongue and jokes, to the indelible mark of this repression of sexual pleasure in the unconscious.

All these philosophers or philosophically-inclined analysts, Marx, Nietzsche and Freud, seem to have identified certain fundamental divisions in modern human societies, divisions of a social, political, economic, or cultural and discursive kind.

Unlike in the ancient or medieval societies, where the human condition was perceived in terms of divisions between a supposedly eternal divine world that was very often mediated and managed by the temporal powers represented by the priests, and a human world that was subordinated to and even subjugated by the former, in the modern world, the divisions were sought to be located within the sphere of the manifest society itself. This is because of the novel understanding that there could not be one human social reality or a single humanity that would manage its own affairs even if it was away from the glare of an almighty god. The new division is essentially a matter of *power*, articulated in one manner or the other, and its order ran within the dominion of man itself. It is to be noted that since the days of Marx, Nietzsche and Freud, our awareness of these divisions based on power has grown almost exponentially. The most important of these, of course, is the archaic power-based division of the gender domain. The otherness of the oppressed feminine gender within the human sexual order, as we know, has served as the basis for the entire social and political movement of the feminists which have swept across many parts of the world since the beginning of the 20th century. It is also worth mentioning that by the fourth quarter of the 20th century, scholarly attention has moved away from merely binary divisions of human social entities to their multipolar understanding and analysis. Individuals are no longer considered as belonging to one or other end of rigid and predefined polarities, but as nodes with a number of defining characteristics in relation to a diversity of plural or multivalent networks or configurations. In a certain sense, human beings and societies can be seen as situated and attending to their affairs in indefinitely plural social and cultural configurations.

***

We can now consider more directly the philosophical treatment of the question of self and the other. We should assume that in recent times this question has been the preserve of phenomenologically-oriented philosophers. As we have noted, in the 19th century, Hegel had suggested that in the forward march of the human mind in history, the self desires for the recognition of the other. Twentieth century phenomenologists have however dealt with the question of the other more extensively. After a brief examination of Husserl's account of the self—other question, we shall introduce Heidegger's and Levinas' analysis of the relationship between self and the other.

In his *Cartesian Meditations*, Husserl reflects on the constitution of an intersubjective 'common' world on the basis of the experience of the self's body, ego and its intentions which enter into a relationship with the other's body, its ego and its intentions. What is formed in the encounters between the self and the other is "the *coexistence of my ego* (...) with the *ego of the other*, of my intentional life with that of his, of my realities with those of his: in short, it is the creation of a *common temporal form*..."[1] Husserl moreover stresses forms of interhuman community higher than that of mere coexistence at the level of common space and common time, which involves a deeper 'intentional penetration' of the other in the self, which in turn, is an 'intentional communion' between one being and another being. This relation which is basically an 'effective communion,' is according to Husserl what makes possible the existence of a world in common, a world of humans and things.[2]

Some of these Husserlian concerns are evidently shared by Heidegger in his *Being and Time*, even if the latter openly deviates from many of his master's key formulations. Not unlike Husserl, Heidegger investigates the nature of a situated living being or *Dasein* or the 'being-there' in terms of its unfolding in time. The essence of a being has to be understood in terms of its existence in time, or more strictly for the living human being in terms of its everyday existence. Between the essential being and the existential everyday being there would be a gap or difference which can be understood only in terms of the authenticity and the totality or the wholeness of the being. Authenticity and totality of being is to be understood in its unfolding in relation to its end, which for the living being is its death. Death is not only that which defines the temporal wholeness (in the sense of completion) of the being, but is also part of the definition of being. Dasein therefore, as far as the living human being is concerned, can only be interpreted as the Being-towards-Death.

Dasein, even while it seeks authenticity and wholeness of its being, is faced with certain difficulties. In the state of its own being and of the possibility of its being, it understands the impossibility of its being at some point of time on the basis of its understanding of the inevitability of death. Through the experience of others' death, Dasein, understands in relation to the current possibility of its own being, the eventual possibility of its not being, or the impossibility of its being. It is in this sense that Heidegger speaks of death as the *possibility of impossibility* (of being). But the other's death can never be genuinely experienced by the self. "*No one can take the Other's death away from him.* ...By its very essence, death is in every sense mine, in so far as it 'is' at all."[3] (This would be true, according to Heidegger even if an individual sacrifices his or her life for the other.) At best, one can have only an inadequate and inauthentic representation of the other's death. The gap between the genuineness of the death of the other on the one hand and the inauthenticity of its representation by the self leads to *anxiety* in the self. It is this anxiety that paves the way towards the transformation of the inauthenticity of the experience of one's being into its authenticity through 'resoluteness.' The state of resoluteness of one's being is a response to the 'call of conscience' that one experiences/ receives. This resoluteness is accompanied at another level, thanks to the call of conscience, by a withdrawal from 'idle talk' or chatter, and a transformation of one's language and discourse, accompanied by the desire for a genuine state of being-with-the-other, or *Mitsein*. In this transformation, chatter is replaced by a concern for truth which Heidegger describes as *aletheia* or 'unconcealedness,' or the disclosure of being (with a small b), which is his definition of truth. For Heidegger, *Mitsein* or being-with is the truth of being in the social and political domain. As we can see, it is Dasein as the being-towards-death, and the experience of the possibility of impossibility of being in death, that lead to the resoluteness as well as the openness of the self's being to the being of the other, that is to say, being-with-the-other (*Mitsein*). Much of Heidegger's existential-political orientation which while eschewing the more traditional questions of freedom and responsibility, places authenticity, resoluteness and *Mitsein* as its central issues. This can be gleaned from the following sentences:

> Resoluteness, as *authentic Being-one's-Self*, does not detach Dasein from its world, nor does it isolate it so that it becomes a free-floating "I". And how should it, when authentic disclosedness, is *authentically* nothing else than *Being-in-the-world*? Resoluteness brings the Self right into its current concernful Being-alongside what is ready-to-hand, and pushes it into solicitous Being-with Others.
>
> In the light of "for-the-sake-of-which" of one's self-chosen potentiality-for-Being, resolute Dasein frees itself for its world? Dasein's resoluteness towards itself is what first makes it possible to let the others who are with it 'be' in their ownmost potentiality-for-Being, and to co-disclose this potentiality in the solicitude that leaps forth and liberates. Where Dasein is resolute, it can become the 'conscience' of Others. Only by being authentically Being-their-Selves in resoluteness can people authentically be with one another—not by ambiguous and jealous stipulations and talkative fraternizing in the "they" and in what "they" want to undertake.[4]

As for Dasein's state of resoluteness, it is not something that is attained on the basis of the knowledge of a specific critical situation. Resoluteness happens in the Situation, just as theory is the result of practice. "As resolute, Dasein is already *taking action.*"[5] And 'action,' Heidegger clarifies, is to be understood more generally so as to include all 'activity' including the 'passivity of resistance.'

Ignoring Sartre's views on the self and the other (for whom famously, 'Hell, is other people'), we shall proceed to an examination of Levinas's texts that deals with our central theme, particularly his chronologically second most important work, *Otherwise Than Being or Beyond Essence*, originally published (in French) in 1974. We should note here *Totality and Infinity, An Essay on Exteriority* (1961) itself had appeared as the culmination of major phenomenological interventions through which Levinas had already sought to bring Ethics to the centre-stage of philosophy, and even as the 'first philosophy.' As a Jewish immigrant from the Russian-speaking Baltic country of Lithuania in Germany first and later in France where he became a permanent resident, Levinas was responding philosophically to the phenomenological and existential works of such 20th century pioneers as Husserl, Heidegger, Sartre and Merleau-Ponty. His own work is pervaded by an extreme sensitivity to the context of the catastrophic wars of the 20th century and the Holocaust (*shoah*) which refers to the mass extermination of the Jewish minority in Europe, and of which he had direct experience. This sensitivity manifests itself in his work as an epochal questioning of the 'hypocrisy' of the Western civilization and of the very basis of its philosophy. Levinas's philosophical starting point is the rejection of the totalizing ontological evidence that is a prerequisite for philosophy. His ethical project was to investigate the very condition of possibility of philosophy itself as a totality. This led him to articulate a specific mode of transcendence which concerns not the nothingness of the ideal realm, but rather the exteriority that refuses the totality and resists totalization. In the preface to his *Totality and Infinity*, Levinas defines the contours of his philosophical goal as follows:

> Without substituting eschatology for philosophy, without philosophically "demonstrating" eschatological "truths," we can proceed from the experience of totality back to a situation where totality breaks up, a situation that conditions the totality itself. Such a situation is the gleam of exteriority or of transcendence in the face of the Other. The rigorously developed concept of this transcendence is expressed by the term infinity.[6]

Levinas was primarily addressing the European philosophical context of the trauma of the great wars, when philosophical discourse had become clogged and constricted. Thought had to overcome its basis in empirical objectivity as well as in an adherence to truth as mere disclosure in the Heideggerian sense. Here, Levinas is evoking a relation with infinity that overflows thought as such. The idea of infinity allows thought to move outside of itself, where it encounters not an alternative truth of disclosure, but the face of the Other. The relation between self and other results not in a truth of knowledge, but in the incessant opening up of an infinite in-between that can never return either to the self or the other, or to their mere togetherness. This idea of infinity is presented as a challenge to thought, because "the relation with infinity cannot ... be stated in terms of experience, for infinity overflows the thought that thinks it."[7] But then this demands at the same time, a different understanding of experience itself, as "a relation with the absolutely other, that is, with that which always overflows thought, [and therefore] the relation with infinity accomplishes experience in the fullest sense of the term."[8] Phenomenology is thus sought to be redefined in terms of the thought or the experience of the infinite encounter with the (face of the) other. In each face-to-face encounter with the other, the latter does not offer itself as a static interiority that is available to the self in its perception or as an image. What prevents the violence between the self and other is the fact that the face of the other offered to the self is other than what it appears to be each time. The face of the other is infinitely other owing to its ineluctable exteriority. This is what leads Levinas to say: "Being is exteriority: the very exercise of its being consists in exteriority, and no thought could better obey being than by allowing itself to be dominated by this exteriority."[9] The 'essence' of being cannot thus be based on the interior feature of being, but is always a passing to its *outside*, and therefore the encounter between the self and other, is never a meeting of essences or of interiorities, but rather an infinite creation of the in-between, exterior to both self and the other. This exterior being can never be an essence, but only an *inter-esse* (being-between). This implies, in fact, the relations of an exponential order between beings in the social space and in historical time. The emphasis is on the infinitely varying relations between beings as exteriority as opposed to the totalizing and homogenizing unity of an internalist logic. This is also the site of the responsibility of the subjective being and the incessantly (and exponentially) multiplying nature of linguistic significations.

In the place of Heidegger's panoramic account of *Mitsein* or being-with and its associated disclosure, Levinas insists on the self's infinite responsibility to the other, where the former is always responding to the 'appeal' of the other (not just the 'call of conscience') by saying 'Here I am' (*me voici*) offering to *substitute* himself for the other in his or her suffering and destitution. It is through such responses that the self maintains its infinite openness to the other, each time offering a new meaning to his relationship with the other and a new sense to the words of language that he utters. The use of language thus, resists thematisation of discourses in terms of the meanings already given, and each time through the self's 'saying' a specific and different signifyingness or sense takes place without allowing the consolidation of the meanings of what is already 'said.' The infinite bursting forth of language from its given totality is not a mere disclosure of the truth of being or that of being-with, but rather a response to the call of the other, that involves an injunction of responsibility which cannot be defined in terms of any ontologically defined situation, but whose very source, according to Levinas, is outside the realm of being.

We notice that while Levinas transforms Heidegger's ontology of subjective being, articulated both in terms of its becoming in time and its status of being-with in relation to other, he also takes issue with Martin Buber's account of inter-subjective relations stated in terms of a certain reciprocal dialogicality and relations of mutuality. While acknowledging the significance of Buber's work, Levinas has emphasized his philosophical differences with the former's classic work *I and Thou.*[10] Buber understands man's place in and relation with the world in terms of the two 'primary words,' *I-Thou* and *I-It*. The primary word *I-thou* signifies a relation of reciprocity and mutuality between two subjects. *I-It*, on the other hand is concerned with the relation between a subject and an object as such. Buber gives priority to the primary word *I-Thou* over the other primary word *I-It*. The former is that which is spoken in the 'original relational event,' and thus precedes, in 'a natural way', the mere *I* which results from 'visualization of forms.'

The other primary word, *I-It* can thus only be posterior to *I-Thou.* It results from the separating out of *I* from the latter relation. The essential distinction between the two is introduced by Buber thus: "The first primary word can be resolved, ... into *I* and *Thou,* but it did not arise from their being set together; by its nature it precedes *I.* The second word arose from the setting together of *I* and *It*: by nature it comes after it."[11] However, there's the possibility of the *I-Thou* relation degenerating into an *I-It* one, as for instance when a person or an object is seen merely as a target of perception or communication. Contrarily, every *I-it* relation can potentially become an *I-Thou* one. For Buber, God is the eternal *Thou,* and since God is the wholly other, only this can be considered as eternal.

Though Levinas does not deny Buber's influence on his own work, he has sought to redefine dialogicality in terms of the sociality of an ethical philosophy, as different from what he rejects as the latter's 'spirituality'. Levinas seems to suggest that the ethical effort required for a more contextual and socialised *I-Thou* relationship is absent in the work of Buber who in his view 'thematizes' this relationship. His critique of Buber therefore focuses on the three main issues, viz. *reciprocity, formality* and *exclusiveness* that according to Levinas, frame Buber's dialogicality. Furthermore, Levinas maintains that the *I-Thou* relation cannot be merely a reciprocal dialogue between two friendly and equal partners occurring in a pure formal space or in an ethereal medium. In his view, Buber's 'reciprocity' does not foreground the dialogue's ethical imperative; the latter's 'formality' is insensitive to the existential context of the dialogue; and further, his 'exclusiveness' "can give rise to no sense of justice necessary in order to go beyond the pure spiritualism of a narcissistic 'I-Thou.'"[12] Levinas therefore insists on a "difference in level between I and Thou."[13] As per his formulation, *I* am already obliged to respond to the call of the other, even before an I-Thou relationship can be established. There is an essential dissymmetry between *I* and *Thou* in the sense that I am responding to the arresting appearance or 'epiphany' of the face of the other. The other has both a 'higher' (more privileged) and 'poorer' (a destitute) status in relation to me, and I am therefore under a prior obligation to respond to his or her call. This obligation precedes and is outside of the ontolological. The otherness of the other thus is not something *a priori*, but is something that emerges in the face-to-face encounter between oneself and the other. Maintaining his philosophical distance from Buber, Levinas says:

> The originality of the [I-Thou] relation lies in the fact that it is not known from the outside but only by the 'I' which realizes the relation. The position of the I, therefore is not interchangeable with that of the Thou. But...if the self becomes an I in saying Thou, as Buber asserts, my position as a self depends on that of my correlated and the relation is no longer different from other relations: it is tantamount to a spectator speaking of the I and Thou in the third person.[14]

Levinas insists on the radical otherness of the Other in the temporal dimension, which naturally opens outward to infinity. Time's openness further ensures that the *I-Thou* relationship remains open. The self's relationship with the other is in and through time, and time is also to be regarded as "an untotalizable diachrony." By 'diachrony', Levinas is referring to its strict sense of the unpredictable and undecidable unfolding of multiple events and entities. As Levinas sees it, "(t)ime means that the other is moreover beyond me, irreducible to the synchrony of the same. The temporality of the interhuman opens up the meaning of otherness and the otherness of meaning."[15]

This alternative approach to language and meaning is characterized by a privileging of 'saying' over that of the 'said'. We may note that it is similar to the one proposed by Merleau-Ponty in an existential context by foregrounding the *parole parlante* ('speaking speech') in relation to the *parole parlé* (spoken speech). Levinas, however, redefines it in an ethical-dialogical manner: "(S)*aying* is irreducible to the ontological definability of the *said*. Saying is what makes the self-exposure to sincerity possible; it is a way of giving everything, of not keeping anything for oneself."[16] He goes on to note that "[l]anguage as *saying* is an ethical openness to the other; as that which is *said*—reduced to a fixed identity or synchronized presence—it is an ontological closure to the other." [17] The basic ethicality of language comes from the fact that *saying* represents a 'pure exposure' as opposed to the 'totalizing closure of the said.' This, according to Levinas, is evident from the undeniable innocence of the child, irrespective of cultural or linguistic factors, for "'(t)he child is a pure exposure of expression in so far as it is pure vulnerability; it has not yet learned to dissemble, deceive, to be insincere."[18]

Levinas's principal concerns are more carefully and clearly worked out in his second major work *Otherwise than Being or Beyond Essence.* The infinite responsibility of the self for the other, in the face of the closure of essence (which he considers as the source of war), remains the predominant issue. The treatment of human subjectivity and language now gains more importance, even when it is still expressed in relation to and against the totalization of being. The idea of a continuous transcendence is still insisted upon, where transcendence is not some sort of an elevation, but the passing over into the 'other than being.' The breaking up of the closure of totality into infinity and the passing of the self's being into its other has to be seen in conjunction as far as Levinas's philosophy is concerned. This essentially is the sense of 'diachrony.' Transcendance is not sought in a mere being-with (*Mitsein* of Heidegger)or a dialogical *I-Thou* of Buber, but in the withdrawal from and an abandonment of being in/to the passivity of the 'otherwise than being' or of the beyond essence, in the time to come. This passivity is a most radical passivity that emerges as a response to the non-cognizable face of the other even in the face of the greatest suffering on the part of the self.

It is important to note that Levinas is setting aside the totality of being's essence, both in space and time, and as subjectivity, and privileging a non-essential 'otherwise than being' where the self is under an (invisible) injunction to respond to the other. The key terms to be understood here are: *saying, proximity* and *substitution.* Proximity implies nearness or neighbourliness of the self in relation the other, irrespective of their actual presence in space or time. Irrespective of language, and even prior to the language of the said, it is 'saying' that brings the self close to the other. Saying is the pre-original language, impossible to be thematically uttered, and imbued with a prior signification, but rather the very basis of the signifyingness of linguistic utterance. This saying is the signifyingness of a 'foreword' that is before or outside of being. As Levinas puts it:

> The original or pre-original saying, what is put forth in the foreword, weaves an intrigue of responsibility. It sets forth an order more grave than being and antecedent to being. By comparison being appears as a game [earlier in the paragraph, we read, 'Saying is not a game.' FM]. Being is play or detente, without responsibility, where everything possible is permitted.[19]

But this 'saying' which has its provenance in the other than being, does gel into a language, where the latter allows itself to be thematized. And conversely, "(l)anguage permits us to utter, be it by betrayal, this *outside of being, this ex-ception* to being, as though being's other were an event of being." But then Levinas goes on to caution us that even a sublime statement of truth in articulated language does not exhaust the responsibility associated with saying:

> ... apophansis does not exhaust what there is in saying. The apophansis presupposes the language that answers with responsibility, and the gravity of this response is beyond the measure of being.[20]

Levinas conceives of an outside of or otherwise than being as the provenance of language as saying, as that which enjoins the subject's responsibility for the other. This saying and this command come from an immemorial past beyond any conceivable history of being. Being has only succeeded (even if not entirely) in suppressing this saying. The outside, the otherwise than being, still continues to haunt being and all that is supposed to be its essence. As we can see, Heidegger's anxiety of the *Dasein* gives over to the haunting horror, and the murmur, of being, beneath all being. The good that one can be is not something that one chooses voluntarily (for, 'no one is good voluntarily') but is commanded to me and ordained on me as my responsibility for the other. It is provoked as my "responsibility against my will, that is, by substituting me for the other as a hostage. All my inwardness is invested in the form of a despite-me, for-another. Despite me for-another is signification par excellence."[21]

In the place of Heidegger's *dasein* (a neologism meaning 'being-there') Levinas introduces his own *il y a* (an ordinary French phrase meaning 'there is') which may be understood as a presence that lurks even in the midst of an eternal absence.[22] If *il y a* in this sense is linked to the existential, it is even more a dialogical notion, for it is the non-existent site of the self's ineluctable contact with the Other. This is how *il y a* is seen as 'existence without existents.' A state of consciousness possessed by the existents (e.g. the human beings) is possible only by being violently torn away from or by repressing the *there is*.

Il y a is the 'otherwise than being' that pervades and penetrates nothingness. It is the impersonal, anonymous presence that murmurs in the depth of nothingness. *Il y a* is described as "an anonymous current of being (that) invades, submerges every subject, person or thing."[23] It cannot be defined as this or that (thing or attribute). Levinas defines it as the presence that takes the place of a universal absence, an absolutely unavoidable presence. It is the negation of all content, and at the same time, not a present content. "As a presence of absence, the *there is* is beyond contradiction."[24]

The night with its obscurity and silence appears as a possible site of *il y a*. It is in the nocturnal space that one may be exposed to the invisible force of the *il y a*. This is what accounts for in us the 'horror of darkness.' "The rustling of the *there is* is horror."[25] The spectres, ghosts, and sorceresses that frequently appear in Shakespeare, says Levinas, "allows him to move constantly towards the limit between being and nothingness, where being insinuates itself even in nothingness."[26]

A glance at the culmination of a subject's temporal

existence, or death, Levinas notes, allows us to have an awareness of this anonymous and impersonal *il y a.* Death comes as the termination of a subject's virility. Death is a reminder of the subject's essential passivity. In death, the subject loses its mastery as a subject: "we are no longer able to be able."[27] The reality of one's own death is entirely beyond the subject's cognitive horizon. One's own death is beyond representation. We cannot assume as ours the event of our death. It is an event that happens to us without our having any prior knowledge of it.

For Levinas, meaning is closely aligned with his central existential notion of the *il y a.* Meaning from this perspective, eludes both the *a priori* and the *a posteriori.* Meaning comes from the outside of the self and of the world. Like *il y a,* it is something that subsists out there as an anonymous presence in the absence, in the potential space of the subject's (ethical) orientation to the other. Furthermore, it is meaning that makes experience possible at all. Meaning is something that comes to the subject from (the site of) an existentially anonymous realm, and not something that the subject produces on its own.

Meaning, therefore, exists before perception. This meaning, or *sense,* is defined in terms of an orientation towards the other. Drawing upon one of the meanings of its French word *'sens,'* Levinas takes the term 'sense' to mean being oriented (directed) towards the other. He prefers to locate 'sense' outside of philosophy. "Does not sense as orientation indicate a leap, an outside-of-oneself toward the other than oneself, whereas philosophy means to reabsorb every other and neutralize alterity?"[28] Sense is orientation, direction, and hence the passage towards the Other. In the cultural world, there is the self's orientation which is a passing from the self towards its outside, toward the Other, which never cease to be other, and therefore absolutely other. This kind of orientation that goes freely from the same to the other, Levinas calls a 'work'. The work involves a 'radical generosity' as well as the 'ingratitude of the other'. It also involves the passage of the same towards the other, which is the master of one's work, and which never returns to the self.

A work is something that is eternally going outside of me; it is the being-for-beyond-my-death. For the public expression of a work, for the signification of the work, and for the celebration of the work, an orientation to the other is a prerequisite. Work is without any remuneration; it is given to the other totally gratuitously. Work is a product of an infinite desire for the other, a desire that cannot be totalized as in the framework of need-satisfaction. Self's expression is devoted to the other even before it is culturalized in any form. In such a dialogical perspective, the other is the 'sense' (direction and meaning) of the self's expression. Levinas notes: "[The other] is neither a cultural signification nor a simple given. He is sense primordially, for he gives sense to expression itself, for it is only by him that a phenomenon as a meaning is, to itself, introduced into being."[29]

The other is primarily manifested in the 'nudity' of his / her face. The self's consciousness withdraws into a state of passivity, and "is called into question by a face." And this calling into question of one's own self, and the passivity in relation to the other's face is a mode of welcoming the absolutely other. In this welcoming, the 'I' goes beyond itself towards the other, in the manner of a passing for which there is no return. This 'unassimilable surplus' of the self, which goes beyond itself in welcoming the other, is also a passage towards the infinity, which links the self and the other. Thus Levinas locates the idea of infinity in the desire for the other. In his own cryptic description: "The idea of infinity is a desire."[30]

The 'disturbing' and fascinating presence of the face of the other, makes it impossible to consider the signifyingness as a mere structural property. The trace of the face, the naked face of the other, comes as an 'irremissible disturbance' from an 'utterly bygone past.' The trace is thus actually not a trace of any real entity, but it is the signifyingness for the self of the face of the other situated on the 'hither side of time.' The time of this self-other dialogicality is not a time of an eternal beyond, but a time that is anterior to and outside of being's existence. "The beyond from which a face comes signifies as a trace."[31] The transcendence of the desire for the other, suggested by

Levinas's notion of signifyingness, would be neutralized in a linear sort of semiotic relationship between a *signifier* and a *signified*. Signifyingness can only belong to a personal 'order' (and not to a structural one) which is 'obliged' by a face, resulting in the trace of the 'beyond being.' This trace of other, which comes from a past that precedes the historical time, "takes on the profile of an '*il*' (he/it)."[32] This 'third person' is a sort of marker of the dialogical existence that comes from the beyond of time that precedes the existents.

We have noted that for Levinas, one's own death is to be understood as *not being able to be able*, the impossibility of possibility. Again unlike Heidegger, one is affected not so much by the dread of the nothingness that lies beyond one's death. But rather one, is haunted by the specter or the '*il y a*' that precedes one. It is in this sense that one assumes responsibility for the death of the other person, one's neighbour. Rather than derive power from the experience of the death of the other for whose death one must consider oneself responsible and whom one might have sacrificed, one can only assume the culpability for his death. The self is indebted to the next person or neighbour who dies. In memory of the victims of the holocaust, in the wake of its trauma, Paul Celan had written: "The world is gone; I must carry you." Since for Levinas, "death is the *no-response*" from the other, the self must remain in relation with the other. "My being affected by the death of the other is ... my relation with his death. It is, in my relation, my deference to someone who no longer responds, already a culpability – the culpability of the survivor."[33] This is what makes the time that remains after the death of the other a different time for me and for my community. Each such instance or instant is a rupture of the historical time in which I live, and therefore the occasion of a renewed diachrony. Death does not empower the self, but transforms the time to come through the passivity of the (culpable) survivor's response!

NOTES

1. Husserl, E., 1958, 108-09; trans. from the French by the present author; italics in the original retained.

2. Ibid., p. 109.
3. Heidegger, M., 1962, p. 284.
4. Ibid., pp. 344-45.
5. Ibid., p. 347.
6. Levinas, E., 1961, pp. 24-5.
7. Ibid., p. 25.
8. Ibid., p. 25.
9. Ibid., p. 290.
10. This discussion on the Levinas-Buber relationship is drawn from Chapter 3 of my book *Literature and Infinity* (2001).
11. Buber, 1958, p. 28.
12. Levinas, 1989, p. 59, See, Seán Hand's introduction to Levinas's essay "Martin Buber and the Theory of Knowledge."
13. Ibid., p. 72.
14. Ibid., p. 72.
15. Cohen, 1986, p. 21, See, "Dialogue with Emmanuel Levinas."
16. Ibid., p. 28.
17. Ibid., p. 29.
18. Ibid., p. 29.
19. Levinas, E., 1992, pp. 5-6.
20. Ibid., p. 6.
21. Ibid., p. 11.
22. The ensuing discussion of 'il y a' is drawn for Chapter 6 of *Literature and Infinity* (Manjali, 2001).
23. In: Levinas, There is: Existence without Existents, 1989, p. 30.
24. Ibid., p. 35.
25. Ibid., p. 32.
26. Ibid., p. 33.
27. In: Levinas, "Time and the Other," Ibid., p. 42.
28. Levinas, 1987, p. 90. In "Meaning and Sense." Levinas's critique of the self-centred Greek philosophy is evident in the following statement: "Philosophy's itinerary remains that of Ulysses whose adventure in the world was only a return to his native island—a complacency in the Same, an unrecognition of the other." (Ibid., p. 91).
29. Ibid., p. 95.
30. Ibid., p. 98.
31. Ibid., p. 103.
32. Ibid., p. 104.
33. Levinas, 2000, p. 12.

3

On Language and the Assumed Unity of the Human Sciences

In this essay I shall be dealing primarily with Lévi-Strauss's treatment of language and linguistics, especially in relation to his project of instituting and developing the 'sciences of man.' Considering the title of the Seminar, at least a part of my contribution is likely to be personal and anecdotal. I hope the readers will bear with me if, there are any excesses on my part in this respect. While paying my homage to Professor Lévi-Strauss on the occasion of his hundredth birthday celebrated in November 2008, I refer to certain significant events in my own intellectual life and acknowledge a few individuals with whom I have in some ways formed a sort of invisible kinship in relation to the famous anthropologist. The latter set in fact, consists, not of anthropologists, but of Professors deeply involved in problems of language and linguistics. They are: my colleague and one of the participants here, Harjeet Singh Gill, Professor Emeritus at Jawaharlal Nehru University; Bernard Pottier, my professor at University of Paris-4 (Sorbonne) during 1987-89, and currently a Member-Secretary at the Institut de France, and therefore a working colleague of Lévi-Strauss till the latter's death in 2009; and Jean-Petitot, a mathematician and philosopher at École des Hautes Etudes en Sciences Sociales, Paris, who is an unrelenting admirer and follower of the naturalistic and mathematicizing project of Lévi-Straussian human sciences.

My own interest in anthropology goes back to 1973 when still a student of the natural sciences in Calicut, I bought for myself a paperback volume of Margaret Mead's *Anthropology —A Human Science*. (It is perhaps worth mentioning here that Lévi-Strauss was never entirely convinced by the work of this American anthropologist.) On reading the book, I remember being fascinated by the field, especially by a chapter called "Warfare: An Invention—Not a Biological Necessity.'[1] I cited a passage from this chapter in an article—my first ever—entitled 'Down with Wars' in a publication that appeared the following year. I shall re-cite it here:

> "...there are peoples even today who have no warfare. Of these the Eskimos are perhaps the most conspicuous example, but the Lepchas of Sikkim are an equally good one. Neither of these peoples understand war, not even the defensive warfare. The idea of warfare is lacking, and this idea is as essential to carrying on war as an alphabet or a syllabary to writing.[2]

Along with my incessant longing for a world free of wars, and my silent admiration for the two warless peoples of the world, what began then as a fleeting fascination for anthropology—perhaps my first academic romance—continued for a long time since my fortuitous first encounter with Mead's book. A few years later in Delhi, I borrowed a copy of Lévi-Strauss's *Structural Anthropology* from Dr Abhilasha Kumari, a sociologist from Jawaharlal Nehru University (JNU). When I went to return the book to her a couple of years later, Abhilasha was indeed so kind as to convert this loan into a gift. Although, I had read this book only in bits and pieces, I have always guarded it as a valuable treasure. Apart from its academic value, my current possession of the book pleases me for somewhat different reasons. The book was bought (possibly by Abhilasha herself, for her name is inscribed in red ball-point ink on the first page) from a second-hand bookshop called 'Hobby Corner' at 41 Hazrat Gunj, in Lucknow. The last page of the book prominently bears the black seal of the Hobby Corner, and on the inner front cover there is the name of its possible first owner and the date of purchase, written in black ink of a fountain-pen: 'Wm Heavey, December 1967, Amherst.' As you can see, one is delighted at this fund of sociological information of other places, times and people, which can invoke the imagination and interest of a bibliophile, or perhaps vice versa.

By the time I bought Vol. 2 of Lévi-Strauss's *Structural Anthropology* in October 1981 (my copy bears this date), I had already developed a somewhat active interest in cultural anthropology by way of an optional course called 'Culture, Society and Personality,' that I did as an MA student at the Centre for the Study of Social Systems at JNU. This course certainly opened my eyes to the significance and the possibility of applying linguistics—a field in which I did my master's and doctoral degrees without ever being fully convinced of its dominant formalist enterprise—in the social sciences. This was a great relief, because it meant that even after having espoused the so-called scientific discipline of linguistics, one could continue one's first, albeit fleeting, relationship with anthropology. I was even more delighted to read at some point, Lévi-Strauss's forceful endorsement of and emphasis on the use of linguistic ideas and methods in anthropology. Thanks to Lévi-Strauss, and following a trajectory contrary to his, I was readily convinced that if linguistics had any use at all, it was in its application in the social sciences, especially anthropology. Having been a student of the natural sciences at the Bachelor's level, desiring to traverse the scientific ambitions of linguistics, and still seeking to avert a wholesale intellectual disenchantment, the following words of Lévi-Strauss provided me if not with so much elation, then at least with a glimmer of hope of being able to move and explore outside one's own 'discipline':

> Structural linguistics will certainly play the same renovating role with respect to the social sciences that nuclear physics, for example, has played for the physical sciences.[3]

I must note here that although the fact this prediction has been subsequently belied, it did not prevent me from titling my first book, with a certain Lévi-Straussian tenor as *Nuclear Semantics —Towards a Theory of Relational Meaning*.[4] I must also note here that at the beginning of the chapter that contains the above citation, Lévi-Strauss expresses his overwhelming enthusiasm for the field of my specialization:

> Linguistics occupies a special place among the social sciences, to whose ranks it unquestionably belongs. It is not merely a social science like the others, but rather, the one in which by far the greatest progress has been made. It is probably the one which can truly claim to be a science and which has achieved both the formulation of an empirical method and an understanding of the nature of the data submitted to its analysis.[5]

Ever since I read these lines in the early 1980s, I have paid sustained and serious attention to these ultimately not-so-prophetic words of Lévi-Strauss concerning the relevance of structural linguistics (and later, its near-antagonistic counterpart, post-structuralism) in the social sciences as well as in cultural and literary studies. This orientation of mine became even more pronounced after Professor H.S. Gill joined JNU in late 1984. A lot of what I have done in my own academic career—even when it was sometimes against his convictions—owes itself to the fortunate relationship I could develop with Professor Gill, first as an informal student and later as a colleague and friend whose views I respected, in the Centre for Linguistics and English at Jawaharlal Nehru University.

Thanks to Gill, the world of structuralism and semiotics on the one hand, and to a lesser extent Sartrean existentialism on the other, opened up before my eyes. Soon, apart from Lévi-Strauss, the other French philosophers or 'theoreticians'—I use this Anglo-Saxon academic term with a certain amusement today—Lacan, Althusser, Barthes, Sartre, Merleau-Ponty, Greimas, Todorov and Kristeva became household names. (By this time, however, the names of the post-structuralist philosophers, Foucault and Derrida, had begun to appear on our intellectual horizon through separate student networks.) The question of existence and signification and their mutual relationship began to pervade every field that one exposed oneself to. In the process, the Anglo-American field of a (mere) formalized Semantics which one studied as part of the Linguistics programme, and around which I wrote a doctoral thesis, began to recede into the background and the French field of Semiotics and related domains emerged in its place.

With hindsight, I can now say that what whetted my appetite during this period was Lévi-Strauss's insistence that social facts are representations, and his invention of the 'human sciences' where anthropology would have a central role, and whose methodological systematization and deepening would require linguistics and semiotics. We know that the Swiss-French linguist Ferdinand de Saussure had proposed semiology as an overarching discipline that studies the 'life of signs in society' based on the core principles of linguistics. We also know that for Lévi-Strauss, there were in fact two different moments when structural linguistics was sought to be made the methodological foundation of anthropology in the creation of the human sciences. The *first* of these involved incorporating into anthropology the theory of 'distinctive features' in phonology initially propounded by the Russian linguists Nikolai Trubetzkoy and Roman Jakobson working under the rubric of the Prague Linguistic Circle, and which Lévi-Strauss had learned from the latter during his sojourn in New York during the 1940s. Though the attractive analogy between phonology and 'nuclear physics' must have been exaggerated, what mattered was the idea that the lowest analytical elements of the two domains, the atom and the phoneme, can be further broken down into subatomic particles or subphonemeic binary features ("pairs of oppositions") respectively. What was important for Lévi-Strauss, however, is that the atom or the phoneme forms part of 'systems', physical in the first, and 'unconscious' mental in the second. By way of extension of this idea, the 'atoms or kinship' form 'unconscious' systems of society:

> Like phonemes, kinship terms are elements of meaning; like phonemes, they acquire meaning only if they are integrated into systems. 'Kinship systems,' like 'phonemic systems,' are built by the mind on the level of the unconscious thought.[6]

Lévi-Strauss's three-fold fascination for structural linguistics is clearly expressed in the above sentence: the shift from a study of conscious phenomena to that of their *unconscious* substructure; the shift from terms to *relations*; and the emphasis on *system*.[7]

The *second* moment, almost simultaneously with the first, was his definition of 'social anthropology' in terms of its equivalence with Saussure's 'Semiology.' The basis of this equivalence is Lévi-Strauss observation that "(f)or anthropology, which is a conversation of man with man, all things are symbol and sign which act as intermediaries between two subjects,"[8] Saussure on his part had viewed language as a 'social institution' which is based in the collective psyche of a society. In his conception of an ordered chain of the human sciences, Linguistics, or the science of language, is a part, albeit the defining one, of semiology, the 'science that studies life of signs in society,' which in turn is a part of 'social psychology,' itself a branch of psychology.

Thus, in his *leçon inaugurale* at Collège de France in January 1960, Lévi-Strauss forcefully announced the affinity and even the equivalence between 'social anthropology' and 'semiology.' Posing himself the question, "What, then, is social anthropology?" he answers:

> Although he did not specifically name it, Ferdinand de Saussure came very close to defining it when he introduced linguistics as part of a science yet to be born, for which he reserved the name "semiology." Its object of study he saw to be the life of signs at the heart of social life. Did he not, furthermore foresee our adherence when he compared language to 'writing, to alphabet of deaf-mutes, to symbolic rites, to forms of politeness, to military signals, etc.? No one would deny that anthropology includes in its own field at least some of these systems of signs, to which it adds many others, such as mythical language, the oral and gestural signs of which ritual is composed, marriage rules, kinship systems, customary laws, and certain forms of economic exchange.[9]

It is worth noting here that it was on the basis of Lévi-Strauss's work and his pronouncements that structuralism and *semiologie* (more popularly 'semiotics', based on an Anglo-American conception of the field) rose to a position of prominence in the French intellectual context in the 1950s and the first half of the 60s.[10] We can find elements of structuralism and semiotics in the works of some of the major French thinkers of the period:

Maurice Merleau-Ponty, Jacques Lacan, Fernand Braudel, Louis Althusser, and particularly Roland Barthes who went on to publish a book called *Eléménts de la Sémiologie* in 1964, and was later appointed as the Professor of Semiology in College de France in 1977. We can also see that Lévi-Strauss was the main inspiration behind Professor Gill's founding a department of Anthropological Linguistics at the University of Patiala, in the Punjab, and later leading a research programme in Semiotics at JNU from 1984 to 2001, the year of his retirement.[11] It is also clearly a Lévi-Straussian inspiration that prompted the present author to introduce an M.Phil. course called *Linguistics and Human Sciences* as a part of JNU's Semiotics programme in 1992.

Lévi-Strauss's articulation of the relation between language and culture at three different levels has been of particular interest to me. The first of these is the relation between a particular language and the corresponding (particular) culture. The point here is that the knowledge of a language and that of a culture can be reciprocally productive. The second is the relation between language as such and culture as such. This has to do with the way in which cultures treat language and conversely how an awareness of culture is encompassed in languages. Lévi-Strauss is more inclined to favour a third level of relation which is 'the relation between linguistics as a scientific discipline and anthropology.'[12] In addition to the usual inclusive relations of either language being a product of culture, or an inclusive part of culture, Lévi-Strauss insists on language being a 'condition of culture.' Here again, it is not just the necessity of language for the acquisition of culture, that Lévi-Strauss was insisting on, but rather the analogical relation between a theoretically-identifiable material of language and the material of culture.

> ... from a ... theoretical point of view; language can be said to be the *condition of culture* because the material out of which language is built is of the same type as the material out of which the whole culture is built: *logical relations, oppositions, correlations,* and the like. Language, from this point of view, may appear as laying a kind of foundation for the more complex structures which correspond to the different aspects of culture.[13]

Through my own interest in a semiotics of narrative, the area of Lévi-Strauss's work that I followed more closely is his structuralist analysis of myths and folktales. In 1958, Lévi-Strauss wrote an influential review of the Russian folklorist Vladimir Propp's work from a strictly structuralist perspective, criticizing the latter's formalist paradigm.[14] In proposing his own method of analysing myths and tales, he highlighted the semantic and contextual aspects which were mostly to be identified in the specific use of the vocabulary.

Here too, as in his analysis of kinship, Lévi Strauss has pointed out the usefulness of the Prague school theory of distinctive features based on the principle of binary oppositions. Further, Lévi-Strauss argues that instead of describing the structure of the folktale, Propp had reduced it to its bare formal framework. Structure, in his view, cannot be divorced from content: "Structure has no distinct content; it is content itself, apprehended in a logical organization as a property of the real."[15]

Propp's tendency to view 'functions' alone as relevant (on the basis of their being constants) and the terms that support this function as arbitrary, is severely criticized. For Lévi-Strauss, it is the vocabulary that conveys specific structural content, both in relation to historical and ethnographic information, and in terms of the relevant oppositions that are significant within the context of a given folktale. For formalism, Lévi-Strauss concludes, "form alone is intelligible, and content is only a residual, deprived of any significant value." While for structuralism,... "there is not something abstract on one side and concrete on the other. Form and content are of the same nature, susceptible to the same analysis. Content draws its reality from its structure and what is called form is the 'structural formation' of the local structure forming the content."[16]

The terms that are part of a function cannot be considered 'variable', because they do have a value in the context where the tale occurs. The terms for the characters may have universal validity, but often they are relative to the social context. For example, a plum tree and an apple tree have different values, since the former is recognized for its `fecundity' while the latter is known for the `strength and depth of its roots.' As a consequence, instead of viewing the characters' performing a function as arbitrary, they have to be seen in their specific value defined positively (e.g. 'fecundity' in the former) or negatively (e.g. 'earth sky transition' in the latter). Plus, in this case both have the 'vegetal' feature in common. Thus, Lévi-Strauss notes, "a universe of the tale will be progressively defined, analysable in pairs of oppositions, diversely combined within each character—which far from constituting a single entity—is a bundle of differential elements, in the manner of the phoneme as conceived by Roman Jakobson."[17] Lévi-Strauss employs in his analysis a set of binary opposites like nature vs. culture, life vs. death, endogamy vs. exogamy, male vs. female, high vs. low, earth vs. sky, day vs. night, animal vs. vegetal, etc.

Following the same principle of 'differential oppositions' or distinctive features, Lévi-Strauss suggests a systematic reduction in the number of Propp's 31 functions. For instance, the functions of 'violation', 'prohibition' and 'injunction' can all be grouped together as one or the other transformation of the same function. Accordingly, 'violation' would be the reverse of 'prohibition' and the latter a negative transformation of the 'injunction'. Similarly, 'departure' of the hero and his 'return' could be considered as the same function of disjunction, positively or negatively defined. The `search' by the hero would be the converse of his 'pursuit,' etc.[18]

Evidently, Lévi-Strauss finds it hard to accept Propp's conception of a grammar of the narrative which does not pay any attention to the specific use of vocabulary and their contextual significations. Even when drawing from a universal set of binary semantic features, the words possess culturally-rooted connotations which it is the job of an ethnographer to identify. It is this 'second power' of words (i.e. functioning as metaphors/metonyms) employed in the narrative that reveal the structural content of the myths and tales.

Following Lévi-Strauss, Greimas in his *Structural Semantics*[19] attempted a grand formalization of the narrative content. Here the latter adopted Lévi-Strauss's idea that the narrative 'functions' can be understood as transformations one of the other, on the basis of which Greimas introduced the concept of the 'semiotic square' which while being a development of the concept of binary oppositions, is introduced to reveal the more complex articulations of a semic category in terms of relations of contrariness, contradiction and implication. Semiotic square is defined as the "visual representation of the logical articulation of any category"[20].

It is indeed a mathematicizable structural logic of language that Lévi-Strauss lays his whole faith in. If, in spite of a range of common interests and concerns shared between linguistics and anthropology, the former has theoretically overtaken the latter, it is because, Lévi-Strauss believes, linguistics has more rapidly adopted the methods of the natural sciences. He exhorts himself and fellow anthropologists 'to learn from the linguists' and to be able to use the latter's 'rigorous' and by far more 'successful' approach. Curiously, the linguists and the anthropologists have sought each other for contradictory reasons. They have even gone after each other in an 'unhappy merry-go-around,' the linguists trying to acquire from anthropology the feature of concreteness for their observation and data, and the anthropologists seeking to systematize the abundance of their concrete data. In Lévi-Strauss's figurative formulation, linguistics has provided the tiny door for approaching the paradise of the natural and exact sciences which scholars in the social and human sciences had thought they can never enter.[21]

It is not difficult to recognize that Lévi-Strauss, a contemporary of some of the most well-known French thinkers of the 20th century, namely, Sartre, Levinas, Blanchot, de Beauvoir and Merleau-Monty (all five of them were born between 1905 and 1908, and are now deceased) was the principal figure behind the formation of a distinctly French field of the *sciences de l'homme*, whose founder, according to Lévi-Strauss, was none other than the 18th century social philosopher, Jean-Jacques Rousseau. Like Rousseau, Lévi-Strauss, dreamt of making the empirical 'man', the anthropological 'man', the centre of philosophy. It was from

Rousseau, he says he learnt the one and 'only' principle on which to base the sciences of man: "To attain acceptance of oneself in others (the goal assigned to human knowledge by the ethnologist), one must first deny the self in oneself."[22] According to Lévi-Strauss, it is neither abstract knowledge nor a Cartesian self-doubt, but an ethnographic exposure to the other in the process of which one may renounce one's own self-knowledge, and deny all other cherished knowledge and ideals, is what constitutes the philosophical attitude of an anthropologist. In this sense, the anthropologist is a 'spontaneous' philosopher.

Despite this dalliance with philosophy as such, linguistics, with its simultaneous treatment of form and meaning and its emphasis on unconscious structure, has remained for Lévi-Strauss, his principal orientation. Elements of kinship and other aspects and artifacts of culture can be expressed as relations, and they have a *meaning* for human beings. Therefore, they can be treated as *signs*—even 'a stone axe can be a sign'—which for the specific system can be on par with the sign system of language. The nature of these relations and the system of their meanings are not evident to the members of the society, because they exist only at an *unconscious* plane of the human mind, but they can be studied by the anthropologist by means of his rigorous methods. What the structural analysis reveals are the universal structures of the unconscious human mind, which manifests differently in specific customs, practices and discourses, but which are related to each other in terms of rules of permutation, combination and other transformations. On the basis of a belief in such unconscious universal structures, Lévi-Strauss is keen to annul the dichotomy between the savage and the civilized man as well as between synchrony and diachrony. Lévi-Strauss: "In anthropology as in linguistics, ...the synchronic can be as unconscious as the diachronic. In this sense ... the divergence between the two is reduced."[23] Further, the structures that encompass both history and society, that is, the structures of the human sciences, would be, from Lévi-Strauss's point of view part of more general naturalistic structures. All phenomena and all structures can thus be naturalized and understood in terms of mutual transformations within a single form. In order to express this ultimate dream of the mathematician, Lévi-Strauss refers us to Goethe:

> All forms are similar, and none is like the others.
> So that their chorus points the way to a hidden law.[24]

As for me, I had sought, from my early undergraduate days, following a contrary trajectory, to escape from the natural sciences into some sort of a philosophical paradise through the tiny door that anthropology seemed to offer me. Since then I have never been keen to return to any field of natural sciences, despite several intimations of it. And ever since I familiarized myself with the intellectual currents that constitute post-structuralism and postmodernism during my stay as a Fellow at the Indian Institute of Advanced Study in Shimla during the late 1990s, I have turned away from Lévi-Straussian anthropology. During this period and later, I have been particularly influenced by a critique of the 'human sciences', based at least in part on a Nietzschean perspective coming from Foucault and Derrida. Although it is not strictly within the purview of the topic of our seminar, I shall submit this critique to a brief discussion.

As early as his *léçon inaugurale* of 1960, Lévi-Strauss was aware of some of the criticisms that were being addressed against the social anthropologist, and he chose to refute them. He refutes the charge of anthropology being an offshoot of colonialism, by stating that it is through the latter that the former has been able to develop a pan-human dimension, that is, "to extend humanism to the measure of humanity."[25] But, as the critics of anthropology have insisted, the problem is essentially this: how can man be both the subject and object of a science? The task of Foucault's *Les mots et les choses—Une Archéologie des Sciences Humaines* is to study the historical emergence of man in his double capacity of a subject and an object of the human sciences. Unlike Lévi-Strauss, Foucault does not believe that the human sciences came into existence as part of a historical continuity of human reason when the latter included man as an object of enquiry. But rather, according to Foucault, human sciences "appeared when man constituted himself in Western culture as both that which must be conceived of and that which must be known." In other words, human sciences emerged as a specific discursive formation with its own objects and rules of analysis. According to Foucault's archaeological analysis, "man is only a recent invention, a figure not yet two centuries old, a new wrinkle in our knowledge, and ... will disappear again as soon as that knowledge has discovered a new form."[26] As for ethnology, Foucault, expressing his misgivings in tune with other post-structuralists (and post-colonialists) observes that it is a field that "can assume its proper dimensions only within the historical sovereignty—always restrained, but always present —of European thought and the relation that can bring it face to face with all other cultures as well as with itself."[27]

Derrida's initial critique of Lévi-Strauss, more direct than that of Foucault, is in the form of a conference paper presented in 1966 at Baltimore in the United States. It is centrally concerned with the problem of structure.[28] The problem of structure is in fact the problem of its centre, or rather, the centring authority. Lévi-Strauss's insistence on naturalistic human sciences, Derrida attempts to show, is based on his adherence to a binary opposition—fundamental in Western culture—between nature and culture, even when it is faced with the 'scandal' concerning incest prohibition which can be deemed as both natural and cultural. Even when Lévi-Strauss exalts the natural 'innocence' of the primitive peoples, he is well-entrenched within the dominant philosophies of the West and its languages which centrally bear the foundational opposition between nature and culture. His decision to favour primitive 'nature' against western 'culture,' *à la* Rousseau, itself proceeds from a determination to arrest the 'play' inherent (and evident, even for Lévi-Strauss!) in any structure, and thus impose on the observational field of ethnology the power of Western science. In a key paragraph in his "Structure, Sign and Play in the Discourse of the Human Sciences," Derrida rejects Lévi-Strauss's plea that structural 'totalization' of the ethnographic domain turns out to be impossible (in spite of the anthropologist's best intentions and efforts) because of the vastness and the unending nature of the ethnographic field and data. He argues instead that this impossibility is because

> ... the nature of the field, that is language, a finite language, excludes totalization. This field is in effect that of *play*, that is to say a field of infinite substitutions only because it is finite, that is to say, because instead of being an inexhaustive field, as in classical hypothesis, instead of being too large, there is something missing from it, namely, a centre which arrests and grounds the play of substitutions.... this movement of play, permitted by the lack or absence of a centre or origin, is the movement of *supplementarity*. One cannot determine the centre and exhaust totalization because the sign which replaces the centre, which supplements it, taking the centre's place in its absence—this sign is added, occurs as a surplus, as a *supplement*.[29]

Thus, in the context of our awareness of the absent origin or absent centre, there can be two contrary versions of interpretations—ethnographic or linguistic—according to Derrida. One is Rousseauistic: 'sad, *negative*, nostalgic, guilty;' the other is Nietzschean, characterized by "*affirmation*, that is the joyous affirmation of the play of the world and of the innocence of becoming, the affirmation of a world of signs without fault, without truth, and without origin which is offered to an active interpretation."[30]

I conclude this essay by dedicating it to the endeavours—intellectual and institutional—that have contributed to the formation, if not of unified human sciences, then of a proliferating field humanities, whose absence, I feel, is acutely felt today in the Indian academic context.

NOTES

1. This was a journal paper, originally published in 1940.
2. Mead, M., 1964, p. 127.
3. Lévi-Strauss, C., 1967, p. 31.
4. Manjali, Franson, 1991. This book is largely based on my post-doctoral work in Paris from 1987 to 1989 in association with Bernard Pottier and Jean Petitot.
5. Lévi-Strauss, C., op. cit., p. 28.

6. Ibid., p. 32. Lévi-Strauss clarifies this analogy further: "We know that to obtain a structural law the linguist analyses phonemes into 'distinctive features,' which he can then group into one or several 'pairs of oppositions.' Following an analogous method, the anthropologist might be tempted to break down analytically the kinship terms of any given system into components.... the term father has positive connotations with respect to sex, relative age, and generation; but it has a zero value on the dimension of collaterality, and it cannot express an affinal relationship." (Ibid., p. 33)
7. Ibid., p. 31.
8. Lévi-Strauss, C., 1973, p. 11.
9. Lévi-Strauss, C., Ibid., p. 9. The inset quotation is from F. de Saussure, *Course in General Linguistics*, 1969, p. 16.
10. Structuralism had become outmoded in France by the time of the May 1968 movement.
11. We note here that this rich and fertile academic programme was abandoned at Jawaharlal Nehru University a few years after Gill's retirement. The shift of interest towards post-structuralism notwithstanding, this is indeed a sad commentary on the Indian academic management.
12. Lévi-Strauss, C., 1973, op. cit., p. 67.
13. Ibid., p. 67.
14. Lévi-Strauss, C., "Structure and Form: Reflections on a Work of Vladimir Propp." Chapter VIII of *Structural Anthropology* 2, op. cit., pp. 115-45. The reference work is Vladimir Propp's *Morphology of the Folktale*.
15. Ibid., p. 115.
16. Ibid., p. 131.
17. Ibid., p. 135.
18. Ibid., p. 137.
19. Greimas, A.-J., 1983.
20. Greimas, A.-J. and J. Courtés, 1979. p. 29
21. Ibid., pp. 68-9.
22. Lévi-Strauss, C., "Jean-Jacques Rousseau, Founder of the Sciences of Man," in *Structural Anthropology* 2, op. cit., p. 36.
23. Lévi-Strauss, C., "The Scope of Anthropology," Ibid., p. 17.
24. Quoted in Lévi-Strauss, C., ibid., p. 18. The suggestion of a Goethean foundation of a naturalistic (topologico-dynamic) structuralism receives an elaborate treatment in a recent work by Jean Petitot, *Morphologie et Esthétique*, 2004. Lévi-Strauss's own naturalist inclinations is said to have originated in his childhood

fascination for geology. "I count among my most precious memories ... a hike along the flank of a limestone plateau in Languedoc to determine the lien of contact between two geological strata." (Lévi-Strauss, C., 'The Making of an Anthropologist,' 1978, p. 68.)

25. Lévi-Strauss, C., 1973, op. cit., p. 32.
26. Foucault, M., 1970. pp. 344-45.
27. Ibid., p. 377.
28. Derrida, J., 1978. "Structure, Sign and Play in the Discourse of the Human Sciences," in *Writing and Difference*, pp. 278-93. For another instance of his critique of Lévi-Strauss, see Part II, I, "The Violence of the Letter: From Lévi-Strauss to Rousseau;" in J. Derrida, *Of Grammatology* 1976, pp. 101-40.
29. Derrida, J., 1978, op. cit., p. 289.
30. Ibid., p. 292.

4

Between Pragmatics and Deconstruction: Wittgenstein, Bakhtin and Derrida

In this essay, I shall begin by referring to at least two of the philosophers of language of the last century, namely L. Wittgenstein and M. Bakhtin. Their works of relevance to us are: *Marxism and the Philosophy of Language,*[1] written under the name of his student, V.N. Voloshinov, and *The Dialogic Imagination*[2] which contains four long essays on language, literature and culture. As for Wittgenstein we shall primarily refer to his *Philosophical Investigations* (*PI*). In the later part of this paper, we shall refer extensively to the philosophical works of J. Derrida.

In *PI*, Wittgenstein introduces us to two or three important metaphors about language. These metaphors, essentially, bring home the point that what we call a 'language' is not static and homogeneous, but a forever-incomplete, evolving and multifaceted phenomenon that we put to different uses, or in the philosopher's words, it is associated with 'forms of life.' The first of these is the metaphor of the 'ancient city.' Language, constantly adds on (or even subtracts from it) domains of use, Wittgenstein notes, such as the 'symbolism of chemistry and the notation of infinitesimal calculus.' And these domains are, according to him, 'new suburbs of our language.' Therefore, he goes on to say:

> Our language can be seen as an ancient city: a maze of little streets and squares, of old and new houses, and of houses with additions from various periods; and this surrounded by a

> multitude of new boroughs with straight regular streets and uniform houses.[3]

According to Wittgenstein there can be different kinds of uses of language, or 'forms of life' such as the one consisting of 'orders and reports in a battle,' or another consisting of only questions and yes-no answers. We have only to think of yet other varieties of languages that coexist in our contemporary world: for example, the language of prayer and the language of slogans which in many contexts have actually tended to replace the former. It should not be difficult to figure out the similarities and differences between these two types or kinds of language-uses, identifiable in terms of the different addresser-addressee relationships. In both the cases we just mentioned, utterances used to indicate one's wishes, are made to a non-present addressee.

Wittgenstein describes these ever-growing types of sentences, as 'language games.' This, as we know, is his most well-known metaphor for language. As he puts it, there are

> ...countless different kinds of use of what we call "symbols", "words", "sentences". And this multiplicity is not something fixed, given once for all; but new types of language, new language-games, as we say, come into existence, and others become obsolete and get forgotten... Here the term "language-*game*" is meant to bring into prominence the fact that the *speaking* of language is part of an activity, or of a form of life.[4]

And moreover, these different uses of language or 'language-games' can be quite distinct, as distinct as a board-game like chess, or a field-game of football or even a video-game that one plays on a mobile or computer screen, for example. But however, just as all games have some features in common, like the members of a family, the language-games also can be recognized by their 'family resemblances.' That is to say, despite their heterogeneity, and their historically evolving character, the language-games bear degrees of organic resemblance to each other. So that the abbreviated language of the SMS on your mobile phone, even if quite distinct from the literary language, is still a form of life, a language-game, bearing a resemblance to the latter.

The later Wittgenstein's ideas on language, we reckon, have greatly contributed to the rejection of the conventional philosophical and theoretical notion of language as a fixed, closed, and static entity, possessing a unique structure and governed by a single set of rules. Within the 'family' of language-games each type of language-use will a have different set of rules, and hence we participate in these 'substructures' of language with different orientations and expectations. Similarly, his 'use' theory of meaning has delivered us from the belief that there is one meaning permanently hinged to one word or sentence. The statement 'Meaning of a word lies in its use,' is, as we know, Wittgenstein's famous motto. This means that the meaning of a word or sentence is not predetermined in the latter, but is the result or the product of the specific way it is put to use in a social or political context. This allows, evidently, a great degree of variability of use and meaning in language, even to the extent that a speaker and a hearer of a language-form does not have to have the same meaning. In other words, the meaning of what is spoken or written need not be what is heard or read. There can always be a non-equivalence or disparity of meaning with regard to the same linguistic elements, between two interlocutors. In post-semiotic terms this means that no signified is permanently hinged to a signifier. There would be a constant slippage or sliding of meaning under the sceptre-like stance of the signifier.

This uncertainty in/of language, the essential inconclusiveness of language, is expressed by Wittgenstein by means of yet another metaphor, that of the 'labyrinth.' "Language is a labyrinth of paths," he says. "You approach from one side and know your way about; you approach the same place from another side and no longer know your way about."[5]

Like Wittgenstein, the Russian philosopher of language, Bakhtin, even before the former, had brought language down from the pure realms of logic into the social milieu. Bakhtin like his contemporary and compatriot psychologist, Lev Vygotsky refused to see language as the secondary manifestation of a thought which the rationalists and logicists took to be primary. From a materialist and historicist point of view, these scholars, under the influence of Marxism, came to view thought (and therefore, meaning) as a consequence and a product of the use of language. Further, they wished to see the linguistic process that takes place between two or more individuals as prior to the cognitive process that takes place in (the mind of) a single individual. This is the essence of the dialogism proposed by Bakhtin. However, proceeding from a deep historical understanding of literature, Voloshinov-Bakhtin had a wider view of what a dialogue is. It is not only "direct, face-to-face vocalized communication between persons, but also linguistic communication of any type whatsoever." Linguistic activity that is embodied in the productive sentential syntactic structure is privileged by Bakhtin against the passive morphological or phonetic forms of language. Even for the founder of structural linguistics, Ferdinand de Saussure, the sentence, ultimately, belongs to *parole*, or the individual and concrete use of language, were as the infra-sentential units belong to the *langue*, or the mere passive structure. Concrete use of language is however not the purely individual and mechanical production of language, manifesting an internal and rational thought. Rather, it is an intersubjective, interlocutive and interactive phenomenon, or more exactly the linguistic response of one individual to the linguistic activity of another. It is essentially and foundationally dialogical. It is from such a perspective that Bakhtin affirms that "signs emerge... only in the process of interaction between one individual consciousness and another" and that "signs can arise only in an inter-individual territory." And moreover, this territory is, strictly speaking, "not natural," for, as Bakhtin sees it, "signs do not arise between any two members of the species *homo sapiens*. It is essential that the two individuals be *organized socially*, that they compose a social unit."[6]

We shall note here that in denying a 'natural' domain of existence for language Bakhtin is eschewing both the objectivist (i.e. positivist) and subjectivist (i.e. mentalist) ideas of language. Language, that is language-use in fact, can only be part of the 'cultural' domain and exist dialogically between individuals who are more or less, and in one manner or the other related. In this context, however, it is important to see, what exactly Bakhtin means by the dialogic. Dialogue, for him, is not the fusion or communication of two different logics held by two different individuals. Such a notion, in fact would fall under the rubric of a structural theory of information and communication, whose main purpose is to arrive at the reduction of 'noise' in communication. By dialogue, Bakhtin means the discourse of an individual that is affected or influenced by the discourse of another. There is an enchaining of discourses among individuals that form a cultural context, and Bakhtin would say, "only the current of verbal intercourse endows a word with the light of meaning." Culturally organized discourses or the utterances of individuals in society are interconnected, and meaning can only be the product of that interlinking. Rather than envisaging an individual speaking about a referential world in all its prelinguistic freshness, or uttering a sentence on the basis of the richness of a cognitive-rational content, Bakhtin argues that what he or she actually does is to talk about a certain given world from his or her own point of view, but with reference to or in terms of the language that he or she is already in the habit of using or given to use. What is suggested here is that language is inevitably self-referential, that is, one is always responding to the speech of the other that one encounters in one's own lived context. Thus, according to Bakthin, there is always this lively interaction between one's own speech and that of the other. (And correspondingly, we may add, between one's world and the world of the other through language.) This is what he calls the 'reported speech' which he defines as: "Speech within speech, utterance within utterance and, at the same time speech about speech and utterance about utterance." And since a word or utterance is produced by individuals who are culturally related in one way or the other, every word is a response to an earlier word, and thus "there is no such thing as a word without evaluative content." Thus the interaction between utterances, which constitutes 'dialogue' in Bakhtin's sense, is not of a merely mechanical kind, but rather it involves the human response of an evaluative or ethical kind. This evaluation of content is present in the syntactic structure of a sentence, but it may be noted more specifically in the 'tone' of one's response.

Bakhtin identifies the 'indirect discourse' as the formal-syntactic structure of such evaluations. The indirect discourse which refers to 'the analytical transmission of someone's utterance' may be either a matter of 'degree' of the authorial response to a direct utterance, or of 'direction.' According to Bakhtin,

> Indirect discourse "hears" a message differently; it actively receives and brings to bear in transmission different factors, different aspects of the message than do other patterns. That is what makes a mechanical, literal transposition of utterances from other patterns into indirect discourse impossible. It is possible only in instances in which the direct utterance itself was somewhat analytically constructed—insofar as direct discourse will tolerate such analysis. Analysis is the heart and soul of indirect discourse.[7]

An indirect discourse, can respond to the referential content of the first utterance, or it can refer to the speaker of that utterance. Thus, both the objective and subjective contents of an utterance are responded to in an indirect discourse. Thus, we can see that Bakhtin abandons the objectivist and the subjectivist orientations to language. Discourse is neither an individual's speaking about an objective or referential world nor is it the natural and spontaneous manifestation of his inner cognitive/emotional states. There is only utterance about utterance, language about language, and infinitely so. Language consists in only this material linguistic chaining, without there being any possibility of moving out of it completely and of comprehensively referring to a world outside, or of exhaustively expressing one's own thoughts or emotions. In their *A Thousand Plateaus*, G. Deleuze and F. Guattari evoke the same point, when they say that

> ...narrative consists not in communicating what one has seen but in transmitting what one has heard, what someone else has said to you. Hearsay.[8]

Derrida's work like that of Bakhtin, is also primarily based on his research on the language of literature. Early in his research career, Derrida encountered and opposed, in the philosophical field, two of the main established positions that prevailed in France during this period, namely phenomenology and structuralism. Taking a cue from Lacanian psychoanalysis, which accorded a privileged place for the 'letter' or the graphic signifier, Derrida went on to investigate how the idealization of language, in Husserlian phenomenology and Saussurean structuralism—which themselves were symptoms of what was always the case in Western philosophy—results in the nullification or effacing of the linguistic signifier, phonic or graphic. Through closely and incisively argued texts, Derrida demonstrated that the constant privileging of the spoken voice in Western metaphysics results from a concomitant privileging of ideal presence as a phenomenological reality. Though language makes use of phonic signifiers, it receives its signifying value only because of its repetitive use in an open-ended system of differential signifiers. A signifier exists not in terms of its assumed 'natural' relationship with a corresponding signified, but as the bearer of traces of other signifiers of the same system. Therefore it is impossible for a signified to exist as a self-present entity bearing a relationship in and for itself. Thus no such thing as a 'sign' really exits, but only *traces* of signifiers standing in relation to each other, all the way. These traces are not marks that exist within a word or sign-like entity, but are always on the exterior, an excess, present only in their exposition to other traces, and to others, and so on, infinitely. This is a very different way of understanding the nature of language. Discourses are no longer seen as possessing an interiority consisting of self-present signifieds originating from a speaking or writing source, but as events participating in an endless play of signifiers. Consequently, there isn't either a phenomenological intentionality that hinges permanently to the agent of a discourse. Any discourse, in Derrida's view can be detached from its supposed original intentionality, and grafted on to other or other's discourses infinitely, so that in spite of one's best intentions, "the letter can always go astray, or fail to arrive at its destination," he says retaining all the pun implied in the word, 'letter.' Just as Derrida substitutes a traditional term like 'sign' of semiology with terms like 'trace,' 'gram,' 'difference' and 'supplement,' he also chooses to emphasize the unconditional iterability of the linguistic signifiers, in the place of the more widely accepted notion of intentionality.

Simultaneously, Derrida is keen to point out the importance of 'signature,' something that is more often considered as a characteristic of the written language and which a speech-act philosopher like J.L. Austin views as equivalent to the originating intentional-source of speech. Contrary to the speech-act perspective, Derrida insists on the "repeatable, iterable, imitable form" of 'signature,' and the fact that it "must be able to be detached from the present and singular intention of its production."[9] Signature is not what remains permanently attached to the intentionality of the speaker or writer, but that which makes a mark in the given language, alters it from within it in terms of his or her specific contribution to or invention in that language. In this context, Derrida refers to the work of the German-Jewish poet-translator Paul Celan, the poet of the *Shoah,* who according to him "attempted a mark, a unique signature which was a counter-signature of the German language and at the same time something that *happens* to German language..."[10]

In nullifying the assumption regarding the self-presence of meaning and the centrality of intentionality, Derrida foregrounds writing as a defining mode of language as such, and serves to diminish the classical opposition between the so-called factual and fictional discourses. The unhinged character of writing with respect to meaning and intentionality is ascribable in the same way and applicable to the same degree to spoken language. And moreover, if self-presence of meaning is clearly not a necessary aspect of the functioning of language, fictional and the so-called true discourses, are only different ways of participating in the play of language. They are both equally susceptible to the play of both presence and absence, as far as their semantics is concerned. They can both be erected one beside the other, mutually affecting and transforming each other, fact, touching and displacing fiction, and contrarily, fiction having the same effect upon fact. Fiction brings forth linguistic signifiers from outside of fact, and fact has to constantly redeem itself of fiction from within it.

The position we have outlined above evidently has serious consequences for philosophy. It is, of course trivial, but yet useful to say that rather than work in the domain of a philosophy of language, Derrida is more concerned with the language of philosophy as such. As long as philosophy is expressed in statements of language, the latter cannot be immune to the forces and effects of language. Philosophy, can after all, be only a product or the result of our use of language. In other words, philosophy, or for that matter science, cannot claim for itself an essential or foundational meaning, but can only be the result of a play of differences that language itself introduces as part of its essential inter-subjective constitution. In order to have any value for what is supposed to be within philosophy, the latter has to constantly bring in alternative discourses from outside itself. It has to allow itself to participate in alternative discursive play, coming from alternative languages, literatures, disciplines, or from sources hitherto regarded as outside philosophy. Philosophy, or the love of wisdom that it etymologically is, has to constantly deconstruct itself in response to its other. It has to constantly listen to other tongues, for 'language' which has its etymology in the Latin word, *lingua* meaning 'tongue,' refers to the articulation of the tongue.

Regarding the relationship between philosophy and its outside, Wittgenstein expressed a similar sentiment, in his *Tractatus Logico-Philosophicus* (the early Wittgenstein) published in 1923. Towards the end of this book, Wittgenstein notes that though philosophical propositions describe the world, and 'are of equal value':

> The sense of the world must lie *outside* the world. In the world everything is as it is, and everything happens as it does happen: *in* it no value exists—and if it did exist, it would have no value.
>
> If there is any value that does have value, it must lie *outside*

> the whole sphere of what happens and is the case. For all that happens and is the case is accidental.
>
> What makes it non-accidental cannot lie *within* the world, since it would itself be accidental.
>
> It must lie *outside* the world.
>
> And so it is impossible for there to be propositions of ethics.
>
> Propositions can express nothing that is higher.
>
> It is clear that ethics cannot be put into word.
>
> Ethics is transcendental.
>
> (Ethics and aesthetics are one and the same.)[11]

We may say that this ethical and aesthetic overcoming of the given language, or sense-making that comes from the outside of the given world is also Derrida's main problem. Literature, because it is an 'institutionless institution,' or an institution that constantly overcomes, undermines or plays with its own limits, is a discursive activity, where it really takes place. Literature is not something that submits to any given law of literature, nor is it something that remains constrained within the given or known genres. For Derrida the term 'literariness' refers to the stretching of the boundaries of what is given as language, or crossing the limits of what is experienced as literature, as in the works of writers like, Joyce, Beckett, Kafka, Mallarmé, Blanchot, Jabbés, Ponge, Celan, etc. Through the ruptures or interruptions that literature introduces, it ceaselessly modifies what we understand as our literary experience.

The activity of translation too, like the fields of language, literature and philosophy that we have already referred, is a limit-phenomenon. It involves, the "double bind" of the necessity of translating as well as the impossibility of translation. This is because, in order to understand, every language has to be translated. But every language finally reduces itself to the specificity of a proper name, or to the confusion of multiple languages. Despite the desire to translate or to be translated, we discover that there is an untranslatable core in every language, or if you like, in every one of us, which is signified by our proper names, and at the same time, there is a plurality of different sublanguages that each language contains. Derrida refers to Jorge Luis Borge's story "Pierre Ménard, Author of the Quixote" and the Biblical story of the

Tower of Babel to illustrate this condition. In both, it is the multiplicity of languages within a singularity that does not render itself to translation. Derrida, in fact, considers the story of the Tower of Babel as some sort of an allegory of deconstruction: god curses the proud people of Shem, a people who are called by the name of name, by uttering his own name, Babel, which is also a common noun meaning 'confusion.' The Shems' dream of reaching God with their tower and making a name for themselves, is destroyed by the uttering of God's name as a curse, whose translation can only result in confusion and endless dissemination. "Translate me and what is more, don't translate me."[12] The double bind of (that is) deconstruction!

Derrida's views on translation maintain close contact with those of Walter Benjamin, presented in the latter's brilliant essay "The Task of the Translator."[13] Translation from this perspective involves neither a reproduction of one language in another nor a communication between two languages. Rather it involves the modification or the augmentation of both. Translation yields not so much the equivalent of one text with respect to another, or of one language in relation to another, but rather the 'supplement' or the 'survival' or the 'overlife' of both. According to Benjamin, though no translation succeeds completely, the event or the performance of translation leads to the possible "reconciliation" of languages. Such reconciliation is what gives us the "presentiment" of a "pure language." Pure language is not a language purified of all faults, but a language that is only promised and a language that stands outside all given representational systems, and of the totalizing schemas of all given languages.

Derrida introduces us to a similar kind of paradox and predicament, when he says in one his later works, "I only have one language; yet it is not mine."[14] His *Monolingualism of the Other* is a very personal essay on the question of language identity, appropriation and belonging. Here, Derrida is, in part, responding to a work by an Algerian writer Abdelkebir Khatibi, entitled *Dü bilinguisme* (On Bilingualism), where the author, among other things, is talking about the "irreparable suffering" that results from "effacing" and "broaching" of local identity associated with one's maternal dialect, when he or she is forced to express himself or herself in alien languages, especially a colonial language like French. Derrida counterposes this account with an account of the linguistic dispossession resulting from the abolition of French citizenship that had been earlier granted to the Sephardic Jewish community in Algeria. After the Nazi-backed French Government of Marshall Petain deprived the Algerian Jews of their French citizenship, they experienced a state of being in a linguistic limbo, with no language to possess, no language to belong to, and no language to mark their identity. Not Hebrew, the language of Jewish religion, not Yiddish, the language of the Ashkenazi Jews of Eastern Europe, neither of which they spoke, and not Arabic, nor Berber, the two more native languages of Algeria, with which they were not socially and politically associated.

A state of thus not having a 'mother tongue' or a 'first language' as a property or as a source of belonging, Derrida notes, is not really a special case applicable only to the Algerian Jews. It can be seen as a more general condition of all situations of relation between language and the self/community. A language cannot be a natural property of any one, just as language itself cannot be anything natural. Since language is never an individual property, and is something inevitably shared by a small or large group of individuals, it is always guided by implicit or explicit laws of interdiction and preservation: "You shall use only the language that is shared by all members of a community, and that in a manner acceptable by all. And correlatively, you shall not introduce as far as possible any foreign elements into your language, and you shall always protect your language from all foreign interference, as well as preserve it and promote its interests." But, where do these laws of linguistic interdiction and preservation come from? They come as part of a hegemonic politics that informs the more or less collective use of every language. The laws regarding what constitutes a language are culturally laid down—in spite of me, outside of me, prior to my entry in it, and for me. And this is moreover simultaneous with a language itself becoming the medium of law. And since the law of one's language comes from elsewhere, and can become the language of law that is imposed on me, one is able to declare: "I have only one language and it is not mine; my 'own' language is, for me, a language that cannot be assimilated. My language, the only one I hear myself speak and agree to speak, is the language of the other."[15]

Now, the most crucial question that Derrida poses for a 'cultural' politics of language is this: how can we, in each act of language, promise a language that does not necessarily fall within the sphere of the language that is imposed as an object of identification and appropriation? How can we promise a language beyond the 'uni-identity' (*unidentité*) of the language that comes to us from outside, and appears as always and already present for us? This can be done, according to Derrida, only by *inventing* in one's own language, by "inventing a language different enough to disallow its own *reappropriation* within the norms, the body, and the law of the given language..."[16], a language that is "*prior-to-the-first* language" which exists only in anticipation. This language would be a 'promised language.'[17]

The other name for this 'invention' in one's own language, of the language of the other, which would also be the 'prior-to-the-first' language, is *translation*. Derrida tends to equate this invention with translation, "the translation of a language that does not as yet exist, and that will never have existed, in any given target language."[18] This is a translation in which there can only be unknown and unforeseen target languages, or languages that are unknown places of arrival, without there ever being a source language, or a language of departure.

In sum, we may say that what unites the 20th century philosophers of language discussed here, as different from their early 19th century counterparts is their refusal to reduce cultural domains like language to some facile naturalistic notions. Language, is not given, it can only be a *gift*. It is not something possessing a universal or particular structure given by some divine or natural design, but permanently an act of giving from the self to the other. It is an unconditional act of giving where nothing is retained by the donor nor nothing is expected in return by him or her. It is an act in which the world is nor represented as it is often supposed to be, but is presented or offered as different from what it is sensed to be. It is an act of inventing in the given language in such a way that this invention results in a better 'sharing of voices'. It is permanently an act of creating new and alternative *sense* (in its multiple senses of meaning, feeling and direction) for and between the self and the other.

NOTES

1. Voloshinov, V.N., 1973.
2. Bakhtin, M.M., 1981.
3. Wittgenstein, L., p. 85.
4. Ibid., p. 11.
5. Ibid., p. 82.
6. See Vikishinov, V.N. 1973, pp. 9-15.
7. Ibid., p. 129.
8. Deleuze, G. and F. Guattari, 1987, p. 76.
9. Derrida, J., "Signature Event Context," 1982, p. 328.
10. In: "La langue n'appartient pas," interview with J. Derrida by Evelyn Grossman in *Europe* 861-62— Paul Celan, p. 83. For English version, see, 'Language is Never Owned,' in Derrida, J., 2005, pp. 97-107.
11. Wittgenstein, L., 1974, 145-46. Italics added by the present author.
12. Derrida, J., "Roundtable on Translation" in *The Ear of the Other*, p. 102.
13. Benjamin, W., 1999. "The Task of the Translator," in *Illuminations*, pp. 70-82.
14. Derrida, J., 1998. *Monolingualism of the Other OR Prosthesis of Origin*, p. 1.
15. Ibid., p. 25.
16. Ibid., p. 66.
17. Ibid., p. 61.
18. Ibid., p. 65.

5

Time, Language and the Destruction of Power

As someone who teaches in a department of linguistics in India, I feel I am twice distanced from the contemporary European discussions on the messianic. Linguistics of our times, unfortunately, as is well known, is a formalistic and (perhaps therefore) an extremely closed discipline, that is to say, not easily amenable to philosophical overtures. The philosophical seriousness of the messianic problem came home to me only during my reading a few years ago of Derrida's *Le monolinguisme de l'autre,* a work I then considered as being of linguistic significance. I have written about it in some of my recent publications. I should also mention here that while speaking about Derrida's suggestion of a 'messianicity without messianism,' during my class lectures at Jawaharlal Nehru University in New Delhi, one of the students, posed to me a most demanding question of the compatibility of the Judeo-Christian notion of the 'messiah' and the Hindu-Buddhist notion of the '*avatara*.' This was something that I had not seriously considered previously, though it might well have been lingering beyond my mental horizon. After a certain amount of research on the problem, I still do not know to what extent the comparison is pertinent and useful. Part of the difficulty is that the 'messiah' is a far more philosophically explored and exposited notion—especially in recent times—whereas 'avatara' still remains a notion discussed mainly by scholars of religion.

However, certain immediate similarities are worth mentioning. Both these divine 'phenomena' are supposed to be capable of making unpredictable, even miraculous appearances, upsetting the continuum of normal life of the people amidst which they are said to manifest. Both messiah and avatara, demand and impose an ethical transformation of the people for whom they might appear, as well as involve an arresting of or a rupture in time, which in certain ways amount to an aesthetic transfiguration. The messiah and the avatara appear in a time and a space distinct from the space and the time normally lived in and experienced by the people. Avatara can in fact manifest wearing a costume and bearing an attitude different from that of the people at large, reminiscent of a skilled theatre artist.[1] However, the messiah and the avatara do not follow the same kind of temporality. The time of the avatara is more or less cyclical and repetitive, suggestive of a mythical endowment, while that of the messiah seems to be singular and linear, unless one interprets him/her[2] in terms of the Nietszchean 'eternal return of the same,' as some people tend to do. And things are further complicated by the fact that the Christian messiah is supposed to have already come, while the Jewish messiah is always 'to come.' The question we can pose is that if the messiah has already come once and if he/she is going to come again (and again), is there a cyclicity involved here? In any case, it is worth noting that there will always be a 'time that remains,' as Agamben puts it, irrespective of whether the time of our existence unfolds linearly or cyclically.

Further, the distinction between the time before the arrival of the messiah, the anointed divine figure, or the avatara and the time after his or her arrival is not only a qualitative distinction, but is also charged with a political significance. The main basis for divine intervention in both cases is to engage in a destruction of power. The alternative time which the coming of the messiah inaugurates is a time in which the locus of power of the previous era will be effectively destroyed. (For example, in the Hindu tradition, Krishna, the avatar of Vishnu destroys the monstrously powerful king Kamsa on a divine stage that is erected on the earth.) The divine time is a time of multiple intervals and interventions, and not a restricted time of linear cause-effect relations within a given structural totality, dictated by forces of political hegemony.

History, Language and Power in Benjamin

We shall try to understand the work of Walter Benjamin in terms of the following three or four main rubrics: language, history or time, power and violence. It is significant that Benjamin's work is suffused with the Judaic idea of messianic time, irrespective of whether he is talking about language, art (theatre) or history. This is amply evident from three of his posthumously published texts written in 1916.[3] In 'On Language as Such and On the Language of Man'[4] Benjamin focuses on the historically-arising disjunction or dissonance between what he calls the 'language of nature' and the 'language of man.' In fact, he tries to trace the metaphysical trajectory between the 'language of god' and the 'language of man' mediated by the 'language of nature' and the 'language of things.'[5]

Benjamin's ideas in the essays we are considering are heavily dependent on the Biblical perspective on language, especially that of the section of Genesis. He places this perspective in a productive encounter with perspectives from linguistics and semiotics of the early 20th century. The key themes that Benjamin discusses in 'On language as Such...' essay are that of (a) naming and names, (b) revelation, (c) lament and mourning, and (d) the movement towards a 'pure language' through translation. Since the Bible begins with the sentence, "In the beginning, there was the verb,"[6] in the point of view developed here, the world is essentially a linguistic problem. Prior to the words of language, there is a language of things that is accessible to the human mind. This ineluctable language of things is communicated by man *in* language, but not *through* it. By extension this would mean that language itself has a language or 'mental being' which is also communicated *in* and not *through* it. Therefore, as far as communication by language is concerned, according to Benjamin only the linguistic being of things can be communicated by language, but their own mental being is already contained in their linguistic being, and only by virtue of this fact, they can at all be communicated. What this implies is a discrepancy between what is communicated *through* language and what is communicated *in* language, the latter being incommensurable with the being of language, and communicable in an infinitely open-ended manner. It follows that the linguistic being of *man* consists not in his language of communication consisting of words, but in his *naming* of other things. Naming by man is not a communicative act in the sense of communication between man and man, but according to Benjamin, *"in the name, the mental being of man communicates itself to God."*[7] (italics in the original). Name is in fact the deep inner core of language, where the fundamental being or property of man (that man uses language) is in touch with the fundamental being or property of language (that language exists by naming). In name, one can say that *"language as such* is the mental being of man."[8] This leads one to say: "man is the namer... and through him pure language speaks." Man's capacity to name things also enables him to know them. This is what gives him power over them. By way of man's naming of things as a culmination of God's act of creation, the name-filled human language has an absolute presence in the world of God's creation, and has universal applicability in the domain of communication.

Now, since it is possible to posit equivalence between the mental and linguistic beings of things, Benjamin goes on to note that what is communicated in a thing is its medium or language itself. This means that the differences between languages is due to the gradual differentiation in the 'density' of accretion of the "communicating (naming) and ... the communicable (name) aspects of communication."[9] Related to this difference in degree is the gap between what is expressible and expressed and what is inexpressible and unexpressed, which is the basis of the concept of revelation. Benjamin says: "The highest mental region of religion is (in the concept of revelation) at the same time the only one that does not know the inexpressible. For it is addressed in the name and expresses itself as revelation."[10] Revelation in religion is distinguished from art and poetry, for the mental being of the former depends solely on man and the language in him, while the latter rests on the "spirit of language in things, even in its consummate beauty."[11]

According to the Biblical account, human language is received from God as a *gift* by a transmission of the latter's breath into the former. The Genesis mentions three consecutive stages of God's creation: letting be, making and naming. With language, creation begins and with language it is finished. "Language is therefore both creative and the finished and creation; it is word and name."[12] Unlike other created things, in man, creation does not end with naming him, but language, the medium of creation, is set free by God. There is a transfer of God's creative power to man. Thus, God's creative power—expressed through the naming of things—is transferred to man as his knowing power. This is what sets up the gap or the difference between word and name, for "all human language is only the reflection of the word in name."[13] And therefore, Benjamin notes that, "the infinity of all human language always remains limited and analytic in nature, in comparison to the absolutely unlimited and creative infinity of the divine word."[14]

The disparity and the proximity between finite human language and the infinite divine word are articulated at the level of the proper name. The proper name—entirely a human creation—is inserted into the creativity of the divine word. And that is why there is more to language than mere signs. Nor is the word a pure representation of a definable essence of things. That accounts for the tension between the properness of the humanly given names and the creativity of the divine word. This arresting of the human name in relation to the divine word, and the consequent presence of the nameless in the name is, according to Benjamin, what necessitates translation. The significance of translation for Benjamin is affirmed in the following terms:

> It is necessary to found the concept of translation at the deepest level of linguistic theory, for it is much too far-reaching and powerful to be treated in any way as an afterthought....

> Translation attains its full meaning in the realization that every evolved language (with the exception of the word of God) can be considered a translation of all the others.... Translation is the crossing from one language to into another through continuum of transformations. Translation passes through continua of transformations, not abstract areas of identity and similarity.[15]

For Benjamin, translation takes place not only from the mute language of things to the language of man, but also from the nameless to the named. From any conceivable beginning till any conceivable end, the world is a process of linguistic transformations of a dialogical kind, that is, of translations. That is, translation also from the human names embedded in the divine word to the pure language that is forever to come. Benjamin's views on translation are more thoroughly elaborated in his "Task of the Translator" (1923). Here, Benjamin notes that languages have a kinship—irrespective of whether they are historically or typologically related—in their 'intention'. He uses the expressions, 'object of intention' and 'mode of intention' to distinguish between the elements of the referential world and the manner in which these elements are understood in a given language.[16] Thus, the German word *Brot* and the French word *pain* have the same object of intention, corresponding to the English word, 'bread', but they have different modes of intention, resulting in a deep semantic disparity and non-interchangeability in the use of these words, in these languages. While the object of intention, or reference remains quite stable with respect to the given languages, the mode of intention is "in a constant state of flux —until it is able to emerge as pure language from the harmony of all the various modes of intention."[17] Thus, in contrast to the intentional or referential use of language, where meanings of words and sentences, though of temporary value, appear to be complete and self-contained for each language, the modes of intention of given languages (e.g. German and French) remain in conflict, but they supplement each with respect to the other language/s infinitely, and thus tend towards a 'pure language,' which is always not yet and different from any given language. The meaning associated with modes of intention, according to

Benjamin, remains 'hidden' till the pure language can appear. The movement along the path towards pure language is however not endlessly linear 'till the end of time'; it is aided and abetted by *translation*. In Benjamin's evocative pronouncement: "It is translation which catches fire on the eternal life of the works and the perpetual renewal of language. Translation keeps putting the hallowed growth of languages to the test: How far removed is their hidden meaning from revelation, how close can it be brought by the knowledge of this remoteness?"[18]

Thus, the 'growth' in the linguistic domain, if at all we can speak of it, is never an isolated affair, never a matter of individual languages, as it was assumed by many philologists of the 19th century. It inevitably involves a process of translation, which "serves the purpose of expressing the reciprocal relationship between languages."[19] And moreover, the 'central kinship of languages' is not something that is always and already available in the constitutive structure of languages (as suggested by a theory of linguistic universals, such as that of Chomsky), but is something liable to manifest, through use, in the future time; it "is marked by a distinctive convergence."[20] "Languages are not strangers to one another, but are, *a priori* and apart from all historical relationships, interrelated in what they *want to express*."[21] (emphasis added). Benjamin goes on to suggest that the linguistic property of 'translatability' of languages is similar to the theory of 'images' associated with cognitive activity. Both are indispensable as far as their respective domains are concerned. Just as there is no thinking without images, there are no languages without translatability. External contact, rather than an internal analysis and comparison, is more relevant for asserting the 'kinship' of languages. Translation aids in the life of languages in one way or the other: "Translation is so far removed from being the sterile equation of two dead languages that of all literary forms it is the one charged with the special mission of watching over the maturing process of the original language and the birth pangs of its [the target language's] own."[22]

Translation is therefore a constant dialogical process,

raising the languages involved to an ever higher plane of existence, into a 'purer linguistic air.' "The task of the translator," according to Benjamin, "consists in finding that intended effect upon the language into which he is translating which produces in it the echo of the original."[23] The translator is someone who is concerned with "integrating many tongues into one true language..."[24] It is not merely to faithfully transfer the content of a text from one language to another, but it is also to keep in view the emergence of a pure language out of the two, or between the two, which will be better amenable to truth as such. It is a language, according to Benjamin, in which "the languages themselves, supplemented and reconciled in their mode of signification, draw together."[25]

This pure language is an in-between language, as well as a language outside all given languages. It is not a stable language, but a transitory language, a language always in transition. Though languages may appear to be closed and self-contained, and their mode of intention seems complete, there is in fact the possibility of their meanings being infinitely supplemented, through translation. A good translation is not pulled by the force of gravity of the original language, by way of the translating language's 'fidelity' to the former, nor does it attempt to remain entirely within the autonomous realm of the latter, through 'licence' or freedom. Rather than aim at equivalence one way or the other with regard to the original, in Benjamin's view, "the language of translation can – in fact, must – let itself go, so that it gives voice to the *intentio* of the original not as reproduction but as harmony, as supplement to the language in which it expresses itself, as its own kind of *intention*."[26] "A real translation ... allows the pure language, as though reinforced by its own medium, to shine upon the original all the more fully."[27]

'Pure language,' as Benjamin sees it, is that uncircumscribable and infinite language not yet realized and not realizable in any given language, and that which cannot be employed in the service of any information or intention. Languages, being the unconscious creation of human life, carry with them, or contains within them all the rubble of particular human—social and political—conditions.[28] Translation aids in overcoming the 'crudeness' of the language of ordinary communication. This movement from the 'crude' to the 'essential' language (in the Mallarméan sense), is indeed politically consequential, according to Benjamin. Thus, "it is the task of the translator to release in one's own language that pure language which is exiled under alien tongues, to liberate the language imprisoned in a work in his re-creation of that work. For the sake of pure language, he breaks through the decayed barriers of one's own language."[29] Users of a language can never sustain the myth of their own perpetual monolingualism, which is often used for the sake of their own political and ideological consolidation and for the subjugation of others.

The mediate character of language, that is, its character between its origin in the name and its culmination in the 'pure language' is also the cause of the plurality of human languages. Ironically, nature is forced to remain mute in the face of human linguistic plurality. This is what makes nature withdraw into a state of 'deep sadness,' and lamentation. The language that mediates between the muteness of nature and the confusion of human tongues is a potential language of lamentation, according to Benjamin. "Lament, however, is the most undifferentiated, impotent expression of language. It contains scarcely more than the sensuous breath; and even where there is only a rustling of plants, there is always a lament. Because it is mute, nature mourns."[30]

Mourning thus involves a movement away from the knowable and the communicable. That which has been named, in its movement from speech to muteness, is clearly more prone to mourning. It would be an even stronger tendency of melancholy when the process takes place in the plurality of overused and name-withered human languages. This involves an 'overnaming' which according to Benjamin is the "deepest linguistic reason for all melancholy." Thus art and poetry vent the speechless speech arising from the tension between the things of nature, still unnamed by man, and the words that humans use in their day-to-day communication. This tension and this overcoming which is also a melancholic overnaming cannot be resolved since the Fall has already happened. It goes on infinitely. It cannot be resolved entirely even in the form of mourning that tragedy is seen to induce. This, according to Benjamin, is the basis of the distinction between Greek tragedy and German *Trauerspiel*. It is also for him the basis of the 'divine violence' which strikes at the root of what is set up as the natural law. It is a non-violent violence, which opens up the space and the voice of art, essentially melancholic, due to the disjunction between the natural and the human, a disjunction which is also that of time, of the messianic time, a time outside of all given time, wherein the above tension cannot be resolved in any presumed dialectical movement of history.

Metaphysics of time in Bhartrhari

In this section, I shall explore the metaphysics of time in a well-known Indian work on the theory of language authored by the 7th century philosopher Bhartrhari. I assume that in the text in question, namely *Vakyapadiyam (On Sentences and Words)*, Bhartrhari (1974) was providing authentic views on time and language in relation to being as they were discussed and debated by the Indian grammatical school. These views pertain neither to the messiah nor to the avatara notion, but some of the sections of the text focus on the transformative powers inherent in the phenomenon of time, and therefore the position or the role that can be adopted in terms of the actions that can be performed by man as the 'means' for doing them.

Bhartrhari's discussion of the 'means' (*sadhana*) of action (*kriya*), and time (kala) appears in the third chapter of his *Vakyapdiyam*, referred to by scholars as the *Padakanda* or *Prakirna*. We shall come to this after we have quickly examined his more general views on meaning and time that appear in the first chapter (*Brahmakanda*) of the work. This chapter, in fact, contains important references to the nature of word and meaning. The form of the word is described as the result of eternal transformations of the *Sabdabrahma* or the eternal-universal word / sound. Meaning is the particular instanciation of the activation, through an explosion or `bursting forth' (*sphota*) in the intellect (*pratibha*) of the perceiver. What is important in these views is the dynamic perspective attached to both meaning and form.

The main feature of Bhartrhari's ideas is the constancy and the omnipresence of transformations in the universe. Both word and the world are the result of manifest transformations and/or apparent differentiations of the cosmic unity, or the *sabdabrahma*. From an eternalist point of view these transformations/differentiations are unreal and illusory. Time, as one of the properties of the unchanging cosmic entity, is the material force which produces these transformations, which can in turn be perceived and cognized as actions of particular things. The *sabdabrahma* is initially differentiated into its mental and material media, and the time force (*kalashakti*) affects both these aspects. These transformations are essentially of the nature of translations (*vivarta*), and not transmutations (*parinama*), in relation to the eternal, unchanging One.

For Bhartrhari, even meaning is governed by the factor of time. As far as the question of form and meaning is concerned, the corresponding terms, *dhwani* and *sphota,* in addition to the usual opposition between the physical (signifier) and the non-physical (signified), capture another opposition, that between the temporally *differentiated* and the *undifferentiated*. As the semantic essence of speech, Sphota, is both unembodied (it is the linguistic centre, the universal) and unmanifested in an all-differentiating and all-diversifying time. Bhartrhari's references to the various analogies employed by other scholars to describe the *sphota* (that of the 'wave,' and that of the 'flame,' and even more pertinently that of the 'seed' or the 'egg') make this amply clear. Owing to the literal meaning of the word, some commentators have also defined *sphota* as the 'bursting forth,' etc. Some have even suggested that *sphota* might actually refer to the bursting forth of meaning in the mind / brain. However, in the present author's view it is indeed useful to retain this very physical sense of the word, rather than quickly reduce it to something cognitive or linguistic, without abandoning the insistence on the undifferentiated character of the *sphota*, in comparison with *dhwani.*

It seems to me that *sphota* is suggestive less of a thing (an undifferentiated or non-differentiable) and more of an action or process of 'spurting.' 'To spurt' according to the dictionary is 'to gush or cause to gush forth in a sudden stream or jet.'[31] If we replace the meaning of the word from that of 'explosion' or mere 'bursting forth' to this 'spurting' meaning, then the meaning of 'sphota' would be much akin to the more natural bodily process of the *spurting* of the menstrual blood or of the semen. It can be seen that this idea that meaning is essentially a fertile principle, or the very principle of intersubjective or interlocutive (linguistic, cultural and ethical) fertilization is in fact also the basis of the Greek notion of the 'sign' or the word *semeion*, whose root *sem*—is shared (even without the wink of an eye) by contemporary English words like 'semen,' 'semantics,' 'semiotics,' or even more pertinently the word, 'seminar.' *Sphota* is an excess or overflow of meaning, the emergence of something over and above the given state of affairs—and note merely its representation. Every utterance of language produces an excess over the being that is already given, and the excess of being of one joins with the excess of being of the other, creating a new linguistic meaning or being. And since what 'spurts' in the sphota, is an expression of the condition of language itself, it can enliven the suppressed language in the self and the other, by means of either a lament or a joyous cry.

Perhaps there's nothing surprising in this suggestively *erotic* (for the purist, the meaning of *sphota* as 'spurt' would be merely a matter of routine repetition, and not that of creation, creativity or even procreation)—in the sense of life-sustaining —sense that we are introducing for one of the central concepts of the Indian philosophy of language. Elsewhere in the literature, while describing the essential principles of word-concatenation, the grammarians—and Bhartrhari prominently among them—talk of *âkânksha*, 'desire' or 'expectancy' between two words or sets of words, in order to form a phrase or a sentence. The other two central syntactic principles for the grammarians are *asatti* or *sannidi* (co-presence or spatio-temporal contiguity) and *yogyata* (conjugability/ conjoinability). All these notions suggest that linguistic creation resulting from erotico-physical dynamics and mutual (dialogical?) contact are the governing principles of language. We may be reminded in this context that the Greek the Greek language uses the word, *symploke* for the interlocking of the noun and the verb, and that in the Latin tradition, the term for the same predicative verb 'to be' is 'copula.'[32]

Essentially, for Bhartrhari time is a metaphysical force which is capable of differentiating everything in the universe. Time is an independent force which acts upon things in the world, perpetually changing their status. It can allow things to emerge, change their form, quantity, or quality, or end their existence. "Time differentiates action and number differentiates everything. It is time, differentiated (though one) which has been declared to be the cause of the origin, existence and destruction of objects which go through these states."[33] The action of time is discernible everywhere in the universe. It 'is the very soul of the universe.'[34]

The action of time on things, induces specific dynamics in their ontology. Consequent to the action of time, things are perceived as *siddha* (accomplished) or *sadhya* (to be accomplished). A thing in the process of accomplishment is perceived as *sadhana*, or the means. Now, time's differentiating force can apply on man's being too. Accordingly, man's life can become healthy or unhealthy, long or short, or good or evil. However, man has the capacity or power to resist unsought differentiations by time by treating himself as *sadhana* or means of action. He can accomplish various skills or states (*siddha*) and yet remain in a state of *sadhya* (to be accomplished) with respect to the infinite time-force. Time acts upon man, accomplishes things upon him, but still with his conscious power, resists his physical and moral destruction, and keeps his self other accomplishments. In this resistance, man recognizes himself to be in a state of *sadhana*. In the state of *sadhana*, man retreats himself from the normal course of actions in time. It is a weak state, having power only to prevent its own accomplishment in time as a *siddha* (completed thing). In this conscious state of being a *sadhana*, in which man is a *sadhu*, there is a double orientation to time. A *sadhu*—often a figure of inexorable melancholy—has, on the one hand, internalized all the experiences of the past, or rather all the events of destruction wrought by time, and on the other hand, he/she is looking forward to the time to come with hope and promise. A *sadhu* is also the one who arrests the unstoppable movement of time, intervenes in it, and creates intervals in it.

NOTES

1. Our reference here is to an article by André Couture, according to which Krishna as an avatar of Vishnu appears on the earth as an actor to play his role on a theatrical stage. See Couture, A., 2001: 313-326. The Hindu avatara can also appear in multiple forms. A standard list of ten avataras of Vishnu is said to include the Fish, the Tortoise, the Boar, the Man-Lion, the Dwarf, Parasurama, Rama, Krishna, the Buddha, and Kalkin.
2. The messiah and the avatara are taken in this article to be gender-unspecified.
3. We are referring to Benjamin's '*Trauerspiel* and Tragedy,' 'The Role of Language in Trauerspiel and Tragedy' and 'On the Language of Man and the Language of Man.' We also refer to his 'Critique of Violence' published in 1921, as well as 'The Task of the Translator' (1923). The references to Benjamin in this chapter are from his *Selected Writings, Volume 1: 1913-1926* (Benjamin 1996).
4. Benjamin, W., 1996, pp. 62-74.
5. Ibid., p. 71-2.
6. We are using here the word, 'verb' and not 'word'. This choice is derived from the Latin version which uses the word, 'verbum' to translate the Greek, 'logos'.
7. Benjamin, W., 1996, p. 65.
8. Ibid., p. 65.
9. Ibid., p. 66.
10. Ibid., p. 67.
11. Ibid., p. 67.
12. Ibid., p. 67.
13. Ibid., p. 68.
14. Ibid., p. 68.
15. Ibid., pp. 69-70.
16. This distinction seems to parallel Gottlob Frege's distinction between 'reference' and 'sense'. According to Frege, the expressions 'evening star' and 'morning star' have different

senses, but the same reference, i.e. the planet Venus). However, while Frege's 'sense' is concerned with synonymy within a given language, and hence intralinguistic, Benjamin's 'mode of intention' seems to be an interlinguistic affair. Nancy's use of the term 'sense' similarly goes beyond the boundary of a given language.

17. Benjamin, 1996, p. 75.
18. Ibid., p. 257.
19. Ibid., p. 255.
20. Ibid., p. 255.
21. Ibid., p. 255.
22. Ibid., p. 256.
23. Ibid., p. 258.
24. Ibid., p. 259.
25. Ibid., p. 259.
26. Ibid., p. 260.
27. Ibid., p. 260.
28. This is what Mallarmé calls the 'crude' language, in opposition to the 'essential' language which is none other than Benjamin's 'pure language'. See a discussion on these notions in Blanchot, 1995, pp. 38-42.
29. Ibid., p. 261.
30. Ibid., p. 73, pp. 38-42, In, "On Language as Such and On the Language of Man."
31. *Collins Concise Dictionary*. We have still to verify whether the Sanskrit verb, 'sphut-' is etymologically related to the English verb 'spurt.' Perhaps not. German word *sputen* means to 'make haste.'
32. Paul Ricœur notes that for the Greek philosophers since Plato, the predicative function—as distinct from the identifying function—of words is characterized by the 'interlacing' (*symploke*) of noun and verb. According to him, "the identifying function ...designates being which exist... while predicative function... concerns the inexistent while aiming at the universal." (1992, pp. 226-27)
33. Bhartrhair, 1974, p. 36.
34. Ibid., p. 39.

6

Kafka: Literature, Law and Language

In our contemporary frames of understanding, we no longer tend to see literature, simply as a mode of representation, albeit of the aesthetic kind. Literature is no more seen as what a writer says about the world, even if we understand by the word 'world,' our social world. For many philosophers today, literature consists neither in the processing of facts that are submitted to a 'faculty of judgment,' in the Kantian sense, nor in the submerged and uncontrollable feelings of awe or fear with regard to that which cannot be subordinated to ordinary language or the artistic field, that is, by invoking a feeling of the 'sublime'. Aesthetics of the sublime, on the other hand, is still be understood in terms of the mediation between the world and the work of art in the human representational faculty

While discussing the intertwining relationship between 'society' and 'literature,' it is useful to consider the two German words having significance for the study of culture, namely, *gesellschaft* and *gemeinschaft*, which may be translated into English as 'society' and 'community' respectively. It is easy for us to see that these words are related to other English words, such as 'social' and 'socialism,' in the first case, and 'communion,' 'communication,' and 'communism' in the second. The word 'society,' it seems to me is suggestive of a 'cohabitation' of and a 'collaboration,' between people while the word 'community' seems to suggest a coming together in a unity, a fusion, a unification, or even a 'communion' where the individual variations, would disappear at least temporarily.

What is to be noticed is that these two terms have their distinct domains of use, though in ordinary language, we often tend to use them interchangeably.

It is worth asking, I feel, what would be the relationship of literature to 'society' on the one hand, and to 'community' on the other. Much of the modern discussions of language and literature have spoken of these domains in terms of 'society.' 'Community' has been somewhat relegated to the background (that is, in spite of 'communism'; it is worth considering the more recent philosophical-literary revival of this term of medieval origin). For instance, in the classic work of modern linguistics, *Course in General Linguistics*, Ferdinand de Saussure speaks of language extensively in relation to society. Saussure proposed the latter as "a science of the life of signs in society." Further, assuming a socially consistent knowledge of the system of signs, including the linguistic signs, Semiology was conceived by de Saussure as a branch of 'social psychology.' Moreover, most of the modern thinkers of the nation, have spoken of the latter, as a 'society.' As for an exception, we know that Benedict Anderson (1991) speaks of the emergence—largely linguistic—of modern nations in terms of 'communities' that were according to him, 'imagined into existence.'

What concerns us here is the question of the coexistence or covariance of the elements of language and the elements of society or community. Following the emergence of modern nations, language is taken to be coextensive with society or community. Thus, it is assumed that within a modern collectivity, national or social, individuals are supposed to be more or less equally competent in the same language and in the same discourses, that is, individuals are socially, linguistically and cognitively competent, more or less to the same degree. We thus (unquestioningly) speak of a shared social knowledge in a shared language. Individual and social variations in use and in communicative competence are often ignored. What is not contested is the assumption of a coextensiveness of a fused society and a fused language and a corresponding fused knowledge. Surprisingly, some tend to have such wrong assumptions not only about small local communities, but also about nation and what is supposed to be the global society.

Once we are able to break out of the above frame, and are able to see that language of a particular collectivity of people is itself nothing natural but a situational and historically continuous invention, then we are already on our way to understanding the relationship between literature and society. Literature, paradoxically, is both an affirmation of the language of a given society or community, and a denial of it. Literature is the transgression of and an invitation to transgress the boundaries that circumscribe the (coextensive) coexistence of language (discourse) and society. Literature is not a mode of repeating or replicating the discourse or the modes of knowledge that is present in the language of a given society. It is, on the other hand, a mode of affirmation or the denial of what is discursively given to a society. It is in this sense that Maurice Blanchot wants us to see that for Kafka literature was a mode of salvation.

Blanchot's early view on this problematic appears in his work, *The Work of Fire* (*La part du feu*, in the French original), a collection of critical essays published in 1949. These texts, along with the essays in an earlier collection, *Faux pas* (1943) represent Blanchot's own transformation from being a religious revolutionary and an existentialist to a faithful of literature. His more mature work on literature was published in 1956 as *The Space of Literature.* Blanchot's primary interest is in an ontological enquiry about writing: What is writing? Why does one write? How does one go about with the act of writing?

The primary condition for literary writing is the solitude of the writer, some sort of cognitive void, and a retreat from language. It is the loss of the language that is given to him that makes a writer write. But paradoxically, "(t)hat which destroys language in him also makes him write."[1] In his solitude and retreat, the writer transports himself to the extremities of his world, where language and its signs are already annihilated. It is in that annihilated or 'neutral' space of literature that the writer affirms himself. And what he affirms in language is in fact no real thing. Literary discourse, like the religious discourse that preceded it, is reaffirmation or an alternative affirmation of language, but it and its predecessor basically affirm nothing real. What it offers in this affirmation of nothing, is nothing but another language, a discourse other than what is 'socially' given, a discourse that belongs to the neutral space of literature.

Blanchot wants us to note that Kafka devoted, and self-consciously so, all his life to literature. In his *Diaries*, Kafka writes: "All I am is literature, and I am not willing to be anything else."[2] In the midst of life's other difficult chores, Kafka, in fact, had to struggle in order to remain in literature. He would write: "My situation is unbearable, because it contradicts my only desire and my only calling: literature."[3] Being religiously involved in literature, his only inspiration and happiness came from the latter. Literature, for Kafka, was a mode of being and, writing, that involved, shall we say, using a Leivnasian expression, the otherwise than being. And therefore, it was never a matter of mere "aesthetic deliberation." Literature, for Kafka, is the mode that leads both being and language towards death, but in it, both being and language remain in a state of impossibility of dying. (In the banality of life, one *survives* or lives on through literature.) Literature opens up towards the exteriority of the given being as well as the otherwise than being as such. It becomes the in-between and the neutral space between the self and the other. It is the dying–undying state of being in language.

Blanchot explains this movement from ordinary language to the 'pure' language of literature in terms of the shift of the personal pronoun 'I' to 'he' or 'it' in literature. 'He' or 'it' is the pronoun of the neutral abstracted from the transactions of everyday life. As he puts it,

> ... literature consists of trying to speak at the moment when speaking becomes most difficult... and consequently necessitates a recourse to a language that is most precise, the most aware, the furthest removed from vagueness and confusion—the literary language.... Literature thus becomes an "assault on the frontiers," a chase that, by the opposing forces of solitude and language, leads us to the extreme limit of this world, 'to the limits of what is generally human.[4]

Writing, like death, is thus characterized by a sense of the impossibility of possibility. Both present themselves to us in their possibility only to let us encounter their impossibility. The existence of language, like death, is possible only in its impossibility. It is the impossibility of language that always makes it a language forever promised, just as it is the impossibility of death that makes possible one's survival.

> If language and, in particular, literary language did not constantly hurl itself eagerly at its death, it would not be possible, since it is this movement toward its impossibility that is its nature and its foundation; it is this movement, that by anticipating its nothingness, determines its potential to be nothingness without actualizing it. In other words, language is real because it can project itself toward non-language, which it is and does not actualize.[5]

From Blanchot's perspective the trajectory that literature takes is very clear. A retreat from one's own subjectivity and the given language and discourse of one's culture, to the apparent possibility of another 'pure' language. But it is here, just as one's own death is an impossibility, that one encounters the impossibility of the language of literature, and of literature itself. This is where, literature can be spoken of as an 'incessant murmur' in and of language, and this is where one can discern the movement of 'language to infinity.'[6]

The same ambivalence of an undying death is starkly present in Kafka's portrayal of his characters. According to Blanchot,

> Kafka probably under the influence of Eastern traditions recognized in the impossibility of dying the extreme curse of man. Man cannot escape unhappiness, because he cannot escape existence, and it is in vain that he heads towards death, that he confronts the anguish and the injustice of it; he dies only to survive.[7]

And thus,

> There is no actual death in Kafka, or more exactly there is never an end. Most of his heroes are engaged in an intermediate moment between life and death, and what they seek is death, and

> what they miss is life, in such a way that one does not know how to characterize their hopes, if they place their hope in the possibility of losing all hope, and how to appreciate their regrets, if these regrets eternalize the condemnation they undergo.[8]

We know Kafka basically as a writer of fiction, short stories and novels, and as the author of his posthumously published *Diaries*. Blanchot, who drew much of his literary inspiration from Kafka (among other literary greats like Mallarmé, Rilke, etc.), was no mean writer himself. Blanchot's initial writings were critical essays, he then wrote fiction, and then went on to write texts, referred to as *récits*, which are indiscernibly literature-philosophy-criticism. This shift in Blanchot's writing comes after having moved from philosophical criticism to philosophical fictions. It is as if Blanchot was reflecting on the ontology of writing, and simultaneously he was also paying attention to the generic division of literature.

Balnchot's enigmatic text *The Madness of the Day*[9] (*La folie du jour)* is an account of a man beginning to tell the story of his fall into a state of decrepitude. This is a short text that Derrida has subjected elsewhere to an extensive reading under the title 'The Law of Genre.' In *The Madness of the Day*, the first person narrator barely speaks of his loss of faith in beings, and his simultaneous inability to die. The doctors try to treat his injury or illness, and in his half-cured state, he sees 'behind their backs' the silhouette of law. The law, rather unexpectedly, is afraid of the man, wants him to acknowledge 'her,' and is strongly critical of his conduct, even when she wants to remain close to him. The doctors are still attentive to the man, and they want him to continue narrating his story. However, when the man recommences his narration, he cannot go beyond the beginning. He realizes that he cannot relate his experiences in a narrative. His speech refuses to translate itself into the genre of a story, even if others presume that he has the competence for it. In his reading of the text, Derrida has observed that this is a narration that fails to be one. A failure, owing to the fact that both the narration and the narrator are heading towards their respective ends, and the law is unable to restore the genericity of either. *The Madness of the Day*, according to

Derrida, narrates the necessary failure of the law of the genre.

In another gesture, Derrida's essay, 'Before the Law' expounds Kafka's parable-like story, also bearing the title, 'Before the Law.' The essay is a deep exposition of the relationship between law and literature. Kafka's story has appeared both separately and as part of his well-known novel *The Trial.* It is the story of a 'countryman' who sets out with many valuable possessions in search of the 'Law' and arrives in front of its gate, guarded by a tall and hefty Tartar with a thick moustache. The guard accepts all his bribes, but refuses to let him into the edifice of law, every time telling him that it is possible for him to enter, but "not now." The countryman is warned that the Law is guarded by many guards inside each more powerful than the preceding ones. He remains before the gate for the rest of his life and grows very old waiting for the permission to enter. As he approaches his death, he wants to know from the guard why no one else has sought to enter it. "Everyone strives to reach the law; so how does it happen that for all these years no one but myself has ever sought admittance?" he asks. The guard replies: "No one else could ever be admitted here, since this gate was made only for you. I am now going to shut it."

Derrida reads this story as portraying the relation between literature and law in both directions: the law of literature as well as the literature of law. Or, better, literature as something legally conditioned, and law as something fictionally founded.

The two principal questions that Derrida poses in his "Before the Law" are the following: what makes a piece of writing literature? And, who decides? These questions are similar to the situation faced by the countryman before the doorkeeper of the Law: what makes him eligible to enter the Law? And who decides? A corollary question that imposes itself on us is the following: can literature and law be said to have surprisingly similar conditions of possibility?

As if to provide an answer to these questions, Derrida makes an inventory of the formal-textual conventions employed in Kafka's story: its specific identity, for example its attribution to a singular author, and the title—also fictional—

spatially separated from the text. And as for the crucial third question above, Derrida is of the view that both the story and the law are made to 'appear' before each other. In his words:

> ... the story, as a certain type of *relating*, is linked to the law that it relates, appearing, in so doing, before that law, which appears before it. And yet ..., nothing really presents itself in this appearance; and just because this is given to us to be read does not mean that we shall have proof or experience of it.[10]

'Before the law' is a story about the fiction of law and the (non-existent) law of literature. The law is often assumed to be without a history, and not reducible to a story. The law excludes narrative. It takes itself to be universal, and it wants others to take it as universal, as natural. Derrida tries to see the interrelationship between law and literature (narrative) as being alluded to by the relationship between the doorkeeper and the countryman. Thus, the narrative wishes to enter the Law, assumed by the countryman to be a general law, and accessible to all. The narrative is before the law, like the countryman waiting for his entry. The Law keeps the narrative waiting, indefinitely. The law is inaccessible to the man in spite of the fact that the gate of the law is 'open as usual.' The law in the form of the series of progressively stronger doorkeepers described in the story, is also something frightening and fantastic, or 'uncanny,' in the sense of Freud. However, the first doorkeeper and the countryman are situated both 'before' and outside the law. Therefore, presumably there is no binary opposition, but only a difference (*'différance'*) between the countryman and the doorkeeper, and thus between the story and the law. As to what exactly is the specific content of the law, the story doesn't permit us to know. Derrida says on this point, following a formulation of Heidegger, that like the truth of the truth that always remains hidden, the law has to always guard itself, its own fictional truth.

According to Derrida, it is the anonymity of the law that is particularly interesting from the point of view of literature. Besides,

> ...it is neutral, beyond sexual and grammatical gender, and

> remains thus indifferent, impassive, little concerned to give an answer as *yes* or *no*. It lets the man freely determine himself, it lets him wait, it abandons him. It is neuter, neither feminine nor masculine, indifferent because we do not know whether it is a (respectable) person or a thing, who or what. The law is produced (...) in the space of this non-knowledge.[11]

The closing of the gate at the end of the story and the closing of the text are both abrupt and simultaneous. Just as the law talks only about itself, the text too talks about itself. In both cases admittance is denied. Derrida views this as the unreadability of the text. Through its play of identity and non-identity, the law and the text neither arrives nor allows anyone to arrive (read). But however, both claim absolute respectability. That the law and the text cannot be trespassed, is something that is ensured by the concerned 'countrymen' (the readers) and 'doorkeepers' (the authorities of the literary institution: publishers, critics, professors, etc.) in the two respective cases.

Derrida reads the last words of the doorkeeper in the narrative, "I am now going to shut it [the gate]" as follows. By declaring itself as 'I', the doorkeeper of Law as well as the text shows themselves up in their performatively-constituted function of being in command of their respective domains. By this declaration, according to Derrida, "the text produces and pronounces the law that protects it and renders it intangible. It does and says, saying what it does by doing what it says."[12] The performative "I" is both inside and outside the text, as it is both outside and inside the gate of the Law.

As for the often-asked question of 'What is literature?' Derrida says that it cannot be answered in any general terms. Each text submitted to its own conditions of possibility with its own implicit movements of 'framing and referentiality.' In relation to these conditions of possibility, each text is surrounded by its own 'law'. And the site of this 'law of literature' is in fact external to literature. Thus, according to Derrida,

> ... the text (for example, the so-called 'literary' text and particularly this story by Kafka) before which we the readers

> appear before as before the law, this text protected by its guardians (author, publisher, critics, academics, archivists, librarians, lawyers, and so on) cannot establish law unless a more powerful system of laws ('a more powerful guardian') guarantees it, in particular the set of laws and social conventions that legitimates all these things.[13]

In a similar vein, Deleuze has argued that literature cannot be undertood in terms of any law of formation, well-formedness of language, but rather in terms of its permanent potential for transformation. Literature shuns the law of language, and "moves in the direction of the ill-formed or the incomplete." Writing is to be located not in relation to already individuated beings of the world, but in relation to the process of individuation. Reflecting on the relation between Literature and Life, Deleuze says:

> Writing is a question of becoming, always incomplete, always in the midst of being formed, and goes beyond the matter of any livable or lived experience. It is a process, that is, a passage of Life that traverses both the livable and the lived. Writing is inseparable from becoming: in writing, one becomes-woman, becomes-animal or -vegetal, becomes molecule, to the point of becoming-imperceptible.[14]

Such a perspective on 'representation' of life in literature, will of necessity have its consequences on the language of literature. Literary language is also something that is constantly becoming, existing only in the constantly deforming and zone of indiscernibility, both in relation to life and to itself. "Language must devote itself to reaching ... feminine, animal, molecular detours, and every detour is a becoming mortal."[15] Like Blanchot again, Deleuze holds that the language of literature exists only when it ceases to refer to real first or second persons, and begins to be associated with powerlessness of an impersonal third person. Literature, he insists,

> ... opens up a kind of foreign language within language, which is neither another language nor a rediscovered patois but a becoming-other of language, a 'minorisation' of this major language, delirium that carries it off, a witch's line that escapes the dominant system.[16]

Deleuze sees in Kafka's works this detachment from the fullness of the language that he is writing in, i.e. the German language. The language of literature, according to Deleuze departs from the *power* of its constant elements to the *potential* of its variables, in creating a minor (literary) language from a major (official) language. It is in creating the minor German language of his writing, that Kafka can be called a minor litterateur. Minor and major languages, according to Deleuze are not two hierarchical forms of a language, but two different 'usages' or treatments of the same. Deleuze:

> Kafka, a Czechoslovakian Jew writing in German, submits German to creative treatments as a minor language, constructing a continuum of variation, negotiating all of the variables both to constrict the constants and to expand the variables; make language stammer, or make it "wail," stretch tensors through all of language, even written language, and draw from it cries, shouts, pitches, durations timbres, accents, intensities.[17]

'Minor literature' exemplified in Kafka's writing, according to Deleuze, can be identified by three major characteristics. Firstly, minor language is *not* the language of a minority. It can only be a transformation wrought within a major language, by a minority. What leads Kafka to construct a minor literature within the major national official language, is linked to the inability of himself and of other Prague Jews to participate in the German national consciousness. Kafka's work represents the survival of language and literature against the oppressive and moribund legal and bureaucratic language of the German nation.

Secondly, it is necessary to notice the pervasively political character of minor literature. Rather than limiting the movement of literature to an individual-psychological level to a social-level as in the major literature, in the 'minor literature' the individual is immediately in touch with the social and the political. For Kafka, as if evident particularly in *The Metamorphosis,* the familial is immediately political. The circle of the family intersects seamlessly with the circle of the bureaucratic in this story. As Gregor Samsa's life is metamorphosed into that of a beetle, the officials of his firm invade the privacy of his home, with the compliance of his father, and his sister begins to flirt with the strangers who come to lodge in their home. Gregor's body, meanwhile, becomes the object of ridicule, insults and assaults, and his voice is reduced to that of mere animal squeak and murmur.

The third important feature of 'minor literature' is the 'collective value' of its statements. The author does not have the role of a master-narrator. This is because, Deleuze believes, an emerging collective consciousness is possible only through literature, and because 'literature is the people's concern.' This is why the text of literature functions like a collective speech. And therefore,

> There isn't a subject, *there are only collective assemblages* of enunciation, and literature expresses these acts insofar as they are not imposed from above and insofar as they exist only as diabolical powers to come or revolutionary forces to be constructed.[18]

This is why it is possible today that writing or literature takes place not within a community, but at its very limit. That is why it is possible to describe it as an *exscription,* in the sense of Jean-Luc Nancy. Literature is always produced as that which ruptures the *immunity* of a people with respect to its outside. It can only be the unworking of the *community* which can exist only as its own contagion with respect to others and the outside, and the otherness *to come* within itself and against its own immanence.

NOTES

1. Blanchot, M., 1943, p. 2.
2. Blanchot, 1995.
3. Ibid.
4. Blanchot, 1949, pp. 17-8.
5. Ibid., p. 20.
6. See for example, Foucault, M., 1977, p. 54. On the relationship between language and death, Foucault writes: "Boundless misfortune, the resounding gift of the gods, marks the point where language begins; but the limit of death opens before language, or rather within language, an infinite space. Before

the imminence of death, language rushes forth, but it also starts again, tells of itself, discovers the story of story and the possibility that interpenetration might never end."

7. Blanchot, M., 1995, p. 81.
8. Ibid., pp. 81-2.
9. Blanchot, 1982b.
10. Derrida, J., 1992: 191.
11. Ibid., 1992, p. 207.
12. Ibid., p. 212.
13. Ibid., p. 214.
14. Deleuze, G., 1977, p. 225.
15. Ibid., pp. 226-27.
16. Ibid., p. 227.
17. Deleuze, G. and F. Guattari, 1987, p. 104.
18. Deleuze, G. and F. Guattari, 1986, p. 18.

7

Blanchot, Writing and the Politico-Religious

I shall focus on three essays by the French critic and writer Maurice Blanchot (1907-2003), which were published between 1931 and 1944. All these essays relate, directly or indirectly, to the Indian context. Only one of these—'On Hindu Thought'—had an early appearance in English translation. The translation of 'Mahatma Gandhi' and a discussion on 'Return to the Source' were published in the October issue of *Journal for Cultural Research* (2012).

All three essays by Blanchot are in the form of review articles, in the sense that they respond through writing, directly or indirectly, to publications that appeared earlier in the French intellectual milieu. The essay, 'Mahatma Gandhi' was published in July 1931 in the last issue of a 'vintage' (that is how Christophe Bident, Blanchot's biographer[1] describes it) journal called *Les cahiers mensuels*. Bident suggests that though Blanchot had written two earlier pieces, this essay is perhaps the first of any serious theoretical consequence. It refers, even if fleetingly, to Romain Rolland's biography of Gandhi, published in 1924 as well as to Gandhi's autobiography, *The Story of My Experiments with Truth*.[2] Significantly, it was in December 1931 that Gandhi, after attending the second Round Table Conference with the British authorities in London, toured Italy where he met Benito Mussolini, and went to Switzerland where he stayed for five days in the residence of Romain Rolland at Villeneuve.[3] The journal, *Les cahiers mensuels* was founded in 1928 by a group of so-called Catholic student revolutionaries, who according to its manifesto, wanted "to kill the modern world by the spiritual violence of sacrifice," and "to be the anarchists of Love."[4]

The second essay, 'Autour de la pensée hindoue' ('On Hindu Thought') appeared in a collection of essays by Maurice Blanchot, entitled *Faux pas* (Gallimard, 1943).[5] It responds to a special issue of *Les Cahiers du Sud* (Marseille, 1941) dedicated to Indian ('Hindu') thought, entitled *Message actuel de l'Inde* (Current Message from India). Several important French writers, including Benjamin Fondane, had participated in this 406-page publication of the journal. The third essay, 'Le pèlerinage aux sources' which appeared in *Journal des débats* in January 1944 is a short review of a work by a French writer of Italian origin, Lanza del Vasto, entitled *Le Pèlerinage aux Sources* (Denoël, Paris, 1943). The English translation of Vasto's work *Return to the Source* by Jean Sidwick, was published by Rider and Company, London, in 1971. The colourful figure of Vasto, a renowned popularizer of Gandhian ideas and ideals and a major campaigner of non-violence in France, also wrote the introduction to the French translation[6] of Gandhi's *Hind Swaraj*, and was a contributor in *Message actuel de l'Inde*.[7]

East and West: Religion, Politics and Modernity

Blanchot's first essay, 'Mahatma Gandhi' can only be read as a youthful rejection, poorly informed and arrogant, of one of the most respected and admired public figures of his time, based on deep prejudices of the Christian religion.[8] In the midst of this prejudicial account, his half-hearted approbation of Gandhi's nationalist politics carries little weight. Blanchot is strangely interested neither in the economic aspects of colonialism against which Gandhi was the most well-known campaigner nor in the ecological issues that much of Gandhi's politics was anchored in. What is significant of the second and third of these essays by Blanchot is that they are *not* just random journalistic articles on a common theme of Indian religious thought as well as its reception and popularization in Europe. There is an attempt here at a systematic understanding of what religious thought or discourse could be, though, still clearly based on a Christian understanding of religion. The first essay, written when the author was only 24 years old, is undeniably marked by an overwhelmingly Christian world-view, and by a certain arrogance and an extreme nationalistic fervour, especially in the concluding paragraphs. The essay primarily addresses European readers from a limited and perhaps still unmediated Christian standpoint, and therefore it says very little of any relevance or value, about Gandhi. The essays cannot contribute to gaining knowledge of the significance of Gandhi, or of Hinduism. At the same time, and that is what I shall attempt here, the specifically 'religious' dimension of the essays helps us to arrive at a more comprehensive understanding of Blanchot and his work. A second point to note is that these texts reflect the author's extreme 'vigilance' towards the European intellectual-political context of the period. Reading these texts, it is possible to discern the aptness of other commentators' description of Blanchot as a philosopher of 'refusal,' the 'extreme contemporary' and an intellectual who never veered from the self-imposed task of 'vigilance.'[9] The third point that can be made, more in the form of a hypothesis that requires for confirmation further research into Blanchot's thought, is the connection between his thoughts on religion and on literature.[10] It has been noted that Blanchot underwent some sort of a personal transformation from religion to literature during the 1930s—precisely the period that concerns us here, which somewhat coincides with the writing of his first novel, *Thomas the Obscure* as well as with the writing of several of the essays in the collection *Faux pas*.[11] But what is interesting here is not only a possible convergence of religion and literature but also the continuity from religious thought to literature, a sort of induction of religion into literary understanding. This continuity, we shall see, is manifested in his discussion of (the impossibility of) *death/dying* and concomitantly of '*passivity*.'

Blanchot's main objection to Gandhi concerns the role of religion in political life. He strongly adheres to the belief that religion cannot be an instrument of purposeful action. His later writings clearly reveal his refusal of the idea (primarily Sartrean) that literature can be used for political action.[12] In the first essay, he reacts to Gandhi's making religion unambiguously the basis of his political activity ("... for me there is no political activity without religion. Political action without religion is merely a trap, for it kills the soul," cited in Blanchot's essay on Gandhi). But, at the same time, Gandhi and Blanchot seem to share a common plank on another major issue: their criticism of modernity. Their critiques however took different trajectories. It is well known that Gandhi was vehemently critical of modernity with its extreme emphasis on mechanization, and he blamed the Western civilization for it. Placing religion on the highest pedestal, he sought a return to the thoughts and practices of the ancient and medieval periods, especially those of India and the East.[13] Gandhi's philosophical thought, in this respect is preceded by that of a host of writers and intellectuals, both from the West and from India, and we know that it continues to inspire a vast number of scholars, scientists and social and political activists,[14] decades after the deeply sorrowful event of his assassination by a religious fanatic in 1948.

Blanchot's critique of modernity, on the other hand, involved a rejection of the modern modes of knowledge and discourses, including the modernized versions of religious thought, and laid its emphasis on a movement towards the 'outside' (neither backward nor forward) which involves the refusal of the existent 'being' in its given historical and ontological reality. His philosophy in most respects parallels and often adheres to that of his close friend and long-term collaborator Emmanuel Levinas. But, in sharp contrast to Blanchot, Levinas's writings display a philosophical vibrancy and clarity (which Blanchot's dense writings often lacked) and his public presence and visibility contrasted with the extraordinarily 'invisible' and ascetic life led by Blanchot.[15] And yet, it is remarkable that Blanchot has been one of the main points of reference in contemporary post-modern thought, having influenced philosophers like Deleuze, Foucault and Derrida. But his opposition to modernity did not lead Blanchot to emphasize religious activity. Rather, unlike Gandhi, Blanchot in his own critical vein distanced himself further from the modern manifestations of religion, even while he retained some of the deeper insights of religion (still, mainly Christian), which were absorbed into his idea and practice of literature, or 'writing.'

Gandhi firmly believed that Western modernity is deprived because it is devoid of or distanced from religion. Thus, a critique of modernity implied for him, and was to be accompanied by, a return to religious activity. Christianity has failed or was unable to check the evil effects of modernity, especially that of mechanisation. The 'failure' of Christianity is something that Gandhi shared with many Western writers, who were his predecessors or contemporaries. Curiously, G.K. Chesterton whose name occurs favourably in Blanchot's essay, was also one of Gandhi's main intellectual heroes.[16] Following Rousseau, many European thinkers of the 19th century had maintained that modernity (with its ill-effects) had emerged because of the failure of the Christian religion, or conversely, the former had succeeded in banishing the latter from European culture. Among these, many of the Orientalist scholars and later the Theosophists had looked upon India and Indian religious thought as the source for a solution to the West's problem of a de-spiritualised culture, where man's humanity and nobility were being increasingly displaced by the rapid progress of mechanization. Theosophists in particular, in association with their co-spiritualists in India, sought to create a new divine discourse which would at least partially substitute for the declining moral authority of Christianity.[17] Gandhi himself was convinced and wrote about the decline of Western civilization while openly appreciating certain aspects of Christianity.[18] But, like many of the theosophists, with whom he was in contact, he would also offer the principles and ideals of Hinduism as a panacea for the ills of Christian religion and of the modern civilization. While often asserting the universality of God and religion, the continuous and unbroken tradition of Hindu spirituality was projected as being capable of making even Christians better Christians. Lanza del Vasto's *Return to the Source* makes it amply clear that he went to live in Gandhi's *ashram* at Wardha in central India, adopted the name of Shanti Das ('Servant of Peace') that Gandhi gave him, walked bare-foot with a stick in his hand in many parts of India, clad only in loin-cloth before reaching close to the source of the sacred river Ganga, not to be converted to Hinduism, but "in order to learn how to be a better Christian."[19]

Conversely, Gandhi's intellectual interest in Eastern religions, at least in the initial phase, was informed by modern European scholars. He had also made efforts in his youth to be an 'English gentleman'[20] before being politically engaged on the basis of religious ideas. Blanchot is suspicious of these double movements in the domain of religion. On the one hand, the movement of the European scholars trying to import particular genres of Indian spirituality, Hindu or Buddhist, in order to revive the Christian ideals, presumed to be affected by internal dissipation. On the other hand, there was the movement of the Indian elites attempting to learn Hinduism and other Eastern religions through the works of the Europeans, Theosophists or others. With respect to this double movement Blanchot's position seems to be this: taking recourse to religion in the political domain does not amount to an encounter with or a resistance to modernity, nor does it spiritualize the modern world; at most, it results in modernizing (and perhaps concomitantly politicizing) religion. This is because religion can be neither a representation nor a mode of conscious action in the world. It is the practical and the applied dimension of making religion an instrument of political activity that Blanchot's critical thought is centrally opposed to. Contrary to Gandhi's idea of the relation between political action and religion, where the latter is the core of the former, Blanchot rejects the idea that religion can at all be a form of action. Blanchot's attempt is to embed what he, along with Levinas perceived as the discursive-spiritual value of opening the self (and the same) to the other, and of seeking an alternative world outside of the given, existent world. Blanchot (unlike Levinas) seems to have identified this process with literary activity, or more exactly with what he called 'writing'; literature here consists not in what is already given, but only as the movement of its own singularity, which is, 'writing.'

This rejection of religious action in modern politics would also turn out to be, at the same time, a rejection of the modern idiom of religion. This would imply that modernity corrupts the purity of religion. To some extent Blanchot seems to be saying this. In other words, if religion is put to work within the closure of modern society and its politics, then it is likely to be corrupted and distorted. Therefore, Blanchot's worry, perhaps rather overstated, is that not only has the Christian religion been distorted by the effects of modernity (on this he would be in agreement with Chesterton), but that Hinduism is also negatively affected by the active engagement of its modern proponents and practitioners, be it Westerners or Indians. In contrast to the decidedly Christian sentiment and an extreme nationalistic fervour that he is unable to relinquish in the first essay, in the essay on 'Hindu thought,' he observes that the 'most elevated forms of Hindu spirituality'[21] are possibly being misunderstood and distorted by the modern, Western scholars, who as foreigners are not intellectually and spiritually equipped to comprehend them. And therefore, the spirituality of those who might have been influenced by these Western or Westernized interpreters of Hinduism must be suspect. It is the facility with which the modern interpreters of Hinduism translate this religion into the modern idiom, and present it as a guaranteed spiritual remedy for successfully countering the ills of modern society and politics that Blanchot essentially questions.

The essay on 'Hindu thought' and the review of Vasto's work deal with the difficulties in translation and communication of religious discourse and thought across cultures and across time. Religious discourse has its own 'profound secrets' which cannot be easily conveyed in our modern languages and by modern modes of communication. Mysteries of one religion cannot be easily transferred to another religion. They cannot be approached casually as many Westerners—Vasto being one case in point—have done in the context of Indian religions. Religious discourse is the result of arduous labour within a given culture, and it does not render itself facilely to the immediate reflection of someone in another culture. Its distance cannot be easily traversed by someone who belongs to a different culture. The appearance of immediate proximity of a religion in another context— be it the Hindu religion in the Western context or the Christian religion in the Indian context—can only be deceptive. Unaware of this deceptive relationship between a religion and its alien cultural and linguistic context, religious discourse is often presented as a quick recipe for spiritual success. Perhaps, it is possible to generalize the sense of what Blanchot says about Hinduism in the Western context:

> ... the doctrine for which the soul has searched through thoroughly pessimistic questioning seems to end up in a strangely optimistic conception of spiritual life. The thought that constantly strove to place itself heroically before the Absolute now has for its ideal only a comfortable laying out of spirituality.[22]

Thus, religious discourses, in Blanchot's view, do not run one parallel to another, neither are they mutually compatible at a surface level. But rather, on the one hand, they hold in their depths 'difficult secrets' and on the other hand, these secrets reveal themselves only at the moment when 'language bursts forth.' Commenting on at least some of the texts that appeared in *Message actuel de l'Inde,* Blanchot writes:

> ... one is struck by the facility with which they establish a bridge between the most elevated forms of Hindu spirituality and readers whom nothing has prepared for such knowledge. It seems, in following these very clear observations, that language easily carries difficult secrets, precisely those that can be known only when language bursts forth: one has the feeling that there are no great difficulties of translation between Sanskrit and Western languages, not only can concepts that already lose a part of their meaning by being expressed at all in the original vocabulary be transferred without new damage into truly foreign languages, but also the highest mystical practices are always communicated, and with the most surprising ease, to any thoughtful reader whatsoever.[23]

The second question that Blanchot poses in a similar vein, is the assumed correspondence between religious thought and nationalistic political discourse. Religious thought from his point of view antedates any modern forms of nationalism and is likely to outlast them. Religious thought or discourse can only 'burst forth' outside of the conditioned discourse of politics and society. In its ideal state, it incessantly and infinitely interrupts and ruptures the political and the social towards the outside of their given totalities. The attempt to force religion to play a political or social role can only make it impure. Blanchot identifies this problem in the approach to modern Hinduism, but we assume that his point of view should be relevant for whatsoever religion in the modern context:

> ...the clearest, purest religious devotion is finally destined to serve national and social claims, those that can best serve as an obstacle to that unity of life founded on a common awareness of profound existence. ... (T)hose are the effects of an unfortunate exegesis and that it would be absurd to make the responsibility for it fall on the Vedanta or the Upanishads. ... (S)piritual problems can only be approached with the greatest rigour and the most severe precautions. Westerners, who, like other peoples, are especially familiar with chatter and palaver, have the particular characteristic of talking nonsense and yet of believing in language.[24]

This rejection of political action in Blanchot should be viewed not as inaction in the political domain, but as the 'retreat of the political' in the sense that Philippe Lacoue-Labarthe and Jean-Luc Nancy have used this expression.[25] It should also be understood in terms of Blanchot's notion of death as 'passivity,' a notion which is related to Levinas's position on death as the 'impossibility of possibility,' in opposition to Heidegger's perspective on death as the 'possibility of impossibility.' Death, as we know, occupies a central position in many of Blanchot's writings on art and literature. A whole long essay, 'Literature and the Right to Death,' in the book *The Work of Fire* is devoted to this question. I shall refer to a shorter account of this problem as it is presented in a section entitled "Two Versions of the Imaginary," that forms part of the Appendix of Blanchot's most well-known work, *The Space of Literature.*

Blanchot, Literature and the Politico-Religious

Though Blanchot's "Two Versions..." is more directly concerned with the artistic image or the art-work, many of his other philosophical reflections converge in it. What is the relation between image and reality/being? Does the former come after the latter or before? The image has a force of its own that cannot be determined or controlled by the humans. One of its functions, Blanchot says, "is to quiet, to humanize the formless nothingness pressed upon us by the indelible residue of being."[26] More than the form which we can consciously perceive, and which may be compared with the object, it is the substance or the force of the image that does not cease to haunt us. It is this substantive dimension of the image that keeps surging towards us, in spite of us, disturbing our relationship with reality as it is given. It is also what Blanchot refers to as "the passivity proper to the image—a passivity which makes us suffer the image even when we ourselves appeal to it... "[27] This force of the image that precedes the object is also what Levinas in his account of the aesthetic domain, calls 'the shadow of reality.'[28]

Even if one were to consider, as in ordinary analysis, the image as secondary to the object, that is, coming after the latter, the image has its own autonomy of being as "that which no one can grasp, the unreal, the impossible."[29] Besides, and perhaps over and above the object, image appears as the thing distanced in its being, "present in its absence, graspable because ungraspable, appearing in so far as disappeared."[30] The surging, autonomous image, with its proliferating possibilities, in its existence as being in non-being, presence in absence, can be more perfect and more refined than the object. It is, as per Blanchot's analysis, what the object has suppressed "in order to be an object—something counter to which it had defined and built itself up." The image as presence in absence, would be for the object, "its presence liberated from existence."[31]

This analysis is the basis of Blanchot's comparison between the image and the corpse. Both have the same kind of 'strangeness.' The image and the corpse belong not to this world, but to a world of their own, a world that is nowhere and here at the same time. Both the image and the cadaver serve to remind us of the world that has been left behind or repressed by the object or by the living person, a world that now surges in its own affirmation. Just as the image is the shadow of reality, the cadaver *resembles* "the impersonal being, distant and inaccessible," a *he* or *it*, which occupies a world of proliferating and indeterminate forms or meanings. Of course, this idea of the image as corpse, and to its passivity is clearly linked to Heidegger's comparison of art to the uselessness of a broken tool.[32] Writing—art or literature —cannot play a direct role in practical and active life. By virtue of the passivity of image's existence, like the corpse, it participates in the unconcealment (*aletheia*) of the given world or the community. It does not actively tell or show the truth of the world. The dead body and the image, rather than actively speak of the truth of the community and the world, passively exposes us to the other of the world and of the community that is always 'unworked' (*désoeuvré*). That is to say, art and literature result in *unconcealment*, in the sense that Heidegger had identified it as a mode of truth.[33]

The image in art and literature, in this perspective, does not participate in the actual world. It subsists passively outside the actual world, as the source for the interruption of and interval in the world in action. It is not a virile force that can change the world, but is itself the result of a retreat from the existent world, into the other of the world of being (and yet not a world beyond). Art is this incessant 'passing' (to) outside the world of being without ever being able to be actively present in the latter, or to have a meaning that can even for once be finalized and intentionally used. This 'passivity,' this 'impossibility' is akin to the impossibility of dying. Death cannot be a resource for knowing the world, and thus for augmenting the world in a temporal transaction. It is in the passivity of death and of the image that the world yields itself to its own other. Thus, the self or the same 'passes' to its other in and through death. The emphasis is not on active transformation, but on incessant passing on to the unpredictable non-being that is yet-to-come, or to the 'otherwise than being' in Levinasian terms, interrupting and opening up the existent being. Blanchot's 'two versions' present themselves

> ... as if the choice between death as understanding's possibility and death as the horror of impossibility had also to be the choice between sterile truth and the prolixity of the non-true.[34]

Correspondingly, the two versions of the imaginary, present themselves as two different possibilities of meaning. As Blanchot puts it:

> ... what speaks in the name of image "sometimes" still speaks of the world, and "sometimes" introduces us into the undetermined milieu of fascination. "Sometimes" it gives us the pwoe to control things in their absence and through fiction, thus maintaining us in a domain rich with meaning, but "sometimes" it removes us to where things are perhaps present, but in their image, and where the image is the movement of passivity, where it has no value either significative or affective, but is the passion of indifference.[35]

Meaning of the image that proceeds from the 'centre of fascination' is however not one of determinate significative contours. But rather, "(h)ere *meaning* does not escape into another meaning, but into the other of all meaning."[36]

How does what Blanchot says about 'writing' compare with his position on religion? We have seen that Blanchot's main vocation is as an astute critical reader of texts. He is concerned with writings and writers on religion, but he himself has no direct involvement in religion. In spite of his one-time participation in a journal run by religious revolutionaries, Blanchot's orientation to religion and 'spirituality' is quite ambiguous and clearly ambivalent. But at the same time, he critically intervenes in written discussions on religion and spirituality. An informed writing of 'god' is not anathema to him. On this theme, Jean-Luc Nancy notes that:

> Now, even if Blanchot's text[37] is devoid of any interest in religion (beyond the fact that a Christian—a specifically Catholic—culture shows through here and there in a remarkable way,...), the name *God* is not simply absent from it.

In his essay Nancy tries to show that for Blanchot the name 'God' is meant to stand for 'absent sense,' or even for 'absenting of sense.' 'God' thus plays hide and seek by both appearing and disappearing in Blanchot. That is to say, the word God as 'absent sense' is thoroughly and consistently ambivalent. For, according to Nancy:

> ... an "absent sense" makes sense in and by its very absenting, in such a way that, in sum, it never stops not "making sense." Thus this is what "writing" designates for Blanchot— ...—, the movement of exposure to the flight of sense that withdraws signification from "sense" in order to give to the very sense of that flight—an élan, an opening, an indefatigable exposure that consequently does not even "flee," that flees flight as well as presence.[38]

Clearly, even when Blanchot names God, a concept of god is eschewed. The absenting of sense that it involves, is also a flight of sense, but at the same time, a tracing of that flight of sense. According to Nancy,

> ... this name does not involve an existence but precisely the nomination (and this is neither designation nor signification) of that absenting... This is why the most precious gift of philosophy is, for Blanchot, not even in the operation of the negation of the existence of God, but in the simple shrinking away, a dissipation of that existence. Thought does not think unless it be from this point of departure.[39]

In his essay, "Atheism and Writing-Humanism and the Cry", Blanchot seeks to situate the place of God in relation to what he views as the ever-opening field of writing, as well as, the position of man and humanism in relation to the latter. The question of God is introduced as an 'absent question' which in its posing can only be 'a surplus of question.' But then, man has somehow displaced God (for instance in Nietzsche's 'overman') and consequently

> ... man is but the pseudonym of a God who dies in order to be reborn in his creature. Humanism is a theological myth.[40]

Blanchot's attempt in the essay is to search for the possibility of an atheism that is neither linked to the 'theological myth' of humanism nor to an atheism which is just a moment in the history of thought or something that is just the "simple project of personal consciousness." The difficulty here is that often atheism does not hesitate to resort to something akin to divine discourse. (We may point out here the fact that Fichte appealed to the German people to consider their language as their divinity. Language or nation, we know has often been divinized.) It is further compounded by the fact that atheists and believers are often prepared to exchange their places. This is because, at one level, the one who is religious might seek the 'other' of his given order, an act which attracts for him the label 'atheist' (the Church has often feared such 'heretics'), and at another level, the one who is atheist may get stuck with a unique value, in a theological mode. (That is how modern political ideologies can be theological, that there can be political theology.) Blanchot formulates the contours of this problem:

> ... seeking the true atheists among the believers (always necessarily idolatrous) and the true believers among those who are radically atheist, we will perhaps, be exchanging one for the other, happily come to lose the two figures they perpetuate.[41]

Even in the modern fields of knowledge, including philosophy, both atheism and theology maintain more or less the same unified discourse, even if they proceed from opposing poles. They cannot evade a founding unity, be it that of a rationally identifiable pattern of sameness or that of a hidden depth, in the theological vein, accessible or not, effable or ineffable. These discursive attempts, Blanchot says, have never been able to go

> ... so far as to offer itself silently to the *Other*: to what would be *excluded* not only from the Same, but also from the *One*. For God can very well be the Other and the Wholly Other, but he remains ever and always the unity of the Unique.[42]

Thus, the critical task according to Blanchot, is to break free of "the domination exercised by the theological even if it is in the humanist form of atheism." And this is where he would like to emphasize an elevated role for 'writing.' Writing, because it is associated with truth as 'unconcealment' of the existing discourse, distances itself from 'light' and makes its way through obscurity (whence the title of Blanchot's first novel, *Thomas the Obscure*). Therefore, in Blanchot's yet uncertain formulation, it is possible to ask

> whether to *write* is not, from the start and before anything else, to interrupt what has not ceased to reach us as *light*: to ask as well if *writing* is not, always from the start and before all else, to hold oneself, by way of interruption, in relation with the *Neutral* (or in a neutral relation): without reference to the Same, without reference the One, outside everything visible and everything invisible.[43]

After displacing both atheism and theology with writing, Blanchot goes on to connect the latter, in a remarkably deft manner, with the 'cry' which is itself viewed as the generic expression of a post-humanist response. Like writing (*l'écriture*), the 'cry' (*le cri*) is that which breaks out of the limits of discourse, and even of language, and its event does not belong to any specific human being or a group of humans. The cry is also marked by an impersonality (like literature, writing), and its voice involves not just the representation of a "subjective interiority, but on the contrary, the reverberation of *space* opening onto the *outside*." The cry is to be distinguished from speech, made up of words, and its voice is associated with the 'impersonal' murmur that preexists before either speech or writing as these are discursively organized.

> The voice that speaks without a word, silently—in the silence of a cry—tends to be, no matter how interior, the voice of no one. What speaks when the voice speaks? It situates itself nowhere, neither in nature nor in culture, but manifests itself in a space of redoubling, of echo and resonance where it is not someone but rather this unknown space—its discordant accord, its vibration—that speaks without speaking.[44]

Conclusion

The attempt here is not to defend or endorse Blanchot's criticism of Gandhi and his European admirers, as well as of the followers of Hindu thought, but to understand the difficult logic of his argumentation, in his own terms. Gandhi was undoubtedly the most revered of the Indian leaders, and indeed of the whole movement against Western colonialism painfully rampant in many parts of the world during the period in question. The list of those who saw him as the saviour of humanity is indeed too long even to be attempted here, though it is worth naming a few great men from across the globe who were inspired by Gandhi: Albert Einstein, Romain Rolland, Martin Luther King Jr., Nelson Mandela, Octavio Paz and of course, Rabindranath Tagore who was his close collaborator in the Indian freedom movement.

Indeed, Blanchot essays a displacement of the political domain, which is also intended to be a retreat from it, a retreat of 'writing.' At heart, Blanchot shares Gandhi's concern about the impoverishment of the modern, especially, the political in the desert from which religion has vanished. But his solution, unlike that of Gandhi, is not to bring religion frontally back into politics, but to diffuse, disseminate and deconstruct both religion and politics, through 'writing'. In the singularity that writing is, we are forever exposed to what is *outside* our immediate historical existence, we encounter the immemorial, and we are open to the infinite future that is to come. And in this 'writing' there is only passivity, or the impossibility of dying, or dying-living, an incessant resurrection, where it is not man who resurrects as per the Christian belief, but death itself is resurrected,[45] everywhere and at every moment. It is towards this post-Christian, post-theological, nay, post-theistic and post-modern world that Blanchot seems to have striven in most of his writings.

NOTES

1. Bident, Christophe, 1998, p. 57.
2. Rolland, Romain, *Mahatma Gandhi,* 1924. English version: *Mahatma Gandhi—The Man Who Became One With the Universal Being* (1924); Gandhi, M.K., *Autobiography OR The Story of My Experiments With Truth* (1927-29).
3. Perhaps it is worth mentioning here that during his Italian visit Gandhi was denied permission to meet the Pope Pius XI. See Mario Prayer (2009) for more details. Prayer also presents a well-documented account of the Catholic Church's strong opposition to Gandhi during the 1930s.

4. Bident, 1998, p. 57.
5. The essay originally appeared in *Journal des débats*, February 17, 1942, p. 3. The English translation of the book *Faux pas* was published by Stanford University Press in 2001.
6. Gandhi, M.K., *Leur civilisation et notre délivrance*, Introduction de Lanza del Vasto, Paris, 1957.
7. According to bibliographic information available, the book contained texts by Jacques Masui, Jean Herbert, René Daumal, Shankaracharya, Chandidas, Ravidas, Ramakrishna, Vivekananda, Aurobindo, Rabindranath Tagore, Mahatma Gandhi, Kabir, Pratima Tagore, Satyarayana, Swami Pavitrananda, Anilbaran Roy, Siddheswarananda, Camille Rao, Akshaya Banerji, K.G. Mashruwala, Dr. G.B., Lizelle Reymond, Louise Morin, Humbert-Sauvageot, L. Barbillion, Emile Dermenghem, Lanza del Vasto, F. Le Lionnais, Jean Grenier and Benjamin Fondane.
8. Commenting on the first two essays, Jean-Luc Nancy says that "they are truly remarkable in that they show Blanchot rigidly clinging ('*crispation*') to a Christian model of religion and a rejection of everything that seemed inauthentic or confused and diffused; for Blanchot, the Christian source of a very "sublime" representation of God, of the "Very High" with its great mysteries (Trinity, Incarnation, Redemption, Resurrection) and the idea of "communion" has always played an important and hidden role." (personal communication).
9. The words in inverted commas are taken from the titles of works on Blanchot: Gerald L. Bruns, *Maurice Blanchot—The Refusal of Philosophy* (1997); Leslie Hill, *Blanchot—Extreme Contemporary* (1997); Lars Iyer, *Blanchot's Vigilance—Literature, Phenomenology and the Ethical* (2005).
10. I use the word 'literature,' which is meant to stand for both literature and art. 'Literature' appears in the title of Blanchot's most popular work, *The Space of Literature*. But more appropriately, one could use Blanchot's preferred word, 'writing' that is meant to denote any politically significant and deconstructive literary or artistic activity.
11. Blanchot, Maurice, 1999. *Thomas the Obscure*. In a short foreword to this work, the author says that he started writing it in 1932, it was delivered to press in May 1940, and was published 1941; Blanchot, Maurice, 1943. *Faux pas*. The title *Faux* pas may be interpreted as the acknowledgement of the wrong step that the author had taken towards religion, or more generally, religion

as the wrong step. Later, in the 1970s, Blanchot wrote a short work entitled, *Pas au-delà* whose English version is translated as *The Step Not Beyond* (1992).

12. This question is too vast to be discussed here. For a useful account, see, Watts, Phillip (1998) *Allegories of the Purge—How Literature Responded to the Post-War Trials of Writers and Intellectuals in France*. See also, Manjali, F. (2008) "Literature, Philosophy and the Discourse of Purity" in: *Language, Discourse and Culture, Contemporary Philosophical Perspectives* (62-72).
13. We cannot, within the space of this chapter, do justice to the variety of issues that have been discussed by philosophers under the rubric of Gandhi's religious thought. For a useful reference, see, Chatterjee, Margaret (1983).
14. It is useful to consider the specifically Gandhian method of 'passive resistance,' also known as *Satyagraha*, or the 'adherence to truth.' Gandhi described passive resistance in terms of the 'soul-force.' See, Chapter XVII of *Hind Swaraj* (Gandhi, 2010: 63-70). It is also tempting to try and compare Gandhi's 'passive resistance' with the Levinas-Blanchot notion of 'passivity,' but this is beyond the scope of this paper.
15. Bident, aptly calls Blanchot the 'invisible partner.' Also, Blanchot, a man of least public presence, was hardly 'represented' in the modern visual medium of photographs; not more than 3 photographs of him are said to have survived for posterity from his long life of 96 years.
16. G.K. Chesterton, journalist and detective fiction writer, was a favourite of many writers of his time. Gandhi admired his writing. In an article entitled "White's Views on Indian Awakening" that appeared in his edited journal *Indian Opinion* (1910) he writes about Chesterton: "Mr. G.K. Chesterton is one of the great writers here. He is an Englishman of a liberal temper. Such is the perfection of his style that his writings are read by millions with great avidity... I too believe what he has said is reasonable." After having quoted profusely from a Chesterton article that appeared in *Illustrated London News* of September 18, 1909, where the author expresses his strong support for an Indian version of the nation's freedom, Gandhi concludes: "Indians must reflect over these views of Mr. Chesterton and consider what they must demand. What is the way to make Indian people happy? May it not be that we advance our own interests in the name of the Indian people? Or, that we have been endeavouring to destroy what the Indian people have carefully nurtured over

thousands of years? I, for one, was led by Mr. Chesterton's article to all these reflections and I place them before the readers of *Indian Opinion*." (From Gujarati, *Indian Opinion*, January 8, 1910) (See *Chesterton Review*, Vol. X1X, February 1993, pp. 92-4). In an afterword to Chesteron's 'allegorical' detective fiction, *The Man Who Was Thursday*, Robert Giddings says: "Although he is now a rather neglected literary figure, G.K. Chesterton was one of the most prolific and influential writers and thinkers of the twentieth century. He was a literary and social critic, historian, playwright, novelist, poet, Catholic theologian and apologist and a tireless debater. His literary output included several hundred poems, five novels, some two hundred short stories, four thousand essays and several plays, but he still considered himself primarily a journalist. His... *The Man Who Was Thursday*— written in 1908 when he was in his mid-thirties—is arguably his best-known novel and, some say, his masterpiece." (Chesterton, 2008: 175).

17. See, Aravamudan (2007), particularly Chapter 3, 'Theosophistries,' for an illuminating account of this spiritual convergence. As per the author's succinct account: "The Theosophical Scoiety was founded ... in New York, in 1875, by Helena P. Blavatsky and Henry S. Olcott. Flirting with Dayananda's Arya Samaj and integrating itself into the Buddhist and Hindu aspects of spiritual tradition, Theopsophy was a cosmopolitan alternative when compared with the parochial nature of the Raj. Founded in the transidiomatic environment generated by the British Empire, Theosophy explored the fungibility of occult practices drawn from plural religious and spiritual traditions." (p. 105).
18. It is to be noted that Gandhi is more directly denouncing the rise of 'modern civilization'. He writes in the Preface to the Hind Swaraj: "The British Government in India constitutes a struggle between the Modern Civilization, which is the Kingdom of Satan, and the Ancient Civilization, which is Kingdom of God. The one is the God of War, the other is the God of Love." (Gandhi, 2010, p. 8) Gandhi appreciated the deeper values, not only of Christianity, but also of all other major religions. Mahadev Desai, his long-term personal assistant writes that Gandhi read out passages from the Koran and the Bible, and interpreted them for the benefit of college students at his Sabarmati Ashram, near Ahmedabad. When he was charged of being a 'Christian in secret' he is reported to have replied: "The charge ... is both a

libel and a compliment—a libel because there are men who can believe me to be capable of being that openly. There's nothing in the world that would keep me from professing Christianity or any other faith, the moment I felt the truth of and the need for it. Where there is fear there is no religion. The charge is a compliment in that it is a reluctant acknowledgement of my capacity for appreciating the beauties of Christianity. ... If I could call myself, say, a Christian, or a Mussalman, with my own interpretation of the Bible or the Quran, I should not hesitate to call myself either. For then, Hindu, Christian, or Mussalman would be synonymous terms." (Desai, 1978: 377-78).

19. Vasto, Lanza del, 1971. p. 97.
20. See the chapter, "Playing the English Gentleman" in Gandhi's autobiography.
21. Blanchot, 2001, p. 33.
22. Ibid., p. 26.
23. Ibid., p. 33.
24. Ibid., p. 36. Commenting on Blanchot's 'On Hindu Thought,' Jean-Luc Nancy says: "This text is less harsh, less aggressive than the other two. It indicates that Blanchot had to change his tone a little bit. His criticism is turned almost entirely against the chattering of the Westerners. In their loose talk (but Gandhi is not excluded, but in any case we no longer talk about him) they drown the real issue, which is one of silence or, more precisely listening to the silence. There are a few Biblical sources for this. Blanchot must have a silent, sublime "spirit" that retreats to an absolute distance... I admit that these texts give me an unpleasant impression of arrogance, not to the East or India, but to a "chatter" certainly rightly criticized (this epoch was very much taken with "Hindu spirituality"...) but also distrusted from a disdainful height that does not explain what it really wants." (personal communication).
25. Lacoue-Labarthe, Philippe and Jean-Luc Nancy, *Retreating the Political* (1996). The original French title of the work, is *Le retrait du politique*, where the word '*retrait*' is intended to mean a retracing and a re-treating of as well as a retreat from the 'political.'
26. Blanchot, 1995, p. 255.
27. Ibid., p. 255. Broadly speaking, the notion of 'passivity' which recurs in Blanchot and in Levinas may be characterized as the incessant surging/appearing in time of the potential within the actual. As absence that interrupts the presence, in a

deconstructive movement, it is considered essentially transformative, of both the subjective and the objective, as well as of the intersubjective. For instance, for Blanchot, literature as incessant murmur, with its provenance in silence, interrupts the given discourse of the world.

28. See Levinas, "Reality and Its Shadow," in: *The Levinas Reader*, (ed.) S. Hand (1989: 129-43).
29. Blanchot, 1955, p. 255.
30. Ibid., p. 256.
31. Ibid.
32. Ibid., p. 257.
33. Heidegger, Martin, "The Origin of the Work of Art," in *Poetry, Language, Thought* (1975, pp. 17-87). Heidegger's notion of unconcealment (*aletheia*) is also developed in this essay.
34. Blanchot, 1955, op. cit., p. 261.
35. Ibid., p. 263.
36. Ibid.
37. Nancy is referring to an essay, "Atheism and Writing: Humanism and the Cry," a chapter in Blanchot's The Infinite Conversation (Blanchot, M., 1992, pp. 246-63). The original French work is *L'entretien infini* (Gallimard, Paris, 1969). See, Nancy, "The Name God in Blanchot" in: *Dis-Enclosure—The Deconstruction of Christianity* (2008, pp. 85-8).
38. Nancy, 2008a, p. 86.
39. Ibid., pp. 86-7.
40. Blanchot, 1992a, p. 248.
41. Ibid., p. 253.
42. Ibid., p. 256.
43. Ibid.
44. Ibid., p. 258.
45. On this point, see Nancy 2008, p. 95.

8

The Discourse of Death

Death—mortality as demanded by the duration of time.

— E. Levinas.

My interest in studying the 'discourse of death' is intellectually motivated by the writings on death by Heidegger, Levinas, Blanchot, Derrida, Nancy and Agamben. It was from these philosophers that I learnt that the questions of language and literature cannot be separated from the question of death. What is attempted here is not a thanatological exercise of understanding what death is. What the philosophers have done is not to provide an explanation of death, but to consider it as the central phenomenon of existence itself. Being can be understood only in relation to death's association with it. At the same time, while working on this essay, I have come to understand that there is great variation in the philosophical, literary and other discourses on death as it has appeared across different historical periods and geographical regions. Though people everywhere have striven to support and sustain life with varying degrees of intensity and to commemorate death, at least that of the members of one's own family or community, death is perceived and spoken of differently in different cultures, and thus seems to be very resistant to yielding a unified picture. It is impossible to judge at this point, whether this diversity in 'the discourses of death' is indeed a positive factor in the sustenance of life in our world. One can only begin to analyse them with the requisite philosophical rigour.

***

One of the most remarkable aspects of our existence on the planet is the fact that human death has been memorialized from ancient times. From the Pyramids in Egypt to the Taj Mahal in India, great monuments and inscriptions bear witness to the extraordinary and even superhuman efforts to erect edifices in memory of human beings who have inevitably and by necessity departed from their lives. Such memorials are a distinct attribute of the humans that mark them out from other species of animals. They are considered as the very basis of human civilization as well as our historical and cultural memory.

In the unfolding of time, what one can notice is a clear asymmetry between birth and death, especially in the case of human beings. Despite modern technologies of reproduction, there are still very limited ways to be born. Death, on the other hand, can occur in many different ways. While inter-human contact involving emotions, knowledge or practical effort can lead to the birth of an infant, a lack or an excess of any of the basic elements, air, water, earth or fire, can result in a person's death. And moreover, while birth can be a more or less well-programmed temporal event, the process of death may not easily submit to any such temporal order or calculation. Death may arrive to a person unannounced, and it can happen anywhere or at any time, owing to natural or non-natural causes. In the case of humanly imposed death or murder, it can become the subject of medico-legal or political discourse. Ironically, only those who strongly believe in the fate's unknown tend to speak of a programmed event of death. It is perhaps this suddenness of death as compared to the slow anticipation of birth that makes the former a matter that is prone to linger indefinitely in our consciousness, memory, discourse, etc.

Though birth and death are regarded as the limit points of an individual's life, it is contestable whether these points can be located respectively at the beginning and the cessation of breathing. Just as 'pre-natal capabilities' in the fœtus have been claimed as an aspect of life, there have been fierce medico-legal discussions regarding the point of death, and thus whether the contemporary notion of a 'brain death' can really be the end-point of biological life. In any case, various religious beliefs, mystical or not, would insist that the cessation of biological life is not the end of a human person, at least in a metaphysical sense. Historically speaking, a discourse about the 'soul' or the 'resurrection' or 'reincarnation' of any person or any living being that has set foot on the earth, has not been the privilege or the prerogative of any particular thought or dogma, Eastern or Western.

***

As with any other aspect of human life, cultures everywhere seem to have proposed practical manuals for dying well. Very often, it was important to learn to die well in order to preserve the purity and integrity of one's soul. Such manuals for learning to 'die well' were common in medieval Europe and in the Eastern traditions. The Christian Last Sacrament may be deemed as one of such aids for a ritually sanctified death. In the East, knowledge of death or knowing how to die well, has always been part of a superior religious life. In the *Katha Upanishad* of the Hindus, Yama, the god of death in his dialogue with Prince Nachiketa reveals the possibility of transcending death and therefore the hardship of life, through the knowledge of *Atman*, the soul that bridges the mortal self with the eternal universe:

> The knowing self is not born; It does not die. It has not risen from anything; nothing has risen from It. Without beginning, eternal, everlasting and ancient, It does not die when the body dies./If the killer thinks he kills and if the killed man thinks he is killed, neither of them apprehends rightly. The Self does not kill, nor is It killed./*Atman*, smaller than the small, greater than the great, is hidden in the hearts of all living creatures. A man who is free from desires beholds the majesty of the self through the tranquillity of the senses and the mind, and becomes free from grief.[1]

The traditional 'Indian' wisdom, be it Hindu or Buddhist, is often individual-directed. A society is not directly referred to, but through an individual's deep knowledge of his own life or death, the society is benefited. In the Mâdhyamaka Buddhism of the Tibetans, the knowledge of the *emptiness* of both life and death, is a means for avoiding the pain of death and to achieve reincarnation. In the *Tibetan Book of the Dead,* death is compared to sleep, and from which evil thoughts that have accumulated in the mind during a person's life can be ritually eliminated through expert mediation, preparing the corpse for purification and subsequent reincarnation. By invoking an everlasting emptiness the Tibetan master assumes the continuity between one's life and his death; and between one life and another life, with purification of the universal consciousness as the chief goal.

The *Book of the Dead* says:

> Thy body being a mental body is incapable of dying even though beheaded and quartered. In reality, thy body is of the nature of emptiness; thou needst not be afraid. The Lords of Death are thine own hallucinations. Thy desire-body is a body of propensities, and void. Emptiness cannot injure Emptiness; the qualityless cannot injure the qualityless. Apart from one's own hallucinations, in reality there are no such things existing outside oneself as Lord of Death, or god, or demon, or the Bull-headed Spirit of Death. Act so as to recognize this.[2]

In certain oriental traditions, such as that of some of the tribal traditions in India, and perhaps in Africa, the soul of the dead is appeased by feeding the animals, such as the crows. Among the Paniyans of south-western India, appeasing the soul/ghost of a dead family member by feeding crows with rice is considered essential for the sanctity and the ethos of the tribal community.

***

A study of the discourse of death, cannot avoid an inquiry into the discourse of suicides. Since Durkheim we have learnt not to view suicides as merely individual acts. Suicides are invariably construed to have familial or social references even if suicide notes—an important genre in itself of discourse of death— when available insist not to have any. Dostoevsky, the great novelist of the social reality of 19th century Russia is said to have created 17 characters who commit suicide, Kirilov being the best-known of these. Death and suicides clearly mark the modern genre of literary discourses, everywhere. Of course, this is not to ignore their precedents in the tragedies in the earlier (pre-modern, baroque and ancient) epochs. We can easily contrast the and-then-they-lived-happily-thereafter ending of a large number of folktales, especially the fairy tales, from the tragic or absurd ends that populate modern literary works.

Certainly, death is a dominant motif in many of the epic tragedies of ancient Greece, and the *Mahabharata*, the great Indian epic is characterized by an avalanche of seemingly senseless killings, resulting from family feuds and wars. The interpretations of these texts have tended to oscillate between the perspectives of a weighty and well-thought cynicism towards life and a heroic and healthy acceptance of death.

The famed suicides in the Japanese context suggest a fluid movement across different axes: individual-social, tradition-modernity, private-public, real-literary. Here and elsewhere, it is often difficult to clearly distinguish martyrdom from suicide, especially when the latter is due to the willing exposure to the danger of being killed. The death of the Samurai is a case in point. We are told that death is the *Way* of the Samurai, for between death and non-death the Samurai must choose the former. It is this and what is perceived as the "nobility of failure" associated with the ideal of the Samurai that makes it facile for him to *eulogize* death and to write his 'death-poems' with equanimity. For example:

> Both the victor/and the vanquished are
> but drops of dew,
> but bolts of lightning—
> thus should we view the world.[3]
>
> (Ôuchi Yoshitaka, 16th century)

Or,

> Holding forth this sword
> I cut vacuity in twain
> In the midst of the great fire,
> a stream of refreshing breeze.[4]
>
> (Shiaku Nyûdo, 14th century)

Into the 20th century, the Japanese society has also witnessed its famous 'literary suicides': that of Dasai Osamu (by drowning in 1948) and that of Mishima Yukio (theatrical '*seppuku*' or splitting one's stomach in 1970). The event of Mishima's spectacular suicide was of a political nature, reacting to the post-Second World War developments in Japan. He is said to have planned his own death in minute detail years in advance, and in tandem with the suicide narratives of his own literary fiction.[5]

***

Martyrdom is strictly a religio-political category, used in the case of forced death or killing of a decidedly innocent person owing to his or her beliefs and convictions. Socrates and Jesus are regarded as the most famous martyrs in the European tradition. Both were put to death for their convictions and not for their crimes. However, we know that the line that separates a conviction from a crime cannot but be a matter of the discourse of death. "What is a true belief?", "Why does one submit oneself to death at the hands of others?" are questions that are never immediately settled, without a long process of interpretation within a given culture. Long before his death at the hands of a fundamentalist assassin, Gandhi in the context of the Indian independence movement had declared his willingness to become a martyr in the cause of non-violence:

> I would suffer humiliation, every torture, absolute ostracism and death itself to prevent the movement from becoming violent or a precursor of violence. (quoted by Romain Rolland)

Sacrifice is perhaps the most primordial mode of executing and interpreting a death. We know since Abraham that killing or the readiness to kill the other sacrificially is at the foundation of ethical questioning in human societies. Man's most precious product within his family or community has to be first excluded or eliminated and then re-included as a value or idea, in a simultaneous operation of sacrifice and consecration. Nancy (2005): "Sacrifice underscores negation, consecration underscores offering: the two together constitute the intimate contradiction of sacrifice."[6]

***

With the advent of modernity, however, man's attitude towards the life and death of other people, and towards death as such have undergone profound and irrevocable transformations. According to Foucault, the biopolitics that informs the modern world is characterized by the replacement of the "ancient right to *take* life and *let* live... by a power to *foster* life or *disallow* it to the point of death." The modern sovereign power is no more eager to impose death on its subjects, but "it is over life, throughout its unfolding that power establishes its domination; death is power's limit, the moment that escapes it; death becomes the most secret aspect of existence, the most 'private'."[7]

It is these transformations in the order of death, aided and abetted not only by biology but also by politics (in short Enlightenment, Revolution and Romantic thought), first in the West and then by contagion in most other parts of the world, that made death a central theme in the modern philosophical, political and literary discourses. Ariès notes in the following terms the transformation in feelings brought about by the 'great romantic revolution': "It was thus this first romantic generation for the first time refused death. It exalted and hypostatized [death] and at the same time, it created, not just of any one, but of a loved being, an inseparable immortal."[8] And at the same time, from a mortal's perspective, Ariès tells us that death was no more to be understood within the religious frame of punishment for the guilt of one's sins, nor as a transitional moment in a life-death continuum, but as sheer absence, a pure and absolute negativity, an infinite and sublime nothingness.[9] This same idea of the negativity of death that stared at man in the beginning of the 19th century prompted Nietzsche a few decades later to shockingly proclaim (and perhaps for the first time ever) the 'death of god' to underscore the nihilism that was clawing at the very roots of a culture of religion.

It is via an understanding of death as negativity and as nothingness that Hegel and Heidegger affirmed their ideas on the relationship between language and death. Hegel declared that in so far as the human is a speaking and mortal being he is a 'negative being' who "is what he is not and is not what he is." That is to say, there is always an unbridgeable gap between his existence in language and the language of his existence. One's own language is not what can identify one's subjectivity in its past or in its future, and one cannot identify oneself in one's language. Man, Heidegger says, is a "place-holder of language."

Hegel understood language and consciousness as continuous movement of the negativity derived from mortality. His notion of '*sublation*' referred to the death or negation of the thing in concept and in language, and its raising to a higher level in the human consciousness. The end-point of this perpetual repressing-and-lifting movement of consciousness is what he viewed as the Absolute Idea. Evidently, and painfully, this idea is clearly not divorced from that of sacrifice—of things as well as peoples in the necessary march of human history as Hegel envisaged it.

Heidegger's *Being and Time* (especially § 50-55) has the most detailed and the most intense discussion on the theme of death appearing in any contemporary philosophical text. The emergence of authentic human subjectivity in the face of the possibility and the inevitability of death and the nothingness that envelops it, is the central concern there. Death that lies in wait for a human person and his dread of death's state of nothingness leads him to authentic existence, according to Heidegger.

This ontology of the human subjectivity based on death as possibility has been staunchly opposed by the post-Heideggerian philosophers. For Levinas, death is the impossibility of a self-possessing subjectivity ready for acting out its predestined historical role. One's own death is *not being able to be able*, the impossibility of possibility. One is affected not as much by the dread of the nothingness of death that awaits one, but as he is haunted by the 'horror' of the spectre or the '*il y a*' that precedes one. It is in this sense that one assumes responsibility for the death of the other person, one's neighbour. Rather than derive power from the death of the other for whose death one is responsible and whom one might have sacrificed, one can only assume culpability for his death. The self is indebted to the next person who dies. In memory of the victims of the holocaust, Paul Celan writes: "The world is gone; I must carry you." Since "death is the *no-response*" from the other, I remain in relation with the other, a relation that is "my deference to someone who no longer responds, already a culpability—the culpability of the survivor." (Levinas) This is what makes the time that remains after the death of the other a different time for me and for my community. Each time, it is a rupture of the historical time in which I live. Death does not empower the self, but transforms the time to come through the response of the survivor.

Blanchot and Nancy have articulated this exposition of the self, and infinite appearance of otherness through death in literature. For Blanchot, literature is the neutral space where the other of our subjective and objective worlds appears incessantly. This implies an incessant negation and death of both the writer and the reader without forever achieving any positivity. For Nancy, a community rather than promoting its own immanence, would be constantly interrupting itself, its 'myth,' through writing. It is a 'compearance' of many others resulting from the death and exposition of their corresponding selves.

More than fiction, perhaps poetry has been traditionally the chosen literary vehicle for a 'discourse of death'. Elegies and threnodies have been the mourning genres in poetry which may be described as such as *'voix endeuillé,'* 'mourned voice' (Michel Deguy). Here is the musically-charged second stanza of *Threnody* written by Ralph Waldo Emerson, the 19th century American philosopher and poet after the death of his five-year-old son:

> I see my empty house,
>
> I see my trees repair their boughs;
> And he, the wondrous child,
>
> Whose silver warble wild
>
> Outvalued every pulsing sound
> Within the ear's cerulean round,—

The hyacinthine boy, for whom

Morn well might break and April bloom,

The gracious boy, who did adorn

The world whereinto he was born,
And by his countenance repay

The favour of the loving Day,—

Has disappeared from the Day's eye;

Far and wide she cannot find him;

My hopes pursue, they cannot bind him.
Returned this day, the South-wind searches,

And finds young pines and budding birches;
But finds not the budding man:

Nature, who lost, cannot remake him;
Fate let him fall, Fate can't retake him;

Nature, Fate, men, him seek in vain.[10]

In a certain way, all writing, all literature, at least from an ethical point of view, is a work of mourning. One leaves behind a certain familiar world, carries it forward to another. Friendship, fidelity gives way to survival. This is what can be referred to as the politics of mourning, which in the case of Derrida was never separated from what he called the 'politics of friendship.' Perhaps there can be no better instance of a philosophical 'discourses of death' than those that appear in Derrida's *The Work of Mourning* first published three years before his own death.

As to the question of what happens to us after our own death, answers have been provided in different traditions in terms of *reincarnation, resurrection,* reviviscence, etc. Socrates himself was a great votary of the idea of resurrection. We read him speaking to Cebes in the dialogue, *Phaedo*:

> ... I am confident that there is truly such a thing as living again, and that the living spring from the dead, and that the souls of the dead are in existence, and that the good souls have a better portion than the evil.[11]

Nancy has recently attempted to revive this very traditional idea of resurrection, though he has given his own interpretation to it. In a beautiful little book, *Noli me tangere* (2003), Nancy avers the centrality of death to human culture and the necessity of a bi-directional *relation* between life and death:

> Without death, there would only be contact, continuity and contagion, cancerous propagation of life which consequently would no longer be life—or rather not *existence*, would only be a life which would not be at the same time *anastasis*. Death opens the relation: that is to say the division (*partage*) of the departure. Each person comes and departs without end, incessantly. That which appears as the end reveals itself without end, incessantly.[12]

NOTES

1. *Katha Upanishad*, Part I, Chapter 2, Section 18, 19 and 20.
2. *The Tibetan Book of the Deed*, Book II, Part 1.
3. Death Poems, www.samurai-archives. com/deathof.html.
4. Ibid.
5. Wolfe, A.S., 1990, p. 36.
6. Nancy, Jean-Luc, 2005a, p. 15.
7. Foucault, M., 1976, p. 15.
8. Faucault, M., 1976, p. 138.
9. Ariès, P., 1977, p. 256.
10. See, Strauss, J., 2000a.
11. In Phaedo, Line 183-186. www. bartleby.com/2/1/32.html
12. Nancy, Jean-Luc, 2003, p. 74.

9

The Body of Sense, the Sense of Body

All our semiologies, all our mimologies, all our aesthetics tend toward this absolute body, toward this oversignifying body, a *body of sense* in the *sense of a body*.[1]

Corpus: all bodies, each outside the others, make up the inorganic body of sense.[2]

In our world, there have been different traditions of the 'body,' which may be based on religions, old or new, or on national cultures. These various traditions evidently imply different beliefs, attitudes towards, practices and treatments of the body. These, in turn may involve personal or social questions of health, hygiene, sacredness, etc., with regard to the body. How one treats one's own body, the other's body, and other living bodies, or for that matter the dead bodies, are often more or less codified in the traditions. This means that bodies are already marked more often than not by a strong cultural meaning. And conversely, meaning itself may or may not be seen as an attribute or extension of the body. For instance, meaning may be construed as akin to a seed—implying a certain fertile power of its dissemination, as the word *'semeion'* in the Greek tradition seems to suggest—or, its occurrence may be viewed as akin to a physical 'bursting forth,' or a 'spurting,' as the term *'sphota'* in the Indian tradition can be interpreted.

Jean-Luc Nancy's work, *Corpus* begins with a consideration of the body in the Western tradition, and particularly in the Christian religion where the sentence, 'This is my body' (*Hoc est enim meum corpus*—in Latin) has acquired a 'cult' status.

Here the body is meant to refer to the God's body, and therefore Nancy notes:

> The body of *that* (God, or the absolute, if you like)—and the fact that "that" *has a body* or that "that" *is* a body (and so we might think that "that" is *the* body, absolutely): that's our obsession.[3]

Is meaning in this tradition the name for the translation of the Absolute body, into and through its contact, with the worldly bodies, especially the human body? Can we speak of a 'world body' or *Corpus*, for which there is no outside (*Il n'y a pas de hors*-Corpus, to parody Derridas's well-known, *'Il n'y a pas de hors-texte'*), and inside of which there is infinite differentiation between sense and body, and of both sense and body? The Western tradition has perhaps oscillated between an idealism of Platonic philosophy and Christianity's desire to have a bodily God or even the body of God. This desire was perhaps for a necessary continuity between the God's body and the personal and the political bodies.[4] The idea of a 'body-politic' as elaborated by Kantorowicz.[5] and discussed by Nancy (more on this later) indeed implies a syntagmatic as well as a paradigmatic relationship with the God's body. Discounting the representational status of the sentence, 'This is my body,' Nancy remarks that, "if [the sentence] says something, it's beyond speech. It is spoken, it's exscribed—with bodily abandon."[6] This body, that is, the Christian body, is perhaps to be seen less as a body of or for knowledge, and more as an artistic body. Religious discourse might very well be taken as aesthetic, having the least representational value. Thus, in *Noli me tangere*, Nancy interprets another well-known Christic sentence, "Do not touch me" that follows the "resurrection" of Christ, in terms of the body's absence and its departure. In the place of a death-and-resurrection, that is often seen as the context of Jesus' utterance, "Do not touch me," Nancy sees there, a "dying indefinitely" and an "incessant parting."[7] Christ's body, in resurrection, as per this view, instead of being in a state of life after death, is rather in a state of permanent departure, and hence not accessible to be touched. According to Nancy, ""resurrection" is "the surrection, the surging of the unavailable, of the other, of the disappearing *in body and as body*."[8]

These remarks have to be understood in relation to the philosopher's treatment of what we may call the body-mind-sense complex. How does he seek to deconstruct not only the Absolute body, but also the particular bodies, and especially the micro-bodies, say, the neurons – bodies, each in permanent physical contact with other bodies – passing through a deconstruction of the human community, both particular, and general, that he calls the 'world'? Furthermore how does he deconstruct sense, not only as semiotic signification, but also the sense that exists in its phenomenological relationship with the body, both of which are invariably considered as a property of the human mind?[9] These are the questions that are examined here.

What is remarkable about 'body' today, Nancy wants us to note, is that there are bodies everywhere in the world, but philosophers have seldom liked to talk about this teeming multiplicity. There are over seven billion bodies in the world,[10] just to talk of the human bodies, without counting the seemingly preponderant variety and number of bodies of other living beings. Human bodies are themselves of a variety of hues and colours, of skin and of hair, differentiated in height, weight and blood-types. Bodies are often displaced in philosophical discourses by a mere conceptual body, or a body that has a more or less unified signification.[11] In relation to the spirit or the idea, often privileged by philosophers, the body is treated, especially in idealistic philosophies, as a subordinate counterpart, made up of mere material substance.

It would not be banal to say that millions of bodies make up our world today, and these millions of bodies are making or involved in making exponentially millions of senses. Millions of bodies are sensing and meaning. Ascribing an agency to all these bodies, we can perhaps see here every body saying, 'We are meaning.'[12] Ours is indeed an epoch of bodies, and of teeming and thronging meanings. Bodies are surging everywhere in our world, by themselves as well as in and as their meanings and images in discourses, and in this universal surge everybody seems to be saying, 'This is my body,' a desacralized version of the sacramental utterance.

The body that is resurrected between the philosophically dominant poles of spirit or idea and matter is not just any body, but a sacralized body, a *corpus*. It is a body in all its ramifications, a laterally and outwardly swerving body, a spurting body, an internally and externally extending and differentiating body. Body, Nancy tells us, is different from a mass, because the former is already internally differentiated and externally formed. It differentiates from itself towards its outside, and this extension towards the outside takes place in the form of further bodies or as thought or sense. Nancy draws our attention to a statement of Freud regarding thought: '*Psyche is extended, but knows nothing of it*.'

By way of its own extension, or through the extension of thought, the body is constantly touching other bodies. It also touches itself, producing more and more variegated same and other selves. The self is always selving, and the other is always further othering and the 'intersubjectivity' between the self and the other, that is, the 'in-between' is always reconstituted. It is the *touch*, directed both internally and externally to the other, that differentiates the body and the bodies, infinitely. Bodies are, at any given point, extending towards the outside, and extending so infinitely. In this extension, they are devoid of any intention of their own. In this endless extension towards the outside, bodies do not permit an entry into their insides, "except through murder or surgery."[13] This is what renders the body infinitely impenetrable. This is also what makes the body a 'secret'. When a body touches another body, it is a touch of extremities and the bodies continue to remain impenetrable to each other. In this touch, a body can *present* itself to the other, but cannot represent itself. That is what makes the 'other' a secret (Derrida: "The other is a secret because it is the other"). At the same time, Nancy clarifies, a secret, in its impenetrability, is like a body (but it can be blown open to scrutiny by violence). In its impenetrability and therefore in its secrecy, the other remains distinct from the self.[14] (Nancy: "Another: if it is an other, it is a body"[15]). The other which manifests itself in its compactness and distinctness can only be a body. "Bodies are first and always other—just as others are first and always bodies."[16] Or, further: "*An other is a body,* because only *a body is an other.*"[17]

Nancy attempts a rapprochement between the body and the mind by introducing a rather surprising notion of the 'weight' of thought, alongside and on par with the weight of the body. There's clearly an experience of the weight of the body, irrespective of whether it is the cause or the consequence of the idea of the Fall. That is to say, there is an ontology of weight. "The body *is* weight.... The body itself weighs."[18] This weight, Nancy seems to say, is not only vertical, but also horizontal. "Our world has inherited the world of gravity: all bodies weigh *on* one another, and *against* one another, heavenly bodies and callous, vitreous bodies and corpuscles."[19]

The body comes with its own weight, but its touch is light, and tender. Every touch further differentiates the body and the bodies, and that is how body touches thought and thought touches body. This touching of extremities is what *writing* essentially is. Body-writing, or *exscription*. Sense is what appears in every finite touch in the infinite contact and the infinite interval between exteriorities. Each time, the bodies, bodies touching, exscribe a different sense, and each time a sense in every sense. Body is what senses, or to put in another way, bodies sense as sensible bodies.[20]

Between the body and the sense, from body to body, and from body to sense, let there be sense, says Nancy. And: "Let there be writing, not *about* the body, but body itself."[21] Nancy:

> Now comes *mundus corpus*, the world as proliferating peopling of (the) body('s) places. What is coming is not at all appearance and spectacle would have us presume (a world of appearances, simulacra, and phantasms, lacking flesh and presence). This kind of discourse is only a Christian discourse on trans-substantiation, but lacking substance ... A ruined discourse: bodies are starting to pass right over it. What's coming is entirely different version, and entirely different articulation of *hoc est enim...* (W)hat is coming is *whatever images show us*. Our billions of images show billions of bodies – as bodies have never been shown before. Crowds, piles, melees, bundles; columns, troops, swarms, armies, bands, stampedes, panics, tiers, processions, collision, massacres, mass graves, communions, dispersions, a spill-over, an

> overflowing of bodies always both in compact masses and in pulverizing dispersions, always collected (in the streets, group housing blocks, megapolises, suburbs, points of transit, of surveillance, business, of treatment, of forgetting) and always abandoned to the stochastic confusion of the same places, to the structuring agitation of their *departure*, to the agitation that structures them, for their endless, generalized *departure*.[22] Ours is an epoch of worldwide departures, there's only the movement *partes extra partes*, nothing above, nothing below, no Subject with a destiny, which takes place only as a prodigious *throng* of bodies.[23]

Nancy's deconstructive quasi-onto-psycho-semiology begins by the consideration that the basic mode of existence of bodies is not presence, but rather their 'birth to presence.' Bodies are in a permanent state of eruption. For any given body, there is it and its outside, which may or may not be another body. Even in the case of Heidegger's examples, 'the stone on the path,' and 'the lizard basking on a stone,' Nancy attributes a contiguity, a contiguity that is characterized by a 'touching.' This 'touching' or '*touching-on*' involves not the possibility of an access, as Heidegger seeks for the ideal touching, but rather a 'passive transitivity.' In other words, Nancy sees there a 'brute entelechy of sense' that is derived from "contact, an absolute difference and an absolute différance."[24] In the touch of the one and the other, there is a *to*-ness or a 'being-toward,' and that is what makes it something more than merely spatial. A mere touch is *touching-on*, just as living is *living-on* or survival. There is the possibility of a *sur-touch*[25] which is more of a temporal dimension of touch, and distinct from a mere touch, that is only spatial. Nancy calls this possibility of a touching-on or a sur-touch, the *passibility*: "the world is passible to sense, it *is* this passibility because it first comes to be in accordance with this— ... atomistic—distancing."[26] Thus for Nancy, touching what really and persistently exists, even if this amounts to saying that there is "no pure space and time. (...) There are only places, which are simultaneously locations and extensions of bodies."[27] This constant passing to sense is also the incessant 'birth to presence,' which is the ceaseless result and consequence of this touching-on. "Presence is what is born, and does not cease to be born" and being born is "transforming, transporting and transiting of all determinations."[28] It is also "finding ourselves ex-posed, existing."[29] And corrollarily, "sense [is], matter forming itself, form making itself firm: exaction and separation of a tact."[30]

Thus, this near-predicative relation between sense and touching[31] implies a kind of morphogenesis of meaning, but a morphogenesis which is rather of a syntagamatic kind, and distinct from the paradigmatic and emergential kind of a 'morphogenesis of meaning' proposed in the works of René Thom and Jean Petitot.[32] It is possible that a social and dialogical sense of touching as well as the idea of sense itself that Nancy develops has more of a Levinasian flavour even before it receives a Heideggerian frame.

Levinas, even while he forcefully asserts ethics as the first philosophy, is indeed a philosopher of sense and sensation,[33] just as he is a philosopher of touch. However, a more or less humanistic framing of both sense and touch is discernible in Levinas, articulated through notions of 'Eros' and 'caress' which are described under the rubric of a certain 'phenomenology of voluptuousness' and mediated by a certain feminine 'mystery.' Caress yields voluptuous sensation, but it however is not constituted by any intentional touch. For Levinas,

> The caress is a mode of the subject's being; where the subject who is in contact with another goes beyond this contact. Contact as sensation is part of the world of light. But what is caressed is not touched, properly speaking. It is not the softness or warmth of the hand given in contact that the caress seeks. The seeking of the caress constitutes its essence by the fact that the caress does not know what it seeks. This 'not knowing,' this fundamental disorder, is the essential.... The caress is the anticipation of this pure future (*avenir*) without content.[34]

While this contact 'beyond' contact is similar to Nancy's touch without touching, or, that which is always in 'parting' or 'departing.' Levinas's 'caress' involves a strong sexual asymmetry, which is also a social polarity. The lover and the beloved that make up the scene of the caress are clearly masculine and feminine respectively. And further, it is the open-ended character of the feminine alterity that is (seemingly) the object of a (supposedly masculine) caress, that makes the "voluptuousness... the very event of future, the future purified of all content, the very mystery of the future..."[35]

In this context, Derrida notices that in Levinas's and Nancy's 'touch without touch' and a 'phenomenology of touch', there's a certain neutralization of the category of touch, which is not without consequences.[36] The distinction between the touchable and the untouchable (that which does not render itself to be touched—and not that which must not be touched as in the Indian caste system) can be made only in the absence of a political, sexual or phenomenological neutrality. It is therefore important to understand the virtualization of touch. (Could virtualization be the body behind the body, the touch behind the touch?) A directly phenomenological approach to touch tends to evade the question of virtualization. Further, touch is not unrelated to law, that is, to the 'force of law.' Does not a law of touch foreclose the possibility of touching the law? Or, in other words, what does one do with the law or inscription that is already there before one touches, be it with, or without touch? Derrida poses the problem sharply:

> One cannot imagine what a law would be in general without something like tact: one must touch without touching. In touching, touching is forbidden: do not touch or tamper with the thing itself, do not touch on what there is to touch. Do not touch what remains to be touched, first of all law itself—which is the untouchable, *before* all the ritual prohibitions that this or that religion or culture may impose on touching..[37]

Nancy addresses the question of sex, and to a certain extent that of Eros, in his work, *L'"il y a" du rapport sexuel*[38] (*The 'there is' of Sexual Relation*). Sex is clearly a domain that involves body, meaning, and the relation between body and meaning. While attempting to deconstruct, two well-known statements of Jacques Lacan, 'There is no sexual relation,' and 'Sexual pleasure/orgasm (*jouissance*) is impossible,' Nancy, presents his own thought on sexuality and touch. The first part of the work is an exposition of the notion of relation, which leads to the notion of a 'relationless of relation.' The absence of relation in a relation is to be understood as the 'in-between' (*entre deux*) which is "the emptiness ... that relates without bringing them [the two related things] together, or which brings together without uniting, or which unites without completing, or which completes without carrying on till the end."[39] Essentially, sex involves an open-ended, or endless relation or activity, and therefore, as Lacan states, there can neither be sexual relation as such, nor a well-identifiable 'orgasm.' Of course, it must be noted that Nancy does not distinguish between masculine and feminine sexuality, or between homosexuality and heterosexuality (unlike Levinas who assumes a masculine-feminine asymmetry, and ignores homosexual relationship in his account of *Eros*.)

Certainly, the question about the sexual relation leads both Levinas and Nancy to its ability to take existence from being to something like an 'other than being' or towards the infinite future. For Levinas, this is essentially a function of 'femininity,' which is "not merely the unknowable, but a mode of being that consists in slipping away from light," and whose way of existing is "hiding," where "this fact of hiding is precisely modesty."[40] While, for Nancy, the 'sexual' cannot be something of a 'predicate' and I can exist only in our ability to identify it as sexual. We identify it each time in its differential occurrence.

> The sexual is its own difference, or its own distinction. To be identified as sex or as sexed, is precisely what constitutes sex or sexuation...[41]

and therefore, Nancy insists, "no one is either man or woman indefinitely, nor is anyone either, homo- or hetero- sexual indefinitely..."[42] Sex, according to Nancy is a result of both internal and external differentiation, that is, by means of a somatic or non-somatic touch involving a 'relation' between one and the other. This relation of the being-together in sex, is further,

> nothing but the unhinging of the identical or of the self-in-self. Sex is really nothing but the unhinging of one-itself: but this one does not pre-exist sex.[43]

In other words, essence of sex, if at all there is one, consists in this touching-unhinging, a division and multiplication, that is, in fact, sexuation. Sex is this endlessly proliferating differentiation itself, and correlatively there is the sexual at the base of all difference or differentiation. He is goes on to claim that even

> Derrida's difference must be sexual. This means that ontological difference is sexual... Thus being is sexed and sexuating. And similarly "god" (masculine or feminine?) of the onto-theological constitution of metaphysics, involved in his sexuating auto-deconstruction.[44]

This 'relationless relation' or this permanent touching-unhinging is the principle of *being-in-common,* according to Nancy, not only for the sexuating *couple,* but also, and perhaps even more so for the *community.* A community consists in the differentiating relations of its always differentiating members. They are devoid of a communal fusion, or a communion. This is clearly where Nancy attempts a political use of the Derridean diffférance. But then the being-in-common of the political/ social realm is articulated in terms of sense, having a deconstructive sense with its provenance both in corporeality and in literature. *Exscription* is Nancy's term for this differentiating being-toward-the-outside of both body and language, that constitutes and deconstitutes the ever singular and ever plural being-in-common of a community, including the community that is often easily designated as 'the world.'

Nancy's notion of difference/différance, though clearly related to Derrida's, is yet carefully distinguished from the latter. Derrida's notion of difference, as we know, arose as part of his criticism of the strong notions of sign and signification in the context of semiotics and structuralism. Différance can be understood as a rather pragmatic articulation of a difference in relation to an existing signification. But it still has a materiality which is expressed by the notion of 'trace', itself partially adopted from Levinas. 'Trace,' for Derrida, allows us to consider signification as 'a formal play of differences,' and it further implies 'a new concept of writing,' which can be called, "*gram* or *différance.*"[45] The 'trace' in this definition, is more of a textual trace, as per which no element of a structure or text can exist without its difference with regard to its other elements "of the chain or system," and which does not a bear a trace of those elements. Therefore no element can be either merely present or absent. And thus, it follows that:

> There are only everywhere, differences and traces of traces. The gram, then, is the most general concept of semiology—which then becomes grammatology—and it covers not only the field of writing in the restricted sense, but also the field of linguistics.[46]

Now, it is interesting to note that it is precisely this 'gram' of Derrida, which is clearly a grammatological and perhaps a graphological notion, that becomes in Nancy, a notion that is additionally endowed with a certain 'weighty cognitive' value.[47] The shift is from a graphological[48] and a textual sense of writing in Derrida to a 'bodily writing' or a 'body writing' in Nancy, which is also inseparable from 'exscription' and the 'weight of a thought.' It seems that while Derrida's infinitizing textuality (*Il n'y a pas de hors-text*; there's no outside of the text.), fails to incorporate the material or the bodily, Nancy's bodily writing and exscription abandons the linguistic from its analytical perspective. For Nancy, the exscription's linguistic that carries the 'weighty cognitive' forward is itself differentiating, both with respect to its own structural elements, and with respect to the bodily and the cognitive. What surges forward to the outside—and everything does—infinitely in the 'corpus' is cognitive, bodily, and semiotic all at the same time. All is thus, exscription, and sense is always the counterpart, produced each time anew in the endless contact of extremities. Exscription is thus the touch of extremities which involves the withdrawal or deconstruction of an already given signification, and the surging to the outside, to an alternative sense, or a sense of the other, each time.

This is in fact, what Nancy speaks of as the 'inoperative community.' Community, from this perspective, is, for ever and always, its own unworking, by means of writing and exscription. Nancy thinks that literature and writing are thus to be seen in their role of interrupting both the community and the binding 'myth' of the community that holds individuals together in a communal or communitarian fusion. Community "takes place always through others and for others." In this sense, it "occupies a *singular* place: it assumes the impossibility of its own immanence, the impossibility of communitarian being in the form of a subject."[49]

Unlike the notion of a liberal community, and which is supposed to consist of individual subjects interacting by means of their interior contents or essences, Nancy's 'inoperative' argument favours a community that is constituted by the exposition (or, ex-*peau*-sition) of singularities. Instead of an emphasis on production and completion, here the relevant notions are interruption, fragmentation and suspension. Nancy: "Community is made up of the interruption of singularities, or the suspension that singular beings are."[50] What this means is that the pre-constituted process / definition of a community always undergoes a shift, a change or an 'interruption.' This sort of an unworking of community, Nancy tells us, is not different from what G. Bataille called the 'unleashing of passions.' Bataille himself had associated this unleashing with a 'contagion' than with a 'communication.' 'Passions' here may be taken in the sense of 'passivity' or responsiveness to the other. According to Nancy, "only exposition to the other unleashes my passions."[51] And further: "Singularity is the passion of being."[52]

In contrast to a community that is mythically founded by fiction, Nancy offers the idea of 'being *in* common.' As being-in-common, the beings are said to 'compear' (present outside together), that is, "they are exposed, presented, or offered to one another."[53] This 'compearance' is the middle way that Nancy seeks between a mythic community and its contrary, the community's disappearance. Community as compearance is the way by which the community resists its 'infinite immanence,' and continually creates an open space within it. The community of compearance comes to be not through a mythic process—which leads to a community as communion – but through the 'interruption of myth.' Nancy notes in *Corpus* that the assumption of the mythic community or the 'body politic' (in the sense of Kantorowicz, or its political-theological equivalents) as a signifying body, has led to a circularity between body and sense.

> The political foundation rests on the absolute signifying circularity: that the community should have body as its sense. Consequently, that the body should have the community—its institution—as its sign, and the community should have the body—of king or assembly—as its sign. Thus there's the infinite presupposition of a body-community...[54]

The connection between deconstruction on the hand and corporeality (plasticity of the human brain, to be more specific) and political community on the other, is further extended in the works of Catherine Malabou.[55] The potential for unworking or inoperativity at the level of subjectivity or of community is comparable with the plasticity inherent in the human brain, which is characterized by continuously developing, modifying and regenerating neuronal connections. Both our world/s and our brains are continuously being recreated.[56] *"Plasticity of the brain is the real image of our world."*[57] The brain is endowed with sense by means of the "being-in-connection" of the neurons, which are continuously being configured and reconfigured, through our mental activities, creating alternative worlds and alternative brains endowed with alternative senses. Through the works of neuroscientists like Jean-Pierre Changeux[58] and Antonio Damasio,[59] it has become increasingly evident that the human mind and brain are made up of images and image-like patterns (which have extension, unlike the point-symbols like the numbers) that are constantly being formed and modified in relation to the images and patterns that we receive from the external world. Thus, neuroplasticity through its poietic and deconstructive activity inherent in the human brain, works against the possibility of any predetermined structure of either the world or the brain. According to Malabou's "biological altermondialism," *"plasticity, far from producing a reflection of the world, is the form of another possible world."*[60] Plasticity, in this sense, has a clear affinity with writing and exscription. For, Malabou notes:

> ...from the graphic to the plastic, the sense of the pure images

can be grasped only in the light of their mutual transformations. Sense, is metamorphosis.[61]

NOTES

1. Nancy, J.-L., 2008, p. 73.
2. Nancy, J.-L., 1997, pp. 62-3.
3. Nancy, J.-L., 2008 op. cit., p. 3.
4. As Nancy puts it: "The anxiety, the desire to see, touch, and eat the body of God; to *be* that body and be *nothing but the that*, forms the principle of Western (un)reason." (Ibid., p. 5)
5. Kantorowicz, E.H. (1957/1997). In this classic work, Kantorowicz, describes the posited conjunction in 'medieval political theology' between the king's body and the body politic. The 'body politic' was in turn indistinct from the 'mystical body,' a notion which maintained a 'crypto-theological' relationship with the body of Christ.
6. Nancy, 2008, op. cit., p. 7. We shall see later in this text, the precise meaning of Nancy's neologism, "exscription".
7. Nancy, J.-L., 2003, p. 31. (my translation)
8. Ibid., p. 29.
9. We are here referring to F. de Saussure's embedding of the realm of semiotics in 'social psychology' and 'general psychology' (*Course in General Linguistics*) and to M. Merleau-Ponty's insistence on the 'embodiment' of mind and meaning (*Phenomenology of Perception*).
10. According to the United States Census Bureau estimate the population of the world was 6.804 billion in February 2010. (Source Wikipedia). In October 2013, the world population has crossed 7.1 billion.
11. Of course, there's no denying the fact that 'body' has recently made a significant return in philosophy. This is particularly evident in the philosophies of Merleau-Ponty, Levinas, Deleuze, Foucault, and certain others. We may also refer to the recent interest in 'embodiment' with or without Merleau-Ponty's inspiration, that is rather widely prevalent in contemporary cognitive science. René Thom's 'morphogenesis' is also concerned with the parallel structural formation in mind, body and language (See, Petitot, J., 2004). Even more meager is the reference to 'flesh' in philosophy. Nancy refers us to Merleau-Ponty's plaint: "What we call flesh, this inwardly worked mass, has no name in philosophy" (quoted in *Corpus*. op. cit., p. 75).

12. This phrase, 'We are meaning,' is the title of a chapter in Nancy 1997. pp. 57-64.
13. Nancy, personal communication.
14. The notion of 'impenetrability' of the body and its relationship with the 'secret' was also explained to me by Jean-Luc Nancy in a personal communication. I am grateful him for his ready help.
15. "Un autre: si c'est un autre, il est un corps," spoken by Nancy in the film, Le corps du philosophe, directed by Marc Grün. 2003. ('An other : if it is an other, it is a body.')
16. Nancy, 2008, op. cit., p. 29.
17. Ibid., p. 31.
18. Ibid., p. 7.
19. Ibid., p. 93.
20. Nancy clarifies this point: "As such, the body is the articulation, or better yet, the *organ* or *organon* of the sign: it is for our entire tradition, that *in which* sense is given and *out of which* sense emerges. But as such, regardless of the perspective used—dualism of body and soul, monism of the flesh, symbolic deciphering of bodies—, the body remains the organon, the instrument o- the incarnation, the mechanism of the work of a *sense* that never stops rushing into it, presenting itself to itself, making itself known as such and wanting to tell itself there. The body, *sense*—in this double sense of the word fascinated Hegel." (Nancy, 1993, p. 192.)
21. Nancy, 2008, p. 9.
22. Ibid., pp. 38-9.
23. Ibid., pp. 40-41. Living in India, I am naturally quite sensitive to the quantitative and the qualitative dimensions of bodies. A land of teeming millions, or more than 1.2 billion bodies currently. Not just these human bodies, but also animal bodies. Living bodies, moving bodies, cadavers, carcasses. There are bodies everywhere: on land, in the sky, in water; in trains, buses, lorries, in cars, in carts, in planes, in boats, in ships; in railway stations, in bus-stands, at bus-stops, in airports; in schools, universities, in hostels, hospitals, hotels; brothels, prisons; in temples, in mosques, in churches, in bazaars, malls, fair-grounds, playgrounds, stadia, theatres, fields, quarries, mines, barracks, wars, rallies, processions, queues, parks, zoos, lawns, streets, on footpaths, on balconies, on beaches, mountains, hill-stations, peaks; on the television, in newspapers, films; at weddings and funerals; in cremation or burial grounds. These bodies, living or dead, are divided qualitatively at least traditionally, into the

touchable and the untouchable bodies. However, in the current post-colonial, post-modern melee of bodies, the untouchables (i.e. in the 'caste' sense of the term), are asserting that they are indeed untouchable, though in the opposite sense of embodying power and importance. The sense of this untouchability may be changing. Those who were previously referred to as untouchable (in one sense) are asserting: "We are untouchable" (in a contrary sense).

24. Nancy, *The Sense of the World*, p. 61.
25. We are using this word as analogous to 'survival', or survie in French, which can also mean 'living-on'.
26. Ibid., p. 62.
27. Nancy, "The Weight of a Thought," p. 77.
28. Nancy, 1993, p. 2.
29. Ibid., p. 3.
30. Nancy, *The Sense of the World*, p. 61.
31. Nancy goes on to say: "In a sense, ... sense *is* touching." (Ibid., p. 63)
32. See, René Thom, *Structural Stability and Morphogenesis*, and Jean Petitot, *Morphogenesis of Meaning*. Without going into the technical details of the differences between the two approaches, we shall simply state that the Thomian morphogenesis involves the dynamic actantial schema or patterns associated with the actions of one or a small number of actants, and hence is based on mimological semiotics, while Nancy's sense is densely material, and bodily, and has to do with the constant interaction of a body with a multiplicity of other bodies, yielding each time and infinitely singular and plural meanings.
33. Especially in "Meaning and Sense," in A. Lingis (ed.) *Emmanuel Levinas—Collected Philosophical Papers*. Dordrecht: Maritnus Nijhoff.
34. Levinas, E., "Time and the Other," (tr) Richard A. Cohen, in *Levinas Reader*, 1993.
35. Ibid.
36. Derrida, J. "The Untouchable, or the Vow of Abstinence," Chapter 4, Part I of *On Touching—Jean-Luc Nancy*, 2005. pp. 66-91. (Fr. Original: *Le toucher—Jean-Luc Nancy*, Galilée, Paris, 2000, p. 82
37. Ibid., p. 66. (emphasis in the original)
38. Nancy, 2001. *L''il y a' du rapport sexuel*, op. cit.
39. Ibid., p. 24 in the original, and p. 5 in the manuscript of the English version.

40. Levinas, 'Time and the Other,' op. cit., p. 49.
41. Nancy, 2001, op. cit., p. 27. (English version, p. 7)
42. Ibid. (English version, ibid).
43. Ibid., p. 28. (English version, p. 7).
44. Ibid., p. 32 (p. 8) footnote.
45. The citations are from the chapter, "Semiology and Grammatology—Interview with Julia Kristeva", In *Positions*, 1981, p. 26.
46. Ibid., pp. 26-7.
47. In 'The Weight of a Thought', Nancy attempts to bring together (etymologically) the senses of the two French words 'pensé' (thought) and pesé (weighing). Even in English, one can say, 'The thought hangs heavy,' suggesting that words like 'pensive' and 'pending'/'pendant' may have a common (Latin) source.
48. From, Gk. *graphein 'writing'*, perhaps from the action of, etching and scratching on rock, or granite.
49. Nancy, J.-L., *The Inoperative Community*. 1991, p. 15. Nancy's main point is that the community is not something calculable or programmable. So, instead of seeing it as an 'operative' entity, it is seen as something to be constantly 'unworked.' The French version of the book, *La communauté désœuvré* was followed by Blanchot's response to it, *La communauté inavouable* (*The Unavowable Community*, 1988).
50. Ibid., p. 31.
51. Ibid., pp. 32-3.
52. Ibid., p. 33.
53. Ibid., p. 58.
54. Nancy, 2008, op. cit., p. 71.
55. See Malabou, C., *Que faire de notre cerveau*? Bayard, Paris. 2004, Eng. tr.: *What Should We Do With Our Brain*? 2008; Also, *La plasticité au soir de l'écriture—Dialectique, Destruction, Déconstruction*, 2005.
56. For Nancy too, this corporeal and worldly creation is related to plasticity: *the body is the plastic material of spacing*, without form or idea. It's the very plasticity of expansion, extension—where existence *takes place*. ... The body's not an image-of. But it's the *coming to presence*... (Nancy, 2008, p. 63.)
57. Malabou, C., 2004, op. cit., p. 82. (emphasis in the original; the citations from this text are translated by the present author)
58. Changeux, J.-P., 1986.
59. For a recent publication, see Damasio, A., 2003.
60. Malabou, 2004, p. 80.
61. Malbaou, 2005, op cit., p. 115.

10

Towards a Philosophy of Image

We shall begin this essay with certain more or less commonplace statements about language and image. The world of image, like the world of language is, historically speaking, nothing static. This follows from the fact that neither of the two phenomena is natural. Secondly, the world of image and the world of language are not independent of each other. In fact, they feed onto each other, ceaselessly. And finally, both image and language have been claimed for and studied in terms of their literary-artistic as well as scientific-documentary ends.

It is a well-established fact today that externalized visual manifestation of the spoken language, that is, *writing*, was historically preceded by and is derived from *drawing*. Therefore, the historical movement of 'representation' could only have been: from *speech* to *image* and then to *writing*. But then, speech itself could be said to be preceded by the non-manifest 'mental image' of the things spoken of. This at least was the perspective adopted by Aristotle, according to whom, "(s)poken words are the symbols of mental experience and written words are the symbols of spoken words. Just as all men have not the same writing, so all men have not the same speech sounds, but the mental experiences, which these directly symbolize, are the same for all, as also are those things of which our experiences are the images." (*On Interpretation*)

We cannot go into the seemingly endless discussions and debates that try to account for the intertwining relationship between language and image. We can only try and identify some of the more recent and contemporary benchmarks on this question. In any case, our purpose in touching upon this question, in the context of understanding the relationship between philosophy and media is only secondary. Our intention is to identify and present some of the philosophical perspectives on image, with as far as possible, a reference to the media.[1]

***

A 'philosophy of image'—indeed a rather vaguely used term—ought to be able to account for the use of the term 'image' beginning from its sense of the 'mental image' to the current proliferation of 'images' in the scientific, artistic, literary and mediatic domains. Aristotle's use of the word 'impression' to speak of the mental image must have been preceded by the existence of seals and other graphological signs and practices in ancient Greece. Today, when the brain scientists take this notion far more seriously, they refer to some sort of a 'reality' that is present in the brain that can be scanned and displayed on a visual monitor. A monitored 'map' of the brain is supposed to simulate in a more or less organized way the somewhat chaotic neuronal activity that corresponds to any mental process.[2] If the image was for Aristotle the form of a representation within us of the outside reality, today this inside reality is said to be mapped and made available to us for further viewing. While a mirror 'reflects' the reality for a viewer in front of it—though with a left-right inversion—on the basis of the luminous rays falling on the latter, the image on a computer 'monitor' involves complex physical mediations between its own properties and the properties of the thing that it simulates. What the monitor 'projects' for our viewing is the technically organized simulation of a reality that is hidden and not given to our viewing.[3]

Since we are accustomed to believing in the images that we perceive on a monitor, or for that matter and more surely, our 'mental images' it is not difficult for us to conclude that the 'image,' whether simulated or not, is *distinct* from the thing. Rather than an exact counterfoil to the real thing, the image is now seen as a node in the chain of visible forms that are available to us, including the thing itself. This means that image is not just a psychological resultant of perception, imagination or thought, but is itself a mode of existence of the real world.

Jean-Paul Sartre in his well-known work, *L'Imaginaire* (1940) had made a clear break with the tradition coming from Hume, which viewed the image or imagination as a pale copy of the mental image or impression resulting from perception. According to him, imagination and perception involve distinct "attitudes of consciousness." The former is 'active,' and in it one gives oneself an image of the object, and the latter is 'passive,' merely letting one to encounter the object in reality. For Sartre, image "is a certain manner in which the object appears to consciousness, or rather, a certain manner in which the consciousness gives itself an object."[4]

Secondly, contrary to perception which manifests only slowly and bit by bit, imagination appears in one bloc and produces the image as a whole and with an immediacy. In this wholeness of the image, the object is however rendered as non-present and non-existing. That is to say, while one can act on the basis of the impression got from perception, the image of an object in imagination does not prompt one's action upon it. Furthermore, according to Sartre, imagination involves a continuous emotive effort on the part of consciousness, while on the contrary, in perception, the object is passively received by it.

This phenomenological position on image has at least two counterpoints in European philosophy. The first of these appeared as a direct critique of Sartre's perspective on 'commitment' in art and literature. Emmanuel Levinas in a short article, 'Reality and Its Shadow' (1948) published in the Sartre-founded journal *Les Temps Modernes* rejects the idea that the (artistic) image can have any value either as representational truth or as manifesting the commitment of the artist. In the image, according to Levinas, there is no transmutation of the object by means of emotive or existential energy. But rather, he argues, it is the image that takes a hold over us and renders us to a fundamental passivity. Levinas:

"An image marks a hold over us rather than our initiative, a fundamental passivity. Possessed, inspired, an artist, we say harkens to a muse. An image is musical."[5] An image detracts us from the secure path of our conceptual reality, and sets us to its own rhythm. Hence, art maintains itself as a realm of sensation (i.e., the 'aesthetic' realm) which can be rendered into conceptual/discursive mode only by means of acts of criticism. In this realm, the image is no longer in contact with reality. In Levinas's words, it, 'disincarnates'[6] the object of representation.

Image also bears a relationship to the object, which is that of 'resemblance,' something which other representational media such as symbol, sign or word cannot have. The thought that is, from a phenomenological point of view, aimed at an object cannot pass the level of image. This is what accounts for the opacity of image, in contrast to the transparency of the sign. This space where conceptual thought is arrested in its quest for reality, is according to Levinas, the shadow of reality, or the image. Image resembles reality not in comparison, nor analogically, but as the shadow that accompanies and resembles the thing. Confronted with the face of a person, one's thought can attain only its caricature, its image. The image precedes the thing. Levinas: "...the thing is itself and its image. ...this relationship between the thing and its image is resemblance."[7]

Thus image is characterized by its own specific temporality. The artistic image is accompanied by a stoppage of time, its inability to participate in real time. Its time is an instant drawn from the real time, separated from it, and destined to last, in its immobility, forever. Levinas: "A statue realizes the paradox of an instant that endures without a future."[8] It is this time of the image that Levinas refers to as the 'meanwhile' or the interval, or even the 'time of interruption.' (Later, Maurice Blanchot will speak of this as the 'time of time's absence' specifically in the context of literature.) Even when an object unfolds or develops in historical time, as image, it may be immobilized as a shadow and an instant of its existence may be immobilized as an interval. The shadow meanwhile (that an image is in relation to its object) is, according to Levinas, "never finished, always enduring—something inhuman and monstrous."[9]

***

A general scepticism towards art and artistic image that seems to lurk in Levinas's work, is not discernible in the works of his one-time teacher Heidegger, and that of his close associate and friend, Maurice Blanchot. Heidegger, as we know, spoke of the artwork in term of its ability to induce truth as 'unconcealment' (*alethia*). In the context of the dynamic flow of the historical world, the artwork is essentially a 'useless object'; it is like a 'broken tool' as he puts it. Broadly speaking , it is this idea that resurfaces in Blanchot's essay, 'The Two Versions of the Imaginary'.[10]

Blanchot, however speaks of the inoperative, and inhuman aspect of the artistic image in somewhat human terms. Here again the image comes not after, but before the object, as the incapacitated shadow that resembles reality. But, Blanchot compares the artistic image not to an inorganic object or tool, but to the organic body, more precisely to the dead body. The image bears a 'cadaverous resemblance'[11] to the thing. Like the dead body, it retreats from the human reality, and occupies a special place as well as a fleeting but enduring time in the human social milieu. The artistic image bears on itself the pompous impersonality and immobility of the dead body. The death of the living body that Blanchot speaks of is not the sublating death of Hegel, nor is it death featured as destinal possibility as in Heidegger. He is instead referring to Levinas's notion of 'death as impossibility'. Blanchot: "It is as if the choice between death as understanding's possibility and death as the horror of impossibility had also to be the choice between sterile truth and the prolixity of the non-true. It is as if comprehension were linked to penury and horror to fecundity."[12] Like the undying death of the other that induces infinite responsibility in the self, the cadaverous absence-presence of the image, induces 'the *other* of all meaning' and due to its ambiguity, 'nothing has meaning, but everything *seems* infinitely meaningful.'[13]

***

Henri Bergson's *Matter and Memory* (1908) antedates Sartre's *L'Imaginaire* by more than three decades. It can be considered as the quintessential work in a philosophy of image. In his materialist account of consciousness, the distinction between matter and consciousness is eliminated by resorting to a universally pervasive notion of images, which act among themselves continuously. Bergson poses the problem frontally in the first paragraph of his work:

> Here I am in the presence of images, ..., images perceived when my senses are opened to them, unperceived when they are closed. All these images act and react upon one another in all their elementary parts according to constant laws of nature, and, as a perfect knowledge of these laws would allow us to calculate and to foresee what will happen in each of these images, the future of the images must be contained in their present and will add to them nothing new.[14]

This naturalistic materialism of images, which mediates the presumed opposition between matter and mind has had its takers and opponents. Levinas rejects it for assuming that there is a natural 'continuity of time to be the very essence of duration'[15] and for not being 'sensitive to the paradox that an instant can stop.'[16] We have seen that for Levinas, image is the shadow of reality, an image arrested in time, the immobile interval.

While for Gilles Deleuze, the Bergsonian perspective of the world as incessant interactive mobility of the material images amounted to a theorization of the cinema, before its time. (Deleuze, G., *Cinema I—Movement-Image*, 1983) This is in spite of the fact that Bergson himself was philosophically sceptical of the artificial movement-image he saw in the nascent cinema of his time. Deleuze's justification for this unexpected Bergsonism in cinema runs as follows:

> The cinema can, with impunity, bring us close to things or take us away from them and revolve around them, it suppresses both the anchoring of the subject and the horizon of the world. Hence it substitutes an implicit knowledge and a second intentionality for the conditions of natural perception. It is not the same in the

> other arts, which aim rather at something unreal through the world, but makes the world itself or a tale [*récit*]. With the cinema, it is the world which becomes its own image, and not an image which becomes world.[17]

***

The second part of Roland Barthes' *Camera Lucida*—a work that is written in homage to Sartre's *L'Imaginaire*—begins with a discussion of the photographs of the then recently deceased mother of the author. What characterizes the photographic image, according to Barthes, is its property of 'it-has-been.'[18] This image, unlike the artistic or the cinematic image, is ultimately *'intractable,'*[19] that is: "what I see has been here, in this place which extends between infinity and the subject (*operator* or *spectator*); it has been here, and yet immediately separated; it has been absolutely, irrefutably present, and yet already deferred."[20] The *referent* of this image was really present in some place and at some time to some consciousness, which may be either the operator (of the camera) or the spectator (of the image).[21] The referent (e.g. of a person, one's mother), *emanates* from the image for the spectator, in one bloc, without giving much scope for personal interpretation. (This is the basis of Barthes' opposition between two contrary qualities of the photograph: *punctum*—that which hits me directly like an arrow, and *studium*—that which permits contemplative study.) And yet, though the photograph refers to a point distanced in space and situated in the past time, the photographic image is *without future.* The photograph is both like a spectre from the past and a sign of one's future death, Barthes would say. In other words, shall we insist, it does not cease to be a caricature, a shadow of reality and the arresting of time?

In the concluding sections of the *Camera Lucida*, Barthes had alluded to this ambivalence in the context of the photographic image. On the one hand, Barthes had noted, the unmediated or immediate evidence of reality that a photograph can give makes it a 'mad' medium. But on the other hand, it is 'tamed' in the attempt to make it into an art such as the cinema or by a banalizing preponderance of it, as is the case in television and other electronic media today. Roland Barthes:

> Mad or tame? Photography can be one or the other: tame if its realism remains relative, tempered by aesthetic or empirical habits (leafing through a magazine at the hairdresser's, the dentist's); mad if this realism is absolute, and so to speak, original, obliging the loving and terrified consciousness to return to the very letter of Time: strictly revulsive movement which reverses the course of the thing, and which I shall call..., the photographic ecstasy.[22]

***

Photography, as we know was a technological invention of the 19th century marking a major transformation in the history of the image. The epoch was also characterized by large-scale developments in the mechanical reproduction of the work of art. While the period leading to the European Renaissance was marked by a proliferation of Christian religious paintings, more or less sacred, the 19th century photographic image and the easy availability of mechanically printed images took away, as Walter Benjamin says, the 'aura' of the artwork,[23] and pushed it closer towards a mere representation of historical reality. Photographic image as a bearer of documented reality, either benign or harmful, is indeed the contemporary mode of its employment and of understanding its use in the media today. Even the neo-realist cinema claimed to present documented historical reality by means of its own specific techniques.

****

Following this historical trajectory, it can be noticed that *from* the medieval images of Jesus' resurrection which are said to have resulted in the 'resurrection' of the image from the monotheistic proscription of divine images *to* the recent attempts to censor the violent media images in the aftermath of the terrorist destruction of the twin towers in New York, the Western civilization seems to have come a full circle. The ambivalent disposition towards the artistic or documentary image perhaps has its provenance in the fact that its presence can be both in the service of man, and a possible source of destructive violence. Unlike the linguistic discourse, the unmediated and immediate character of the image has been a source of concern both in the mediation between man and god, and between man and man. *Can images kill?*[24] is the title of a recent work by Marie-José Mondzain, a contemporary philosopher of image. Similarly, 'Image and Violence' is a central chapter in Jean-Luc Nancy's book, *The Ground of the Image*.[25] We shall dwell on these two works in the remaining part of this essay.

Both Nancy and Mondzain are concerned in the texts mentioned above with the question of the relationship between image and violence. But, while Nancy approaches it in terms of a deconstruction of the ontology of image, Mondzain inquires into the relationship between the image and the spectator that is always in the process of being constituted and reconstituted both from the end of production and that of reception of images.

Both are also concerned, at least as a starting point, with the sacredness of images, and even if not entirely, with the sacred image. The 'sacred,' Nancy clarifies, is that which is separated, cut off, from the rest of the objects. It is 'distinct' from them. The distinctness of the image, comes from its being both present and absent, and at the same time, neither present nor absent. In Mondzain's technically more precise definition, "image (is) a certain category of vaguely designated objects like the visible objects which are strictly speaking neither objects like other objects, nor are they signs like other signs, but some sort of specific appearances (*apparitions*), available only to the power of the eyes and not to any other organ."[26] Further, from a more closely spectator-oriented perspective, she would say, 'image (is) is all that makes a seeing subject a subject capable of maintaining a spectatorial relation with the visible.'[27]

An associated feature of the image is that whether it is created by the human hand or not, it cannot be touched. It is that which is untouchable. It maintains its 'sacred' distance from us, even when it is exposed to us in its intimacy. It can exert a sacred, even a violent, force over us. Though sacred,

Nancy says, the image is not something that can be sacrificed. In its simultaneous separation and intimacy, the image maintains a pompous and violent domination over us. It remains present for what is absent, and its distinct presence cannot be made absent, either by sacrifice or by consumption. This is what gives the image its power over us, its power to engulf us, to render us passive, even when it is we who are looking at it. Hence the fear and the concomitant question, 'Can images kill?' An answer to this question is indeed not difficult to find, for no violent image as such can lead to a correlated violence, just as any number of images of virtue cannot, in themselves make us non-violent and virtuous. Clearly, it is not the violent or virtuous contents of the image that make us respectively violent or virtuous, but it is the unmediated character of the images that can hold us in their violent sway.

According to Nancy, in its monstrous intimacy, in being an indelible excess over a given a field of forces, the image is akin to violence. This excess is also not different from and is parallel to the excess of the scopic drive in us whereby we wish to *see* over and above as well as behind what we see. According to Mondzain, this principle has been profitably exploited in the 'violent history of images.'[28] That is how, as per her account, the Byzantine church authorities, rejected the iconoclasts' demand for (re-)enforcing a ban on divine images, even while they were not in favour of religious idolatry. Rather than prevent the believers from seeing the divine image in accordance with the monotheistic God's decree to Moses, the officials decided that it was even better if the former were allowed to be in visual contact with the figure of the Christ 'incarnated' in images.

What the medieval church sought to achieve was the elimination of the brute and violent power of the images as such, by claiming that the divine figure is incarnated in them, that is, they took the place of or represented an absent god. The strategy they employed was to both ward off the substantiality of the 'incarnated' images and to 'incorporate' the followers into the body of the church. Mondzain, speaks of this complex move made to re-establish the authority of the

Church even when it was faced with the vexing question of the proliferation of images:

> Only the image can incarnate, such is the main contribution of Christian thought. Image is not a sign among other signs, it has the specific power of making one see, of pictorially realizing forms, spaces, and bodies that it offers to the view. Since the Christian incarnation is nothing but the coming to the visible of the visage of God, incarnation is nothing other than the becoming image of the unfigurable. To incarnate means to become an image, and more precisely an image of passion. But this power of appeasement, is it the case with every image whatever be its form and its content? Indeed not... Only the image which has the force to transform violence into critical freedom, is the image that incarnates. Incarnation is not imitation, reproduction or simulation. The Christian messiah is not God's clone. It is also not enough to produce a new reality to be offered to the idolators' eyes. The image is fundamentally unreal, and it is in this that rests its force, in the revolt against all substantialization of its content. Incarnation means giving flesh, and not giving body. It is to function in the absence of things. Image gives flesh, that is to say, *carnation* [flesh-tint] and visibility to an absence, in an insurmountable distance from what is designated. To give body, on the other hand, is to incorporate, to propose the consumable substance of something real and true to the members of a community, who come to be and who will disappear in the body with which they are identified. To commune in and by the image is to lack incarnation of a visibility without substance and without truth.[29]

The Byzantine church thus claimed the incarnation of Christ in the non-substantial but visible image, but at the same time it sought to incorporate the believers in its own body by means of their communion in and through the substance of his image. The power and the violence of the image is thus contained by invoking the absence of any substantial presence behind it, but at the same time the substantial image is employed to incorporate the faithful into a common, and potentially violent body in and through their exposure to the visible image. In our own day, perhaps this is how, the preponderant and seemingly endless stream of images, even though harmless in themselves, and in their contents—since there is no causal connection between images of violence and acts of violence—, incarnate one or other kind of absent realities, incorporate and confuse the viewers who are exposed to them through the public or private media into a common, nay, communal body, ready for violence.

In the modern technologies of media, especially in film and television, the role of the screen is to offer a determined place of the subject with respect to the voice of the master, that is, to organize the spectator's look. The screen is that which divides the visible space into two: that of the 'director' and that of the 'spectator.' The directorial 'voice' directs the course of the visible image for the spectator who is reduced to the silence of scopophilic desire, and is 'incorporated' into the master discourse. The spectator's body that fuses with the body in which he or she is incorporated, is also led by the imaginary personhood of the latter body. This is how the television or the cinema screen induces a *personification* of the guiding body of the visual discourse that keeps unfolding there. The violence that the screen-image may induce is not due to the contents of what appears there, but due to the suppression of the body, the voice and the thought of the spectator himself/herself who is 'guided' by the director. Since the image and its power is essentially unchannelizable, the operations of *incarnation, incorporation* and *personification* that take place can be resisted only by opening it to a non-directed and open-ended critical discourse, or shall we say, an endless deconstruction of the visual discourse. In Mondzain's words: "The visible does not kill in the field of an ever active speech."[30]

However, it is worth asking if language itself is immune from any play of violence. And in what is image necessarily manifested as violence? Jean-Luc Nancy explores these questions, in his text, 'Image and Violence.'[31] There is indeed a 'truth of violence,' where the latter is straightaway a display of force, over and above the given play or equilibrium of forces, leaving behind tell-tale signs of destruction. He insists too, in a rather deconstructive vein, that 'truth' itself—whether in language or not—cannot be dissociated from a certain violence. (Though this violence is quite different from the violence of the image.) Truth, he says, "cannot irrupt without tearing apart an established order."[32] Truth breaks open towards the outside of any given system, it involves acts and the reality of transgression. There's a difference between the two kinds of truths, and between the two kinds of violence, according to Nancy. The 'true truth is violent because it's true'[33] while truth of violence is true only because it is violent. Similarly, the truth of violence is both destructive and self-destructive,[34] while the violence of truth is that which "withdraws even as it irrupts and ... that [which] opens and frees a space for the manifest presentation of the true."[35]

Similarly, Nancy observes that image and violence also share certain common features. Violence communicates itself to its beholders only by leaving an image of itself. It renders itself visible by authorizing its own action upon the surroundings. Image, is similarly an excess upon what is already given to view. Violence, truth and image, all these involve the appearance of a certain alterity in relation to the given self. In other words, a self-manifestation of the other. Both truth and violence, involve some kind of showing: a *demonstration* in the former and a *monstration* in the latter. That is why, the image is a continuous and unstoppable eruption in relation to the placid stability of the given order. A 'dynamic and energetic metamorphosis' that it is, the image cannot be completely separated from blood-stained cruelty. The image, in Nancy's words "is the prodigious force-sign of an improbable presence erupting from the heart of a restlessness on which nothing can be built."[36]

NOTES

1. An earlier version of this paper was presented at a conference on 'Philosophy and Media' organized by the Department of Philosophy, University of Poona, Pune, in March 2008.
2. In his now classic work, *The Neuronal Man* (1983) Jean-Pierre Changeux insists on the 'materiality' of the mental images, and hence what scanning reveals are the reproductions of these 'images' in the brain. The 'mental images,' according to him, 'arise spontaneously and voluntarily in the physical absence of

the original object.' (Changeux, 1985 edn., p. 130) This is because 'the image is an 'autonomous and transient memory object...' (Ibid., p. 138).

3. In a recent note, Claudine Tiercelin provides us with an account of the new and recent developments in response to the question 'What is an image?': Firstly the proliferation of images of every kind, but even more, the appearance of new types of images (photographs, films, videos, synthesized images, virtual images and digital images, etc.) and the galloping complexification of networks and medias within which they are inserted. And then, the appearance of new techniques of imagery and among them cerebral functional imagery intended to establish the mapping of brain in its functioning. She notes that there has been, "thanks to these new technologies, a transformation of the methods of cognitive science, cognitive psychology and the philosophy of mind," and it "becomes possible not only to obtain structural information relating to the anatomy of the brain (MRI, X-ray) but with the aid of techniques such as electroencephalography (EEG), positron emission tomography (PET), functional magnetic resonance imagery (fMRI) or the magneto-encephalography (MEG) to observe in vivo the brain involved in cognitive activities, such as, notably that of imagery" (text translated from an Internet site in French by the present author).
4. Sartre, J.-P., 1986 edn. p. 21. (translation by the present author).
5. Levinas, E., 1989, p. 132.
6. Ibid., p. 136.
7. Ibid., p. 135.
8. Ibid., p. 138.
9. Ibid., p. 141.
10. Blanchot, M., *The Space of Literature*, Appendix 2. pp. 254-63.
11. Ibid., p. 257.
12. Ibid., p. 261.
13. Ibid., p. 262.
14. Bergson, Henri, 1962 edn., p. 1.
15. Levinas, op. cit., p. 140.
16. Ibid.
17. Deleuze, 1986 edn., p. 57.
18. Barthes, R., 2000 edn., p. 77
19. Ibid.
20. Ibid.
21. This notion of the 'intractable' has been questioned since the advent of the digital images, which allows for distortion and

manipulation of the image shot by the camera. See especially, criticism by B. Stiegler, 'The Discrete Image' in *Echographies of Television* (2002). Stiegler says: "... discretization radically affects the chain of memorial light, the Barthesian luminance; and by extension the *belief* we have in the image, since it was only this chain *and the intuitive knowledge we have of it* that led to this belief" (p. 154).

22. Barthes, op. cit., p. 119.
23. Benjamin, Walter, 1968 edn. According to Benjamin, the mechanical reproduction of art, since it produces multiple copies of the same object, destroys the authentic place that artwork occupies in a tradition: "...that which withers in the age of mechanical reproduction is the aura of the work of art.... The technique of reproduction detaches the reproduced object from the domain of tradition" (p. 221).
24. *L'image, peut-elle tuer*? (Paris, Bayard, 2002) is the French title of Mondzain's book. Citations from this text are translated by the present author.
25. The first six chapters of Nancy's *The Ground of the Image* (New York, Fordham University Press, 2005) are a translation of *Au fond des images* (Paris, Galilée, 2003). We shall be referring to only the first two chapters of the English version, viz., 'The Image —the Distinct' and 'Image and Violence.'
26. Mondzain, Marie José, *Homo spectator*, Paris, Bayard, 2007, p. 13.
27. Ibid., p. 13.
28. Mondzain, 2002. See Chapter 1, pp. 13-60. Images, Mondzain notes, "are situated midway between things and dreams, in an in-between world, a quasi-world, where we perhaps experience our servitudes and our freedoms. Thinking the image in this perspective allows us to inquire into the paradox of its insignificance as well its powers" (p. 14).
29. Mondzain, Ibid., pp. 31-2.
30. Ibid., p. 59.
31. Chapter 2, *The Ground of the Image* (Tr.) Jeff Fort. New York: Fordham University Press, 2005.
32. Ibid., p. 18.
33. Ibid.
34. Ibid.
35. Ibid.
36. Ibid., p. 23.

11

Culture and Politics in the Novel: *On the Banks of the River Mahe*[1]

'Forgetting' is first of all and technically an unconscious and individual mental phenomenon.[2] It is akin to leaving something (object or experience) behind, which one has already had, or not having something that one once had. One cannot forget consciously, for then it is a case of 'ignoring.' 'Amnesia' on the other hand, is a somewhat pathological condition where one suffers from habitual forgetting. One also speaks of, by extension, a collective forgetting or amnesia, where a whole community has forgotten, left behind or no longer possesses, certain 'experiences' it previously had. 'Collective amnesia,' thus, refers more to experiences than to objects as such.

History is a discursive construct in which one tries to trace the lived experience of a people in time. Writing of history is invariably confronted with the question of whether one can include in a conscious and linear discourse all the experiences of a community in historical time. Historical discourse is often the discourse of a dominant few, where the discourses of a minor and marginalized people do not find an adequate place. Historical discourse inevitably involves procedures of selection and rejection, and therefore much of everyday experiences of the people tend to be ignored. This neglect of certain aspects of the history of a people may also be due to the limitations of human consciousness and memory, i.e. due to forgetting. It is virtually impossible for history to record the contents of everybody's consciousness or memory of every experience in historical time.

Another question concerns the kind of structuring that history can submit people's experiences to. In its anxiety to have a scientific history, can its discourse adopt a formula-like structure? Or, is a narrative structure inevitable when it is a question of historical writing? We tend to think that this is the case.

A further question is that of the differential experience of discontinuities. Different sections of people have different experiences towards breaks or discontinuities in history. This is probably because different people are differently oriented towards the major events that constitute or lead towards an historical break, such as a revolution. It is in this context a linear temporal notion of history becomes least acceptable. These breaks, in fact, involve a break with the run of history, that is, with the linear flow of time. A disjointedness of time is introduced, towards which different sections of people, that is, especially the dominant and the dominated would respond differently.

***

Such differences in historical perspectives are also the basis of the differences between 'major' and 'minor' histories. 'Major' and 'minor' are construed here as markers of power rather than in terms of any association with a majority or minority of people constructing their histories. Thus, there can be a 'major' history of a minority as well as a 'minor' history of a majority. One can say with reference to the Indian context that the colonial and nationalist histories represent major histories of two different minorities, and one may ask whether the 'subaltern' histories on the other hand, represent minor histories of a majority of people of India.

It is worth asking whether 'major' and 'minor' histories would be differentiated in terms of their mode of constitution. Would a major history be written in a mode that pays attention to its own scientificity, while a minor history would not take care to eliminate its own narrative mode? In other words, is it the case that a minority that is major in terms of power can afford a scientific mode of discourse, with its own emphasis own rationality, while the majority that remains minor tends to adopt the narrative mode, retaining for itself what would be perceived as raw emotive content?

It is in the convergence of the meaning of history as a scientific construct with the meaning of history as narrative, that the question of literature becomes relevant for us. What is the relationship between literary narrative and history, major or minor? Is the discourse of literature, when the latter presents a historical narrative, historical enough to satisfy the demands of historiography in the strict sense of the term? Can the narrative of literary history be sufficiently conscious to account for all the relevant events that academic history would be concerned with? Is the unconscious aspect of certain literary historical narratives prone to biases and prejudices that are patently unscientific? Are the events of literary history acceptable as events of academic history? Do literary and academic histories make use of the same sources, e.g. personal accounts, media, and archives of official and unofficial documents? What kind of discursive and linguistic transformations are to be expected in the two different kinds of histories? Are the conscious and unconscious contents of the two kinds of history compatible? What is the relationship between these two kinds of history on the one hand and the unconscious and conscious aspects of our experience, on the other? Taking these questions and possible responses to them into consideration, is it appropriate to set up a hierarchy of academic history and literary history, in which the latter is thought of as a 'minor' history, where the term 'minor' refers not to absolute insignificance but to its own powerlessness?

Literature, as 'minor history,' would thus be marked by its own impotence. It would be devoid of any administrative-political or pedagogical role. It would remain in its own passivity, which as Blanchot reminds us is the mark of the 'space of literature.' But literature in its passivity is both absent and present, and thus it is simultaneously infinitely powerless and enormously powerful. It is absent in the sense that it cannot participate in the speech acts that characterize our everyday life. It is present to the extent that it can move and affect the persons who happen to read it. And moreover, the more literature tries to shun power, the more unforeseeable, unacknowledged and unclaimed power it tends to accrue.

As linguistic acts, all literature may be thought of as minor discourses and some among these may even be minor histories. However, according to Gilles Deleuze's perspective, literature may be either or major or minor, and the philosopher evidently privileges the latter. Kafka is a 'minor litterateur' according to Deleuze, and his works are instances of what the latter calls minor literature, which firstly "is not that of a minor language, rather what a minority does in a major language;" secondly, in minor literatures, "everything is political"; and thirdly "everything there takes on collective value."[3]

***

It is in this sense that Malayalam writer, M. Mukundan's novel, *On the Banks of the River Mahe*, can be viewed as an instance of minor literature. This novel is indeed regarded as a major novel, written in a 'minor' literary language of the world, viz. Malayalam (i.e. it is hardly known on the global literary scene), a language spoken by over 30 million people belonging to or originating from the state of Kerala in south-west India. At the same time, it (the novel) qualifies to be considered as a 'minor literature' in the Malayalam language itself, since it is written in a non-standard dialect of northern Kerala, and is interspersed with occasional words and sentences in French. Perhaps it is the only novel in Malayalam, which contains so many linguistic elements in a European language other than English. French, a major world language, appears in this novel as a minor language, transliterated and transcribed into a minor world language (i.e. Malayalam) itself written in a minor and non-standard dialect.

It is also worth noting that for the author of the present essay, reading the novel in the original language involved an experience of returning to a language that is now a minor language for him, and which in fact was the major language of his childhood. (The author's first language, at least autobiographically, is Malayalam, and currently, two of his main working languages are English and French.) That is to say, reading the novel in the original Malayalam, has brought him face-to-face with his personal history of certain linguistic forgetting, which of course, has been at least partially overcome by the very act of reading and working on the novel.

***

The relevance of this novel for the theme of the colloquium has to do with its central narrative of the event of 'liberation' of the tiny territory of Mahe from French rule in 1954. The narrative brought this event out into the open, by resisting its forgetting, in the context of other major and more significant narratives about India's obtaining independence from British rule in 1947. The novel has successfully overcome the forgetting of the event of Mahe's liberation in the wake of a preponderant number of discourses in English and other languages dealing with the greater event of the Indian independence movement. The liberation of Mahe, as well as the events and people surrounding it, receive in this novel a major literary treatment, but the novel remains an instance of minor literature as it is written in a minor dialect of Malayalam, with a notable flavouring of French language.

***

In this narrative of liberation of Mahe, Dasan, a character perfectly well-educated in French institutions at Mahe and Pondicherry (where he completes his Baccalauréat), is the main character. The discourse of the novel consists of interconnected narratives, some of which are taken from real life, while others are mythical and fictional. The function of these narratives is perhaps to resist the forgetting of the politically and culturally significant real events, as well as to rearticulate the somewhat mythified 'memory' of the historical or quasi-historical events that have affected the community. The novel's main task is to fictionally portray the life of the people of Mahe before and immediately after its liberation. It was written about 15 years after this major event. It captures more or less faithfully the often intertwining lives of the members of a small community of French and Franco-Keralan métis, and those of the local Keralans and other Indians living in the territory of Mahe. The territory is administered by a French administrator who is referred to as *Mooppan Saivu* (Grand Sahib) in the novel.[4] He is the first person to possess a car in the town.[5] The other French or half-French individuals of the town are: David, a bachelor, who has the local prostitute Kunhichirutha as his stable mistress; Edouard, a school-teacher; Lorraine, the commissar, who has a moustache like Stalin; Leslie, the notary, and his wife who is simply known as 'Missie,' and their two sons, Albert and Gaston. Leslie is the son of Clément, who was a wine-shop owner and who claimed to be a descendant of the Count of Lally who fought against the British; and Missie is the daughter of Armand, who was a spice-merchant. Clément wanted a 'pure' French bride for his son, and when he saw Missie, "he felt as if his eyes had seen the golden sun and became dazzled." She was said to have "shining blue eyes" and "curly golden hair." When Leslie and Missie were seen walking along the beach hand in hand, the folk of Mahe would remark that they were truly "made for each other."[6]

However, after the disgraceful exit of their elder son Albert, and his presumed disappearance in a French legion in Indo-China, Leslie is glad to arrange the marriage of his younger son Gaston with Térèse, the daughter of a former mayor of Pondicherry, Chévalier Ignace. But this marriage would soon end in tragic failure due to Gaston's impotence. The parents are heart-broken when Gaston returns home from his honeymoon with an indelible shame and decides to shut himself up in his upstairs room with only a guitar and dolorous music for company for the rest of his life.

Leslie and Missie maintain the most amicable relations with the local Malayali people of the town, especially with the family of Dasan.[7] Kurambi, Dasan's grandmother, is a source of great solace and perhaps (at one time) sexual gratification for Leslie, and he visits her every evening to get a pinch of intoxicating tobacco powder ('snuff'). She hardly knows any French, but just enough to say *"Oui, monsieur,"* to Leslie's query, "*Ça va*"? Gaston and Damu, Kurambi's son and Dasan's father, who worked as a scribe, were also classmates and childhood friends.

The other noteworthy characters associated with the administration are: Chekku Mooppar, the Mayor, who is black as teakwood, and his French wife; *Sergeant en retraite* Kunhikannan, who has fought in Kampuchea; Karunan, the *Secrétaire*; and Sukumaran, the clerk.

***

Among the interlacing narratives of the novel, the most prominent are that of the vicissitudes of the French rule in Mahe and that of the rise to prominence of Dasan followed by his desolation and tragic disappearance. Dasan becomes the intellectual and moral force of the liberation movement. Under the able guidance of his teacher Kunhanandan, a determined communist (who adorned his house with pictures of Marx, Lenin and Stalin), nourished by the writings of French writers like Jean-Jacques Rousseau (*Le Contrat Social*), Victor Hugo (*Hernani*), de Beaumarchais (*Le mariage de Figaro*), Balzac and André Gide,[8] and in spite of opposition from his grandmother Kurambi and his father Damu, the scribe, Dasan organizes the young men of Mahe in a political struggle against the French, which is eventually successful. In the process, however, Dasan, has to defiantly forego a comfortable career in the French administration, which is offered to him on a platter as it were, by Grand Sahib, and is forced to end his amorous relationship with his childhood friend, Chandrika, who unable to bear the sorrow of the break-up, presumably takes her own life. In spite of the success of the liberation struggle, which culminates in the French administration deciding to quit Mahe for good, Dasan's youthful life is mutilated by despair, and he ends up wasting his life until his premature death on the banks of the river Mahe. Dasan's story is indeed told in a tragic mode as neither does the liberation that he and his friends spearheaded seem to be able to sustain the spirit of the Mahe people, nor would Chandrika's father allow Dasan to unite in marriage with his beloved.

The novel's fictional description and an independent

historian's account,[9] both articulate the fact that the liberation of Mahe was the consequence of a daring 'revolt' by the local people in 1948. Chapter 23 of the novel gives a detailed account of the revolt which involved the capture of many French establishments in Mahe. The revolt, according to the novel, started when some of Dasan's friends and their sympathizers, who were active in the liberation struggle, were refused their voter cards before an impending referendum on the status of the French territories in India. They forced their entry into the office of the Mayor, Raman, by pushing him aside. They shouted: "All those who have a right to vote must be given their cards. Give us our cards." The revolt turned unruly. "They pulled open the almirah doors, took out the voter cards stacked inside and threw them on the floor. The ground was soon scattered with old, faded papers. Chairs and tables lay turned over. The rebels heaped the papers on the road and set fire to them."[10] Soon Dasan arrived on the scene and large sections of people, including teachers and students of La Bourdonnais College, and clerks in the offices, came out and marched through the main streets of Mahe shouting cries of victory. The rebels then went to the Residence of Grand Sahib, who faced the events with stoic calm. "Grand Sahib stood at the arched glass window, binoculars in hand, watching the unfolding drama silently. His eyes, bluer than the sea crashing against his ancient bungalow, blurred with tears."[11] "Don't shoot," he ordered the policemen who were waiting "to pull the triggers of their rifles, as the rioters entered the forbidden territory." Soon, "innumerable flags with the saffron, white and green started fluttering over Mayyazhi."[12]

***

In spite of the event of 'liberation,' a large part of the novel in fact narrates tragic existential stories. There are few characters who survive the onslaught of time, both in the main fictional narrative, and in the secondary narratives. Perhaps, the story of Dasan is intended to be elevated to that of a martyr of the land, similar to the tragic-heroic story of Jeanne d'Arc that Kurambi, Dasan's grandmother, is fond of narrating, and which the entire people of Mahe are sorrowfully aware of. "No grandmother in Mayyazhi could tell the story of Jeanne d'Arc without weeping. Every child in Mayyazhi had grown up with the story and wept over the tragic fate of the shepherd girl who was burnt to death."[13] On hearing the story of Jeanne d'Arc from Kurambi, Dasan himself "thought of the pyre in the plaza of Vieux Marché and the shepherd girl standing with joined palms in the middle of it. Tears flowed unchecked from his eyes."[14]

Kurambi is also a treasure-house of Mahe's tales which she is fond of narrating to her grandchildren, Dasan and his sister Girija. Her husband Kelu Achan died of snake-bite while he was toiling as usual in the field during the monsoon. Kurambi's reaction when she heard of the snake-bite was to turn towards the cross on the clock-tower of the church of the Virgin, and pray: "Save my man."[15] But neither the Mother of Mahe (the Virgin) nor Malayan Kudungan, whose magical powers could draw out any poison, is able to save Kelu from dying.

Kurambi's first story is a mythical account of how Kunjakkan and his ancestors of two previous generations became lame. Kurumbachan, the grandfather of Kunjakkan had taken to drinking early in his youth. One day, in order to keep up his drinking spree and to retrieve his coconut-scraper that he had pawned in the arrack shop on a previous occasion, he stole a bunch of bananas from a tree in the temple precincts. While he was returning home blissfully after trading the banana-bunch in the arrack-shop, with the coconut-scraper secure under his arm, he is attacked by Gulikan, the goddess's dancer, who demanded his temple bananas back.

> Kurumbachan heard the sound of dancing bells as he reached the temple. A pale figure loomed out of the dark. Kurumbachan's heart beat fast. He stood with his eyes popping out.
>
> 'Where are my bananas?'
>
> Gulikan stepped out of the temple, wearing anklets and a skirt of palm fronds. Kurumbachan's hair stood on end.
>
> 'Where are the bananas?' repeated the apparition.
>
> 'Forgive this creature!' Kurumabachan fell at his feet.

> The deity kicked Kurumbachan and ran back, hooting into the darkness of the temple. Kurumbachan lay dumbstruck among the fallen hibiscus flowers. The scraper shot out of his hand. He did not know how long he lay there. When he got up, he found that his right foot had gone lame.
>
> Kurumbachan's son, Kunhikutti, was born lame as well, in his right foot. And Kunhikutti's son Kunjakkan was also lame in his right foot.[16]

Kurambi's second story about life in Mahe, though again mythically-framed is perhaps even more morally charged. It is a story that she would tell only to Dasan. It is the story of how Vaisravanan Chettiar, a prosperous, itinerant silk-vendor of Mahe was enticed by Kunhimanikkam, the prettiest damsel of the town.

> Her skin colour was of beaten gold. The thought of Kunhimanikkam, decked in jewels and wearing *kasavu mundu*, haunted the men of Mayyazhi while they slept. Even the white men were disturbed by her. As their ships neared the shore, they would be impatient to be with her.[17]

Whenever Vaisravanan sought permission to visit her, she excused herself by telling him she already had as visitor, one or other white man. Once it was Bernard Sahib, the next day it was Antony Sahib, then it was Francis Sahib, and so on. Expecting an entry into her chamber, Vaisrvanan sacrificed for her all his valuable possessions, precious silks and gold jewellery. Gradually, he lost interest in his business and wilted away. "And he soon drew his last breath without ever having possessed Kunhimanikkam."[18]

But later, while she was having her elaborate bath in a flower-scented pond nearby, a serpent approached her on three successive days accompanied by a whistle. "It stopped by the side of the pond, spread out its hood and devoured Kunhimanikkam's beauty."[19]

In spite of Kunhuraman's best magical chants and medicinal remedies to ward off the serpent, it kept coming back to her house insistently. The serpent forces itself one night in an intimate encounter with the courtesan Kunhimanikkam, which results in her violent death. The scene, in which both the beauty and the beast perish, is described in a tragic frame followed by a mystical explanation.

> Dawn broke. Crows cawed loudly and beat their wings noisily as they flew over Kunhimanikkam's house. Covered with jewels, she lay lifeless on her silk mattress. The serpent lay dead as well, its hood on her bare breasts.
>
> 'Do you know who that serpent was?' Kurambi Amma took a pinch of snuff from her box, inhaled it and went on, 'It was Vaisravanan Chettiar.'[20]

***

Mahe's story (again mythical) of the battle between St. Sebastien (referred to as Veluthachan, literally the 'white father') and Vasoori Amma (the Hindu goddess associated with the eruption of small-pox), at a time when the disease raged in the town is narrated to Kurambi Amma by bandman Kanari. According to the authorial narrative: "When oracles and sorcerers failed to control the disease, devotees brought Veluthachan out from the church. The procession bearing his idol wound slowly through the streets. The church bells chimed sadly."[21] This event is further mythically modified and exaggerated by the bandman Kanari, who claims that he saw with his own eyes "the battle between Veluthachan and Vasoori Amma."[22] According to Kanari's awestricken account,

> ...the battle had taken place in the vicinity of the Church of the Virgin the previous night. Veluthachan had been on a white horse and was armed with a lance while Vasoori Amma had worn a white sari and had her hair streaming over her back.[23]

Dasan, however, refuses to believe that the spread of small-pox in the town is due to the presence of the black goddess of Vasoori. He tries to explain to Kurambi Amma, who places a pot of cow-dung mixed with water on her doorstep, for keeping the goddess of small-pox away: "It's a virus that brings the small-pox, not Vasoori Amma."[24]

***

The authorial narrative also tells the reader of the conflict between the young and politically conscious men of Mahe and its traditional folk in the context of a temple ritual. After the death of Malayan Kurumban, the responsibility of performing the most important Thira ritual at the Meetala temple, falls on his son, Uthaman. Uthaman, in the company of his young friends, is already known to be a communist, and is keen "to educate himself and find a respectable job."[25] But due to poverty, he is forced to take up the temple rituals, including the performance of Thira. But Uthaman is not ready to follow the requisite codes of personal hygiene. He refuses to keep the regimen of not eating meat or fish, and of observing celibacy during the festival period. Being progressive, he must defy the traditional rules of the temple. On the eve of Thira, he cooks himself a basketful of sardines and eats them and then goes to Kallu the prostitute to satisfy his sexual desire.

> The next day in the temple, he is dressed up as the local god Gulikan, wearing a long headgear, and begins to dance.
>
> As the dance grew faster, the balancing sticks were discarded. Gulikan began to dip and sway in the yellow light, his enormous headgear caught in the whirlwind movement of the ritual dance. The headgear dipped and rose against the skyline. At the climax of the ritual dance, Uthaman faltered and fell on his face.
>
> ...
>
> In the flickering lamplight, Uthaman could be seen writhing, his neck broken under the weight of the towering headgear.[26]

***

We observe that the French citizens of the town are on the whole portrayed in their friendly and cordial relations with the local people of Mahe. The Administrator, the Grand Sahib or Mooppan Saivu, is seen to bear goodwill towards them. This is best evident when Dasan is invited to meet him in his residence (adorned with Van Gogh's *Le champ de blé*) after he had passed the brevet examination of the *cours complémentaire*. Grand Sahib utters these kind words to Dasan:

> *L'état se réjouit de ton succès...*
> *Poursuit tes études...*
> *Va à Pondichérry...*

> *L'état t'accord une bourse...*
> *L'état s'occupe désormais de toi.*

But Dasan rejects the offer. Later, however, when the liberation movement was gaining momentum and when Dasan and the other leader of the movement, Kanaran were invited to meet him, Grand Sahib is decidedly very curt, and tries to threaten them with military action. He was sitting in office chair with a pair of binoculars in his hand.

> 'What do you want?" he asked, without turning around.
> 'Freedom,' said Dasan.
> Grand Sahib still had his back to them. ...
> 'Freedom?'
> 'Yes.'
> Grand Sahib pushed open the windows.
> 'Look my friends...'
> He pointed to the sea. The silhouettes of battleships were etched against the horizon. They were moving towards Mahe.[27]

But, on the day of deliverance, that is on the day of the final handing of charge to the people of Mahe, on July 14, 1954, the Grand Sahib, in a friendly gesture, places his right hand on Kanaran's shoulder and tells him:

> *Mahé... c'est à vous.* [28]

***

The Silvery Rock (*Velliyan Kallu*), situated in the distant sea, barely visible from the shore of Mahe, plays the role of a transcendental bearer of memory, in this novel. The distant rock-island is metaphysically the transit zone for all the souls coming into and going out of Mahe and it is capable of resisting all forgetting. It is also the source of all life-sustaining creativity of this land. Dasan is told by his grandmother, Kurambi, that before he was born he existed on the Silvery Rock, which is described in the novel as a "cluster of rocks... that lay far out in sea like a bright tear drop." "All Mahe's children had come from there. The souls waiting to be born in Mahe fluttered over the sun-bright rocks as dragonflies."[29] This was the place for the transmigration of the souls, according to Hindu beliefs. When Dasan first looked at it as a child: "*Velliyan Kallu* could be seen in the distance as if in a dream, the souls fluttering over it like dragonflies. Souls that were waiting to be born or reborn, souls taking a brief rest from the cycle of birth and rebirth."[30]

Later, when he has become an adult, in a moment of self-reflection, he would tell himself that, "Once upon a time, my soul was a dragonfly, fluttering over the Silvery Rock. He was lost in thought for a moment, full of the mystery of life and death."[31] Dasan was becoming aware of a profound exteriority to which his existence was linked, from which his being and his consciousness could not be detached. The Velliyan Kallu also becomes for him a metaphysical source of inspiration during his troubled and anxiety-ridden political development. "... Where was Mahe's freedom?" He reflects. "As far away as Velliyan Rock, where unborn souls hovered like dragonflies..."[32] And finally, when the people of Mahe revolted, leading to the capture of many French government offices and hoisting of Indian national flags on many of them, the narrative says: "A breeze blew in from the distant Velliyan Kallu, the abode of Mayyazhi's souls.... Mayyazhi was free."[33]

Thought about the Velliyan Kallu would keep returning to Dasan, whether he was exerting himself during the political struggle, or when he is in self-exile outside Mahe, or when he thought of his beloved Chandrika. When he realized that Chandrika had disappeared for ever from the house that her father had built specially for her to live with a bride he had arranged for her against her own wishes, only Dasan knew where she was. "The breeze blowing from Velliyan Rock carried Chandrika's voice to him. 'When I grow up, Dasetta, will you marry me?'... Only he knew. That she was on Velliyan Rock where souls fluttered like dragonflies."[34]

And finally, at the very end of the novel, Dasan also disappears, after having spent his last days listlessly on the banks of the river Mahe, deeply immersed in multiple sorrows. He had perhaps returned to the place of his origins, the place of the origin and return of all those who belonged to Mahe. For those who sought him, Dasan couldn't be found. But: "Across the water, the Silvery Rock could be seen like a teardrop. Souls fluttered over it like dragonflies. One of these dragonflies was Dasan."[35]

NOTES

1. M. Mukundan, 1974. *Mayyazhipuzhayude Theerangalil.* Malayalam novel, first appeared as a serial in 33 issues of *Mathrubhumi* weekly from November 5, 1972 to June 1973. It was published as a book in 1974. The author of the present article has consulted D.C. Books (Kottayam) edition, 1992. English translation, *On the Banks of the Mayyazhi* by Gita Krishnankutty, Chennai: East West Books, 1999. French translation of the English version, *Sur les rives du fleuve Mahé* by Sophie Bastide-Foltz, Paris: Actes Sud, 2002. The English version which contains 36 chapters is a shortened and modified (apparently in collaboration with the author) version of the original which runs into 43 chapters. The French version is a near-faithful translation of the English version of the novel.
2. The French version of this paper (entitled "Culture et politique franco-keralaise dans le roman 'Sur les rives du fleuve Mahé") was presented at a conference on "L'Histoire de l'oubli" (The History of Forgetting) held at the University of Primorska, Koper (Capodistria), Slovenia, and organized in collaboration with l'Agence Universitaire de la Francophonie, Paris, on October 24-25, 2008.
3. Deleuze, G., 1975, pp. 29-31.
4. Administrator's real name was Deschamps. See, Ajit K. Neogy, 1997. *Decolonization of French India—Liberation Movement and Indo-French Relations 1947-1954*, Pondicherry: Institut Français de Pondicherry.
5. The town is criss-crossed by a few streets bearing distinctly French names: Rue de la Résidence, Rue de la Prison, Rue du Gouvernement, Rue de la Cimetière, Rue de l'Église, Rue de la Gare. There are also a few French schools: l'École des garçons, l'École des filles, Cours Supplémentaire, and Collège La Bourdonnais. The court, or Palais de Justice and Mairie are in the centre of the town which is also dotted with a prominent church of the Virgin Mary situated on a hillock and the Meethala temple dedicated to goddess Bhagwati.
6. *On the Banks of the Mayyazhi*, p. 8. (The English translation refers to Mahe as Mayyazhi, the local name of the town in Malayalam. In this paper, we use the two names interchangeably.)
7. Missie, we read, "spoke Malayalam as fluently as anyone in Mahe," Ibid., p. 14.
8. One of Dasan's close associates, Pappan, is never satisfied with the pacifist trajectory of the liberation struggle. In his urge for

violent activism, he thinks of Gide's motto, "*vivez dangereusement*." (Ibid., p. 194).

9. Ajit K. Neogy, op. cit.
10. Mukundan, *On the Banks of the River Mayyazhi*, pp. 152-53.
11. Ibid., p. 154.
12. Ibid., p. 154. As per Neogy's more recent historical account, on October 21, 1948, after having waited till late afternoon, to get their identity cards, "a large number of people led by Kumaran [real leader of the movement] marched to the residence of the Mayor and finding him unhelpful, returned and resorted to picketing in the municipal office [*Mairie*] demanding the distribution of the cards. Kumaran (who was a sitting municipal counsellor) had a sharp exchange of words with the Police Commissioner who was there. The latter became violent and assaulted Kumaran. N. Narayanan Nair, a Praja Socialist Party worker was also manhandled. This provoked the wrath of the people and the situation degenerated. Those assembled there were joined by a large crowd including fisherman...They ransacked the municipal office, seized the electoral rolls and burnt them. The Police Commissioner was roughed up. Records of civil and criminal cases were removed from the court and destroyed. The Residency was besieged. The Administrator and his family became prisoners. The armed guards of the Administrator's office surrendered. (Neogy, op. cit., p. 112)
13. Ibid., p. 37.
14. Ibid., p. 37.
15. Ibid., p. 10
16. Ibid., pp. 38-9.
17. Ibid., p. 40.
18. Ibid., p. 12.
19. Ibid., p. 42.
20. Ibid., p. 42.
21. Ibid., p. 59.
22. Ibid., p. 59.
23. Ibid., p. 59.
24. Ibid., p. 60.
25. Ibid., p. 90.
26. Ibid., p. 98.
27. Historian Neogy writes that it was the Gouverneur de l'Inde Français, Baron, who had instructed to send a battleship, *Commandant Bory* to rush immediately to Mahe "for rescuing the beleaguered Administrator and his family and reconquer

Mahe and re-establish French sovereignty there." (Neogy, p. 113) Baron had "announced that France would protect by all means the people of French India so that they might freely express their wishes in a democratic manner." However, things happened contrary to his intentions. "The arrival of 'Commandant Bory' had created panic in Mahe. The Administrator and his family were taken away by the nationalists to an unknown destination. Other Frenchman had fled. Nearly 75 per cent of the people of Mahe also left the town with their families for fear of reprisals by the French troops." (Ibid., p. 114)

28. According to Neogy, several political and administrative factors, led to a volatile and unmanageable state of affairs in Mahe in July 1954. Finally, "the Mahe Administrator found himself unable to maintain order and solicited permission from the Paris authorities for evacuating the pocket. Accordingly on 16 July Deschamps, Mahe Administrator, handed over de facto governmental power to the people of Mahe. I.K. Kumaran, President of the Mahajana Sabha and Joint Action Committee, took over charge of the Mahe administration on behalf of the people. He hoisted the national flag on the Government House. Wishing happiness and prosperity of the people, Deschamps left Mahe that same afternoon. In Mahe, the French government had not really transferred power to Indian hands. France was, in fact, compelled to retire." (Neogy, op. cit., p. 261) In the novel, the Grand Sahib's departure by ship is described as a sorrowful event for both sides. Large numbers of Mahe people waited in the blazing sun to have a final glimpse of Grand Sahib. As he came down from his bungalow: "Grand Sahib's blue eyes hovered over each of his subjects, standing in rows on the seashore. '*Adieu, mes enfants*!' He raised his right hand slowly. Kurambi Amma... broke into sobs.... The ship's anchor was raised. All Mayyazhi wept as the ship moved away. Their tears moistened the burning sand." (*On the banks of the Mayyazhi*, p. 231)
29. Ibid., p. 27.
30. Ibid., p. 27.
31. Ibid., p. 56.
32. Ibid., p. 120.
33. Ibid., p. 154.
34. Ibid., pp. 253-54.
35. Ibid., p. 255.

12

Globalization of English and the Indian Linguistic Context

Languages or, the linguistic context of India, may be said to have entered the modern age when in 1786 Sir William Jones declared in his third annual lecture at the Asiatic Society of Bengal in Calcutta that Sanskrit, a language of Indian antiquity had a common ancestry with the so-called classical languages of Europe, namely Latin and Greek, that all three must have "sprung from some common source."[1] Later in 1835, Indians, at least a substantially large number of them, were destined to become users of the English language, when Lord T.B. Macaulay vigorously proposed the introduction of the English language for public instruction in British India with the aim of forming "a class who may be interpreters between us and the millions we govern—a class of persons, Indians in blood and colour, but English in taste, in opinion, in morals and in intellect."[2] In 2006, according to the proud account of the British linguist, David Crystal, 700 million of the over 1.4 billion estimated users of the English language globally, lived in the South Asian region.

During the colonial period of the 19th century the major contexts of English use by Indians were the law courts, bureaucracy (including petitions), education, journalism (including letters to the editor, some of which were in the form of petitions to the British authorities), and to a limited extent, creative writing and literature. Though there was growing political aversion for the use of the colonisers' language throughout the protracted struggle for independence it is a fact that the Indian leaders, especially M.K. Gandhi and Jawaharlal Nehru, wrote extensively in English in order to promote their anti-colonial campaigns. Even when some of Gandhi's writings, including his autobiography, were initially written in Gujarati, they were soon available through English translations. In this context, it will not be incorrect to say that English writings of major nationalist leaders, Gandhi and Nehru inspired many Indian elites to emulate them and to write adulatory works about them in English.[3]

According to the Indian Constitution, Hindi, written in Devnagari script, is the language of official communication of the Indian Union. It also states that English is an 'associate official language', to be retained in that capacity, as long as the people of India so desired.[4] In addition to these two languages of the Union, the Constitution initially adopted 14 regional languages as official languages of different Indian states. These are referred to as languages of the '8th Schedule' of the Indian constitution, which has since been expanded and currently consists of 22 languages.[5] These only roughly correspond to the 28 states of the Indian Union, with the correspondence having become less exact since 1956 when the 'linguistic reorganization' of the Indian states was completed.

In spite of the political significance of Hindi as the union official language and of the other official languages of the states of India, in practice, especially for the educated and professional classes of India, English is the most important working language. It is widely used in every domain of social and cultural life: administration, business and industry, politics, military, media and entertainment, education and technology, tourism, sports, etc. English is, for Indians, the language of inter-regional communication, and as it is for people of many other parts of the world, the language of international communication. It is a major source of employment for large sections of people, especially in the tertiary sector, in contexts both national and international where substantial Indian presence is widely acknowledged. India is also a major centre for English language teaching, conducted in universities as well as private institutions or 'teaching shops.' More than a decade ago, according to *Newsweek* magazine, the English language teaching business in India was worth more than $ 100 million. With the policy of economic liberalization of successive federal Indian governments, the number of English language users has been growing at a rapid rate. The popular absorption of English began to gain momentum under the economic liberalization programme initiated in the early 1990s, under the leadership of then Finance Minister of India, Dr. Manmohan Singh, currently the Indian Prime Minister.

At the same time, the English of India today has distanced itself from the one that Macaulay promoted in order to produce a people who were supposed to be culturally and intellectually transformed under British domination by means of the English language. It has been steadily drifting away from the standard British English, and has acquired a clear identity of its own. The Indian English today—and perhaps beginning with the end of the Second World War—can be said to be one of a variety of 'world Englishes' dominated and led by American English.[6]

What interests us in the paper are a range of theoretical questions posed by the spread and prevalence of English in India. What is the effect of plunging the English language in the vast population of Indians? What can in fact be noticed is a two-way transformation of the language scene in the subcontinent. Along with the Indianization of English which involves the grafting of Indian forms upon the English language used in India, there is the equally evident corresponding process of a reverse hybridization involving what is referred to as the Englishization of Indian languages. (It will not be wrong to say that English is only the recent major addition to the 'melting pot' of languages in South Asia.) In this context, the question that interests us is that of the 'identity' of languages. Can languages be said to 'exist' with a well-defined identity? Do languages have clear-cut boundaries analogous to national boundaries? Can languages be superposed on identifiable geographical territories and corresponding communities of people? Some useful answers have been provided to such questions, including the notion of 'hyperlanguages' proposed by Sylvain Auroux and others in the French context.[7] A comparable notion is present in the 'integrational linguistics'of Roy Harris, which is guided by the principle of 'co-temporality.'[8] The idea that most languages that one encounters are historically and culturally 'mixed languages' is equally interesting.[9] The 'habitat model' is yet another relevant idea.

In general, we welcome the suggestion that there is, really or potentially, a 'continuous creation' in language use and therefore a continuous, even if slow, historical variation of language. Though 'communication' and communicability are overriding in determining the identity and the structure of given languages, in specific historical situations, linguistic creation often results in overcoming the limits and the boundaries that are constitutively part of the definition of a language in any given period of time. Communication can be seen as a dynamic, creative and structurally interactive process in which ever new cultural-linguistic-cognitive worlds are created in ways that are not always predictable. A 'language' is a virtual entity that can be actualized through undecidable and unpremeditated creative modifications of it both internally and in relation to (the virtuality of) other languages. To describe this process, we may usefully employ Deleuze's expression 'continuous variation,' or Derrida's 'monolingualism of the other,' or even Benjamin's 'pure language' (through infinite translation).

Thanks to an infinite 'potentiality,' every language seeks to get out of, or is in the process of getting outside of itself, in relation to either its own structure and constitution or other language/s. We may describe this linguistic movement towards the outside, as an *exolinguistic* process inherent in every language. Perhaps every language, in its unbounded and creative state, tends to be its own *'exolanguage.'* While the philologist and the linguist may be concerned with knowledge of the past existence of a language, we may say that the poet and the philosopher are concerned with the making of its future.

It is tempting to view this relation with otherness, both within and across languages, as some sort of aesthetic and ethical relation, involving an excess and a desire that describes not only communication in general, but more importantly, the process of literature, especially poetry. That is how, if we follow Salman Rushdie's suggestion regarding Urdu that in a situation of language contact "a poet's language [is] born out of soldiers' mouths."[10] The poetic language of Shakespeare with part of its ancestry in the language of the barbaric Vikings, could be regarded as one of the best examples of such a process.

Growth and Development of 'Impure' or Hybrid Languages

Rushdie was writing of the emergence of Urdu in the South Asian context. That is, the transformation of the language of the Mongols into a language that had acquired sophistication and poetic sensibility. In this context it is useful to inquire into a similar process of embedding of the English language in the Indian cultural context. We obtain a sample of this process in the efforts involving the publication of Henry Yule and A.C. Burnell's *Hobson-Jobson: A Glossary of Colloquial Anglo-Indian Words and Phrases, and of Kindred Terms, Etymological, Historical, Geographical and Discursive.* (The first edition of this book appeared in 1886.) In their Introduction, Yule and Burnell refer to Governor Sir Charles Napier, who in 1844 requested his subordinates to "indite their various papers in English, larded with as small potion of the to him unknown tongues as they conveniently can, instead of those he generally receives—namely Hindostanee larded with occasional words in English." The work is described as "a historical dictionary of words current in 'Anglo-Indian' and on the Eastern trade routes, from the sixteenth to the end of the nineteenth century. Illustrative quotations, in date order, are drawn from travel narratives and other literature in numerous languages: those in Arabic and other Asian languages are given in translation. In the second edition Crooke added a few entries and some further quotations, and corrected some etymologies. Entries are under Anglicized (sometimes laughably Anglicized) Victorian spellings." (See Andrew Dalby *A Guide to World Language*

Dictionaries. London: Library Association Publishing, 1998.)

It should be mentioned here of the publication of a more recent Indo-English glossary authored by Nigel B. Hankin under the title *Hanklyn-Janklin, or, A Stranger's Rumble-tumble Guide to Some Words, Customs and Quiddities, Indian and Indo-British* (1994). What is interesting about the titles of the two glossaries referred to above is the deployment of reduplicative structure, abundant in a majority of Indian languages. Hankin, who lived in Delhi for many decades, seems to have invented a reduplicative pun of his own name, whereas 'Hobson-Jobson,' according to the authors, is derived from a festive Muslim lament.[11]

In spite of this early attempt to record the mixing of English and Indian languages/s, Indians have always wanted to speak (and write) pure English language. Or at least they have sought themselves to be seen as speaking or writing the standard variety of British English, even if this was seldom the case. This tension between the presumed necessity of using correct English and the desire to invent an Indian idiom of that language has been most evident in the writing of English literary works by Indian authors. Some of them have self-consciously interrogated this existential-linguistic tension. For example, the reputed Indian writer of English fiction, Raja Rao (who studied in France between 1929 and 1933) noted the difficulty of writing in English in the 'Foreword' to his novel, *Kanthapura* (1939) in the following terms:

> The telling [of the story] has not been easy. One has to convey in a language that is not one's own the spirit that is one's own. One has to convey the various shades and omissions of a certain thought-moment that looks maltreated in an alien language. I use the word 'alien,' yet English is not really an alien language to us. English is the language of our intellectual make-up. We are all instinctively bilingual, many of us writing in our own language and in English. We cannot write like the English. We should not. We cannot write only as Indians. We have grown to look at the large world as a part of us. *Our method of expression has to be a dialect which will some day prove to be as distinctive and colourful as the Irish or American*. Time alone will justify us. (italics mine)

In *Kanthapura,* Raja Rao can be seen to use unabashedly the following hybrid expressions (among others): pariah-polluter (p. 8), 'Mahatma Gandhi ki jai'; 'Gandhi Mahatma ki jai' (p. 10); police-inspector: 'Give them a shoe-shower' (p. 11); Khadi-shop Dasappa (p. 13). Even before, the appearance of Raja Rao's *Kanthapura,* Mulk Raj Anand had experimented with Indian expressions in his English novel, *Coolie* (1936): 'Salaam Huzoor' (p. 12); 'Ohe, you son of an owl' said the chota Babu 'have you dried your feet before entering the room.' (p. 21); 'Shabash, Shabash' (p. 22). However it can be argued that it was in the work of G.V. Desani (*All About H. Hatterr* 1948), that an institutionalized and caricatured use of hybrid Indian English had made its authentic first appearance. Desani was also self-conscious about his language-crossing venture, but he was clearly irreverent about the process and its product. His innovation of unbroken, contiguous word associations, like, 'Furgoodnessakes' (p. 16) (which later became the hallmark of a Rushdiesque writing beginning with his *Midnight's Children*) could be seen to legitimize itself (and contrast with standard English) through his character's lighthearted remark : 'I write rigmarole English, staining your goodly godly tongue, may be: but friend, I forsook my Form, School and Head, while you stuck to yours, learning reading, 'riting and 'rithmetic.' (p. 37)

Desani could bring in model's descriptions of Indian feminine aesthetic perfection through seemingly convoluted Indian English constructions: "...Meanwhile let us enjoy the idea of maiden perfection."...

> ...(H)er nails matching the red Malabar sunset, the lobes of her ears as sweet as Kulu peaches! Her ankles as nimble as those of a fawn! Her wistful as that of a babe! Mother, O mother, hearken! The parting of her hair as straight as the road to Mandalay, her walk as graceful as that of an amorous peacock, her ankles-adorned feet as musical as the temple bells! Her face as tender as a lotus! Her lips enshaming molten copper! Her toes like jasmine-petals![13]

Rushdie has openly acknowledged Desani's writing as the inspiration for twisting the rectitude of English. Contemporary readers should be more familiar with this style of Indian

English. We provide here a few examples from his most famous work, *Midnight's Children* (1981):

From the character Padma:

> 'Eat, na, food is spoiling.'
>
> 'What is so precious... to need all this writing-shiting.' (involving an Indian mode of reduplication - FM)
>
> 'Okay, starve, starve, who cares two pice?'
>
> 'I tell you, my child, that girl is so sickly from too much soft living only.'
>
> 'Too much sweetmeats and spoiling, because of the absence of a mother's firm hand. But go, take care of your invisible patient, your mother is all right with her little nothing of a headache.'

From Aziz:

> '... is it lady's time of the month?'

Etc...

With the success of Rushdie's master work of fiction, *Midnight's Children* in which the English language was marked by generous and wholesale use of literary Indianisms, it was only natural that the ordinary Indians' confidence with their own variety of English grew by leaps and bounds. From Raja Rao's apparent linguistic angst to Rushdie's Indianist exultation, Indian English had travelled a long way. Meenakshi Mukherjee eloquently describes this transformation:

> Salman Rushdie's *Midnight's Children* (1981) [represented] ... "the confidence and effervescence of a new generation which no longer agonises about the choice of language nor seems overtly self-conscious about 'Indianness'. The number of Indian English novels published every year has steadily grown, and at the turn of the century it has become a virtual flood.... It is no longer possible to keep track of all the new titles and new novelists emerging almost every month.[14]

Mukherjee also noted a shift in the site of the production of Indian English literature. The works of Indian English fiction were now increasingly being published outside India. As she put it:

> Not all of these recent writers reside in India. Some have moved away form the country to a more developed world, as part of the larger demographic shift that characterizes the migratory pattern of the late twentieth century. Consequently the newly coined category called 'diasporic writers' has begun to gain currency.."[15]

What Mukherjee effectively noted was two stages in the development of confidence in the specifically Indian use of English. The first had to do with a shift in historical time and the corresponding change in the political attitude of the English-educated Indians. The second had to do with the shift in spatial setting or diasporic movement of the Indian writers as indicated above. The first had to do with the tacit declaration of independence from the colonial masters insofar as the Indians' use of English is concerned:

> In the novels written in the last two decades [of the 20th century] language has been used in many more innovative and experimental ways.... And one of the most noticeable shifts is that somewhere along the way English seems to have lost its alienness. The present generation of novelists was born much after the country became independent and, for many of these urban and socially privileged people, English has very often been an everyday peer-group language used casually and informally, and therefore capable of being used in playful, irreverent and impure ways mixed with other Indian languages. Such mixing was constantly being done in college campuses, coffee houses and playgrounds even in the fifties and sixties.."[16]

At the same time, linguists have noted not only an infusing of Indian words in English, but also an even larger phenomenon of incorporation of English words in Indian languages. We should assume that the latter process has been going on for more than two centuries, and it has gained even stronger momentum in the last two or three decades, especially with the massive spread of vocabulary from the domain of information technology. It is useful to refer in this context to an important paper by B.N. Patnaik who accounts for the "Englishization of Oriya' on the basis of 'texts of sports, reports, film journals, advertisements, thrillers, popular and scholarly writings on political and economic topics.' Patnaik focuses on Englishization at the levels of lexicon, syntax, linguistic etiquette, and pronunciation.[17] He also provides examples of substantive or nominalized words: e.g. *Rama* pass *karichi*; *Hari* phel *haichi*; Settle, lecture, etc. He also notes, perhaps correctly, that the extensive use of English numerals in Indian languages is "mainly due to the national enthusiasm for cricket."

In spite of the evidently hybrid or mixed character of the formation of languages in general and particularly of English in India, some commentators have tended to characterize it, on the other hand, as a distinct 'variety' of English. Braj K. Kachru, for instance, tries to understand the problem not in terms of a continuous variation of languages, but rather in terms of the traditional and static notion of the 'mother tongue.' Rather than deconstruct the current notion of a 'language' as an entity with definite internal substance and contours and consequently assuming a clear definition of English, Kachru refers to the current global spread of that language in terms of 'Englishes.' Thus, according to him the three 'concentric circles' 'representing the spread and stratification' of English are the following:

1) The 'Inner Circle': countries that have a traditional base of English (e.g. USA, UK, Canada, etc.).

2) The 'Outer Circle': countries where English is institutionalized as an additional language (e.g. Ghana, Pakistan, Singapore, India, Philippines, etc.).

3) The 'Expanding Circle': countries where English is used as primarily a foreign language (e.g. China, Japan, USSR, etc.) (See "Overview" by Jody Stoffels, Hiedi Hecker, Roshawn Sook, Claudia Reeve, Joyce Pham Chapter 9 in Braj B. Kachru, *World Englishes: Approaches, Issues, and Resources.*)

Kachru's approach is thus ambivalent: on the one hand he glorifies the great global march of English, but at the same time and on the other hand, he attributes distinctness of the Englishes used in the non-native regions. He is less interested in the inexorable instability and hybridity of the language phenomenon, and therefore especially of the fractal dispersion of what we understand as the current global English.

Global English has at the same time been the target of outright refusal on the part of linguists and scholars living in currently English-speaking regions. There is a fear about the menacing and all-conquering global march of English. The following text written by Nkonko M. Kamwangamalu, a South African linguist, will give us some idea of the overwhelming sense of anxiety that has pervaded at least some of the culturally and linguistically conscious scholars in that part of the world.

> Whichever theory one espouses, the fact remains that, in the context of South Africa, English is spreading like wildfire and has even infiltrated the family domain, particularly in urban black communities. This spread of English has been welcomed by some, especially the elite, who cash in on their knowledge of the language. However, it has caused a lot of anxiety and agony for others including the purists on the one hand, who believe that the language is being mutilated through nativization by its new users (i.e. non-native speakers); and, on the other hand, African language activists and community leaders, who see the spread of English into the family domain as a threat to the maintenance and a prelude to the demise of the indigenous languages. This concern about the fate of the African languages against the spread of English is exacerbated by the fact that South Africa has a well-documented history of language demise (Lanham and Prinsloo 1978), a history which is evident from the disappearance of the Khoisan languages and the Indian languages from the country's languages map. Not surprisingly, the speakers of African languages feel, as we will see later, that if the current trend towards unilingualism in English continues, the African languages will face attrition and death, much as the Indian languages and the Khoisan languages did.[18]

In the remaining part of the paper, we shall argue in favour of the idea that historically languages exists never in isolation, but always in terms of superposing and mingling of more than one language. Unconscious or conscious hybridity and even 'marriage' between languages, is the way of life of language. 'Interlanguage' is more of a language than mere 'language' or mono-language, which is, historically shortlived and artificial in its existence. This is so, in our view, because below the surface manifestation or 'actualization' of a language, there is always its virtual existence. The association between what is assumed as a well-bounded (state of) language and the associated people is rather ephemeral. What is linguistically real is the continuous 'variation' or 'creation' of the virtual resources that are always and already available for the users of a given language. From this dynamic perspective, staticity of language and the corresponding monolingualism of national or other communities can only be a myth.

Gustave Guillaume, an exceptional though little-known French linguist of the first half of the 20th century, had insisted on understanding the virtual nature of language before attempting to study the structure of language. According to him:

> To study language in conditions which would be as close as possible to the real conditions of its use, we must start, as speaking subject, from the language in its *virtual state* and accomplish with it the actualization (realization) of the virtual with which it is made up. .... The virtual (in this book) is considered here as the depository in us, not only of the concepts which are used to express the material part of thought, but also the entire mechanism for the use of these concepts.[19]

Similarly, Emile Benveniste, a better known linguist of a generation later had suggested that "(i)t is more productive to conceive of the mind as a virtuality than as a framework; as a dynamism than as structure." And correlatively, "a linguistic system—precisely because it is synchronic—has only a virtual existence in sequential time; a language really exists only when a speaker takes over and actualizes it."[20] The question of the virtual has received a slightly different treatment in the work of Jacques Derrida. He does not see it as the equivalent of potentiality, but as a kind of structure that pervades the transactions at the level of the actual. It is that which refuses to stop impinging on the actual, and that on which the task of deconstruction is meant to be directed.

> I would insist ...above all on a concept of virtuality (virtual image, virtual space, and so virtual event) that can doubtless no longer

> be opposed, in perfect philosophical serenity, to the actual reality in the way that philosophers used to distinguish between potential and act, *dynamis* and *energeia*, the potentiality of a material and the defining form of a *telos*, and therefore of a progress, etc. This virtuality makes its mark even on the structure of the produced event, it affects both the time and space of the image, discourse, "information," in short everything that refers us to this so-called actuality...

This notion of the virtual is in some ways contrasted with that of the promise 'in language). It is the promise that takes language outside itself, outside oneself, it is promise that goes back and forth between the self and other in and through language. It is promise that refuses a monolanguage of the self and that incessantly makes appear the language of the other, the other language, or as we have suggested earlier, the *exolanguage*. We can contend thus that all poetic or literary language is an *exo-language*, and all poetics, the ideal source as well as the target of all linguistics, would be an *exo-linguistics*.

Perhaps, one should go to the extent of saying that there really is no such entity as 'language'. Or, rather there is no substance of language, either to begin with or as an end. There are only intermediary languages, only modes of speaking, writing or communicating with others. The 'monolanguage of the other' is this non-existent 'language' of a non-finalized subject or of an 'unvowable community' in the sense of Maurice Blanchot). In other words, there are only hybrid, 'mixed' or 'inter' languages, and thus there can be national or community languages only artificially, that is, by force. In present-day linguistics, there are many ways of understanding this hybridity or mixture. We shall present here at least one theoretical formulation on 'mixed languages.'

> One seldom encounters a language that is not, in some way mixed, in the sense that it has not been influenced to some point in its history by another language, and employs some structure or form that derives from that language. In ... Mixed Languages, we are concerned... with varieties that emerged in situations of community bilingualism, and whose structures show an

> etymological split that is not marginal, but dominant, so that it is difficult to define the variety's linguistic parentage as involving just one ancestor language. This definition—a bilingual mixture, with split ancestry—is the one most commonly applied in the literature of mixed languages.[21]

In this work, the authors give an account of the emergence of Michif, a language "spoken by several hundred Métis, descendants of French-Canadian fur traders and Amerindian women.... The language combines verbs form Plains Cree and noun phrases from French." According to Bakker, mixed languages, appear as a result of 'intertwining,' characterized by a "single and predetermined process involving mixed populations, by which the grammar (bound morphemes and some free grammatical morphemes) of one language, typically that spoken by native women (or, in the case of nomadic populations, the, surrounding majority language), combines with the lexicon of another, usually a colonial language spoken by men (or in the case of nomadic populations, the ancestral language). The intertwining model views both contributing languages as hierarchically equivalent. The process by which they are combined is viewed as a rapid process, and quite often one that is intrinsically connected to the process of formation of a new ethnic identity." (Ibid.) Further, according to Bakker, 'the intertwined languages are created 'more or less consciously.'

From the context of the history of Indian languages, Malayalam offers an excellent example of a self-conscious creation of a mixed or hybrid language. Malayalam, is said to have been developed from the conscious mixing, in the late 14th century, of Western Tamil (which provided its grammatical structure) and Sanskrit (providing mostly lexicon) resulting in 'Manipravalam' (= pearl-and-precious stone) style of poetic composition, that preceded the formation of a language currently spoken by more than 30 million people. The grammatical text of Manipravalam style of poetry, *Lilathilakam*, was devoted to describing/prescribing the poetic style of/for the language. Similarly, historical processes of 'mixing' are said to have resulted in the formation of Yiddish (Eastern German and Hebrew) and Ladino (Hispano-Hebrew) in the European Jewish context.

Gerard Leitner has given a slightly different picture of the same process. According to his sociolinguistic 'habitat model' (*Australia's Many Voices*, 2004)

> contact [is] a multiplex process involving partners in multidialectal and multilingual contexts, and recasts entire language habitats. .... The introduction of English (or of any other transplanted language) leads to the unsettling of an established language habitat and of the social and linguistic texture of local languages. Responses to contact are the 'modification' of languages, the creation of contact language, and the increase and subsequent decrease of multilingualism. ....Non-dominant migrant languages are typically reduced to informal, often family-friendship functions and modification means stylistic improvement and syntactic change in the direction of English.

We shall make a brief reference to Roy Harris's Integrational Linguistics, relevant for our discussion of the hybridization of languages. According to Harris, "(l)inguistic acts are assumed to be immediately relevant to the current situation, unless there is reason to suppose otherwise, just as non-linguistic acts are. ... The principle of chronological integration between linguistic and non-linguistic events plays an important part in our picture of human rationality." In order to connect the linguistic and non-linguistic acts under a common domain, he has proposed the notion of 'co-temporality' in lingusitcs. Harris notes: "Linguistic acts could ... be said to be cotemporal in our experience with non-linguistic events and circumstances of all kinds." And further, "(i)t is cotemporality which allows non-linguistic acts to combine freely with speech in the organization of interpersonal exchanges..."[22]

Adopting such a perspective, Harris is persuaded to propose an alternative linguistics, what he calls, 'integrational linguistics,' which in its role as "a demythologized linguistics would be an investigation of the renewal of language as a continuously creative process."[23] Integrational linguistics is not only meant to be an alternative to how the field of linguistics is practised, but also to radically modify our understanding of what a language is. A language can from such a perspective, be seen and defined, not as what it is, but only as what it is now becoming through the interaction of its speakers, and by way of the (contingent) integration of their ambient world. From the perspective of integrational linguistics, according to Harris, "language is continuously created by the interaction of individuals in specific communication situations."

It is worth adding in conclusion, that a new communication situation has unfolded before us in the last 20 years or so in the form of cyber-communication. The old ordered patterns of language, supported and moulded by nation-states and ethnic cultures, have been subjected to rapid transformations. Computers, internet, and mobile phones have radically transformed today's languages, both internally and under the influence of other languages. Words and other elements from English, the dominant language today of 'information technology' have further (that is over and above its forceful spread the colonial period) penetrated all the languages of the world. Users of many languages, especially Indian, find that it was convenient to adopt words and phrases, and even more commonly the Roman alphabet as used in English, when they communicate by e-mail or other internet media. Mobile phone SMS messages have been up to now dominated by the use of English and the Roman alphabet with English values. Even more interesting is the reduction and modification of English spellings and vocabulary. Short Message Service (SMS) and Twitter messages require known or innovative abbreviations of words and sentences. Within a short span of time, communicators in these new media have become adept at creating and deciphering abbreviated messages. Redundant spellings, especially in languages like English and French, as in words like 'tough' and 'should' (which become 'tuf' and 'shud' or 'shd') in English, or 'beau' (which becomes 'bo') in French are easily transformed, making the earlier forms seem archaic.

Perhaps it is right to say that the digitality of the Information Technology domain has had a concurrent effect of digitalizing portions of our languages. For example, it is common to substitute the English prepositions 'to' and 'for' by the figures 2 and 4. Or, an office, a commercial establishment or a television channel may be said to function '24/7' a substitute for expressions like 'daily' and 'round-the-clock.' Such digitalization of language, is also perhaps the motivation for referring to the date of major natural or human catastrophes in terms of the digitalized dates of their occurrence – e.g. 9/11 to refer to the destruction of the twin towers of the World Trade Centre in New York in 2001, and 26/12 to refer to the date of the great tsunami that struck many regions of South and Southeast Asia in 2004. All these suggest the endless suppleness and mutability of language use in previously unthought of ways.

NOTES

1. In the words of William Jones: "The *Sanscrit* language, whatever be its antiquity, is of a wonderful structure; more perfect than the *Greek*, and more copious than the *Latin*, and more exquisitely refined than either, yet bearing to both of them a stronger affinity, both in the roots of verbs and in the forms of grammar, than could possibly have been produced by accident; so strong indeed, that no philologer could examine them all three, without believing them to have sprung from a common source, which, perhaps, no longer exists: there is a similar reason, though not quite forcible, for supposing that both the *Gothick* and the *Celtick*, though blended with a very different idiom, had the same origin with the *Sanscrit*..." See Bagchee, M., (ed.) *Sir William Jones—Discourses and Essays*, 1984.
2. Thomas Babington Macaulay's Minutes from which this quote is excerpted was approved by Lord William Bentinck on March 7, 1835.
3. See, John, B.K., 2007.
4. According to a report in the *The Hindu* newspaper of August 8, 1959, the Indian Prime Minister Jawaharlal Nehru, said in the Lok Sabha (the People's House of the Parliament) on August 7 that he was "against imposition of any language on the people. The Prime Minister categorically stated that English would continue as an associate or additional language in the country for an indefinite period or as long as the non-Hindi-speaking people wanted it. The decision as to how long it should continue

as an associate language, Mr. Nehru emphasised amidst cheers, should be left to the non-Hindi-speaking people and not the Hindi-speaking people. He added that English would serve as a useful key to modern scientific and technical knowledge, and in short as a 'window to the modern world.' As such, they could not afford to shut out English except at their peril. Of the many foreign languages which helped them to study scientific and technical subjects, they should naturally prefer English because they had already learnt it. It had been the medium of instruction in schools and colleges for generations." (From 'This Day That Age' of *The Hindu* dated August 8, 2009.)

5. These languages are: Assamese, Oriya, Urdu, Kannada, Kashmiri, Gujarati, Tamil, Telugu, Punjabi, Bengali, Marathi, Malayalam, Sanskrit, Hindi (the initial 14), Sindhi, Nepali, Konkani, Manipuri, Bodo, Santali, Maithili, Dogri (subsequently added in three different stages).
6. This could be attributed to the post-Second World War global spread of American English through the media (magazines, films, music, radio and television), publishing (books), academic and scholarly journals). A liberated space for the use of English came to be during the 1950's and 60s of the last century. During the phase of American cultural-mediatic domination, the sense of shame associated with English at least among the politically enlightened during the colonial period was replaced by a more casual and playful use of English from the late 1960s.
7. F. Mazière and S. Auroux, 2006, pp. 7-18.
8. See a discussion on this, in Manjali, F., 2004, pp. 71-80.
9. See, for instance, the discussions in Matras, Y. and P. Bakker (eds.), 2003, p. 1.
10. Rushdie, S., 2008, p. 34.
11. The glossary entry says: HOBSON-JOBSON, s. A native festal excitement ... This phrase may be taken as a typical one of the most highly assimilated class of Anglo-Indian argot ... peculiar to the British soldier and his surroundings ... an Anglo-Saxon version of the wailings of the Mahommedans as they beat their breasts in the procession of the Moharram—"Yâ Hasan! Yâ Hosain!"
12. See, John, B.K., 2007.
13. Desani, 1948, p. 244.
14. Mukherjee, M.,
15. Ibid.
16. Ibid.

17. Here are Patnaik's examples of incorporation of English lexical items in English: Daily life: torch, battery, brush, lantern, switch, glass, cigarette, book; furniture: desk, bench, table, stool, dressing table, fan; Crockery: cup, plate, dish; Cooked food and related items: omelette, cutlet, chop, mutton, biscuit, chicken, peppermint, dinner, breakfast, dining table, buffet, hotel; Fashion (clothes and accessories): pant, short, coat, skirt, earring, ring, powder, blouse, snow, hairpin, fason; Games: hockey, cricket, football.... Names of diseases: typhoid, cholera, cancer, fever, cough....
18. Kamwangamalu, N.M., 2003, pp. 65-81.
19. Guillaume, G., 1929/1984, p. 121.
20. Benveniste, E., 1966, p. 73.
21. Matras, Y. and Bakker, P. (eds.), 2003, p. 1.
22. Harris, R., 1981. See Chapter 6, "Language Demythologised?"
23. Ibid., p. 164.

13

Beginnings of Modern Linguistics and the Colonial Context: Perspectives from History, Culture and Religion[1]

Scientific rationality defines itself as it constructs the subject matter and methodology of each new discipline. In the human sciences, moreover, there is no virgin territory to explore; the fields of investigation are continents mapped by tradition and explored by religious thought.

Jean-Pierre Vernant[2]

Among the unstated facts of 'modern linguistics,' its intricate and enduring relationship with colonialism has an important and ineradicable place. The history of 'colonial linguistics' is said to have begun with the Spaniard Anton de Nebrija's recommendation of his newly published grammar of Castillian (1492) to the Queen Isabel with the observation that "language was always the companion of empire... language and empire began, increased, and flourished together."[3] From that moment to that of Jacques Derrida's enigmatic assertion that opens his *Monolingualism of the Other; or, The Prosthesis of an Origin* (1998), "I only have one language; it is not mine,"[4] scholars have struggled to grapple with the nature of the relationship between linguistics and (colonial) politics. We make our own modest attempt here by focusing on the works of Sir William Jones and our project could be extended to analyse the works of other linguistically-oriented philosophers like Johann G. Herder and Max Müller, who advanced historical, cultural, civilizational and religious perspectives on languages. We examine here more closely the founding of the idea of the 'Indo-European' which was often, and at least initially, nothing but racially (and therefore politically) motivated. We also present a tentative hypothesis regarding the intellectual currents that the Indo-European hypothesis possibly gave rise to, especially as it concerns the fate of the so-called Semitic peoples, the Jews and the Muslims, in Europe and the South Asian region, respectively. We go on to provide a working understanding of the colonial use of languages and linguistics, both outside and within India, in relation to Bernard Cohn's (1997) apt description of the British authorities' project of developing 'the command of language, and the language of command.' Through these attempts, we also seek, in a post-colonial vein, to breach the avowed political neutrality of contemporary linguistics.

In his well-known work, *Imagined Communities*, Benedict Anderson (1983/1991) describes how in the context of the emergence of capitalism and print-technology, the European vernaculars were assembled into 'print-languages' and how the latter with the aid of 'print-capitalism' became the basis for the emergence of national consciousnesses. This process, he notes, further entailed:

(a) The creation of "unified fields of exchange and communication below Latin and above the vernaculars."
(b) Providing "a new fixity to language, which ... helped to build the image of antiquity so central to the idea of the nation."
(c) The creation of new " 'languages of power' of a kind different from the older administrative vernaculars."[5]

Anderson emphasizes that "the fixing of print-languages and the differentiation of status between them were *largely unselfconscious* processes resulting from the explosive interaction between capitalism, technology and the human linguistic diversity."[6] (italics mine)

The historical period that Anderson is concerned with is that of early European modernity, which somewhat coincides with what Foucault calls the 'classical' period, that is, the period preceding that of 'Enlightenment,' or the 'modern' period. Foucault, in his *Order of Things – An Archaeology of the Human Sciences* (1966), sees the fourth quarter of the 18th century in Europe as the period of 'comparison' of languages and study of their historical changes. This, as we know, is the period of comparative philology, which in many ways paved the way for modern linguistics (i.e. of the 19th and 20th centuries).

Foucauldian 'archaeology' sees the emergence of comparatism and historicism as a 'discontinuity' in European linguistic thought (along with other similar discontinuities in economics and biology). This discontinuity from the classical to the modern period is characterized by the shift from understanding language as 'representation' by means of *signs*, to the study of the historical changes in the *form* of languages, by way of comparison. As Foucault states it:

> In the last quarter of the 18th century, the horizontal comparison of languages... no longer makes it possible to know what each language may still preserve of its ancestral memory, what marks from before Babel have been preserved in the sounds of its words, but it should make it possible to measure the extent to which languages resemble one another, the density of their similitudes, the limits within which they are transparent to one another.[7]

Such comparisons between languages, he goes on to say, involves 'great confrontations between various languages' which sometimes reflect 'pressures of political motive'...[8]

In relation to this 'confrontation' between languages' Foucault rightly identifies 'inflection' as the "form intermediary between articulation of contents and the value of roots."[9] We note here that the grammatical property of 'inflection' became the basis of the comparison between and the so-called classical languages, Sanskrit, Greek and Latin, by Gaston Cœurdoux and Sir William Jones, and particularly the basis of the latter's claim regarding the superiority (and for some, the near-perfection) of Sanskrit even among these 'classical languages.' Foucault is not interested in the ideological elevation of these classical 'Indo-European' (for some, 'Aryan') languages, but he rightly notes the decisive role played by 'inflection' in the birth of modern linguistics.[10] By the end of the 18th century:

> ... through the inflectional system, the dimension of the purely grammatical is appearing: language no longer consists of representations and of sounds that in turn represent the representations and are ordered among them as the links of thought require; it consists also of formal elements, grouped into a system, which impose upon the sounds, syllable and roots an organization that is not that of representation. Thus an element has been introduced into the analysis of language that is not reducible to it.[11]

Right as he is about the emergence of modern 'scientific' linguistics, Foucault's 'archaeology' is decidedly averse to focusing on the *ideological* dimensions that accompany this discontinuity. Edward Said (still inadequately) and others have focused on the central role that philology played in the formation of the bourgeoning field of 'Orientalism.' Said quotes Benjamin Disraeli at the start of his book: 'The East is a career.'[12] It could be added that the 'Orient' was perhaps a lucrative career for the European bourgeoisie in the late 18th and early 19th centuries. And moreover, they were clearly motivated by cultural-political and religious ideologies in the wake of the economic gains that colonialism had begun to accrue.

Undoubtedly, the prodigious British scholar, Sir William Jones, also known to his admirers as 'Oriental' Jones, was the most important figure here. Born in 1746, he was knighted in 1783, and soon after left for Calcutta to take up his dream job as a puisne judge at the Calcutta High Court. The very next year, he founded the Asiatick Society of Bengal on the model of the Royal Society in London.[13] He had instituted the Society's anniversary lectures which were given by himself beginning, February 1784. It is a brief passage in the third anniversary discourse of 1786, 'On the Hindus,' that made a lasting impression in the world of Orientalist scholarship. The often quoted text can very well be regarded as the jewel in the Orientalist crown:

> The Sanscrit language, whatever be its antiquity, is of a wonderful structure; more perfect than the Greek, more copious than the Latin, and more exquisitely refined than either, yet bearing to both of them a stronger affinity, both in the roots of verbs and in the forms of grammar, than could possibly have been produced by accident; so strong indeed, that no philologer could examine all three, without believing them to have sprung from some common source, which, perhaps, no longer exists: there is a similar reason, though not quite so forcible, for supposing that both the Gothic and the Celtic, though blended with a very different idiom, had the same origin with the Sanscrit; and the old Persian might be added to the same family, if this were the place for discussing any question concerning the antiquities of Persia.[14]

This passage also marks the official birth of the notion of the Indo-European 'family' which has been deemed as the most important of all the world's language-families, within what emerged as historical linguistics in the 19th century. Note that Jones' 'discourse' was made within a year of his having embarked on learning Sanskrit (in order to translate and codify the Hindu laws) after he met a pandit in Benares, the previous year. Besides, Jones was not the only European to be acquainted with Sanskrit and other Indian languages at that time, nor was he the first to propose a relationship between it and the European classical languages.[15]

Jones' discourses and essays (that appeared in the publication *Asiatick Researches*) have to be seen in relation to the works not only of linguistically oriented scholars like Gaston Cœurdoux and Abraham H. Anquetil-Duperron, but also in relation to the overall intellectual climate of Europe of the period marked by Enlightenment thought and the Romanticist critical response to it. Jones knew such luminaries as the German writer Goethe and the French philosopher of Enlightenment, Voltaire, and his work in certain respects bears affinity to those of the pre-Romantic German philosopher Johann Gottfried Herder, who was his contemporary. Goethe greatly admired Kalidasa's *Shakuntala* that reached Germany via Jones' English translation of the work in 1789. Some scholars believe that Jones' contribution to the European understanding of Oriental literatures by way of his translations from Persian, Arabic and Sanskrit is as important as his contribution to linguistics.

William Jones' philosophical position bears a remarkable affinity to that of Johann Herder. Herder, the 'greatest' and once the favourite student of Kant, had turned away from his master and from Enlightenment thought under the influence of Georg Hamann, a wayward philosopher compared with the disciplined Kant, but yet one of the pioneering thinkers of early German Romanticism.[16] The idea of a universal reason that is transcendentally available to man according to the Enlightenment philosophy was rejected by Hamann and his followers like Herder and they replaced it with the *volkgeist* (folk spirit) that was manifested in ordinary people's language, literature, history, and religion. According to Herder, humans everywhere start with the same mental abilities but their practical living in specific conditions and contexts, as well as their specific historical experiences, form their mentalities differently. These mental differentiations, in turn, are manifested in their differential creative outputs, that is, in their languages, literatures, and religious thoughts and beliefs.

Herder's main merit, according to many scholars, is in having favoured cultural pluralism, but a pluralism that sometimes verged on relativism.[17] Unlike the rationalists and the earlier votaries of religion, Herder foregrounds language in human history and human existence. Human beings are made of language, their nature is 'a tissue of language.'[18] Human reason needs language to articulate itself. The grammatical form of any language, whether simple or complex, reflects the experience of the world as impressed in language. Unlike Voltaire,[19] who as a major philosopher of Enlightenment despised religious texts, both Jewish and Christian, Herder in a properly Romantic vein admired the Hebrew poetry for its simplicity and spiritual richness that reflected a paradisiacal innocence.

Herder, as a historian of humanity, attempted to trace its progress through time in terms of the acquiring density and complexification of language in different nations or cultures which were in turn the product of human interaction and sense-making. Human societies are all equally endowed and they progressed in history according to the *zeitgeist* or time-spirit of each, but at the same time, the succession of epochs in the universal human history is predetermined as per the Divine plan, that is, it is a matter of Providence. Effectively, Herder pursued the thought of a cultural pluralism, where every culture is historically progressing in terms of its own singularity, but ultimately, this human history is subordinated to a Providential intent. From such a perspective, since each nation had its own internal progressive force and destiny, Herder was opposed to any form of religious conversion. As Olender relates Herder's position: "To convert a nation to Christianity by imposing on it a new way of life is to compel it to betray its own values, to lose its own identity, and thus to imperil its spiritual and political integrity."[20]

But yet, for Herder, understanding the creative unfolding of human history—even if humans are sense-making agents—is possible only as "an art of uncovering the divine order hidden in the Bible."[21] A historian, Herder would expect, to be "a prophet of the past," a poet whose work is based on an "aesthetics of Providence."[22] Olender has noted that if Herder subordinates a secular 'cultural history respecting national and spiritual diversities' to a Lutheran 'providential anthropology,' that's because, for him ultimately only the Bible provides "Revelation in the proper sense of the word." Other religions can only provide mythology, liturgy or high morality. Herder's final *coup de grace* is directed at Judaism whose holy scriptures, the prayers and moral judgments, in his view, are "sublime writings," but in spite of that Providence itself had made a decision in favour of Christianity as the "unique design for our species."[23] Herder is dismissive of the Jewish religion as a 'parasitic plant'; and goes on to predict that they will be assimilated and will begin "to live according to European laws."[24]

This brief excursus into Herder's thought was necessary for us to be able to understand better the intricacies of William Jones' historical-civilizational claims. A recent work on Jones' texts has focused on his rootedness in an 'antique theology' that overruns Jones' reputation as an orientalist scholar with a liberal and progressive worldview. The Swiss author of *The Birth of Orientalism*,[25] Urs App's main criticism of Jones in another text, runs as follows:

> While the volumes of the *Asiatick Researches* stunned their European readership by their utterly secular and objective outlook on Asia and thus propagated a new kind of orientalism that was no more the hand-maiden of theology, [William]Jones's yearly discourses show how even the erudite and coolheaded founder of the Asiatick Society remained chained to Europe's time-honoured religious ideology with its peculiar vision of an extremely short history dominated by a God who kindly instructed his first creatures, drowned most of their descendants in the deluge, and had three sons of Noah populate the entire world in a couple of thousand years. While Jones's papers on a wide range of oriental subjects, his letters, and his editorship of the *Asiatick Researches* show him as a pivotal figure in the move towards orientalism's emancipation from theology, his yearly discourses demonstrate a surprisingly deep attachment to Bible-inspired chronology, sacred history, and ancient theology. Edward Said was right in stating that Jones was ideology-driven; but the nature of that ideology as well as its connection to European colonialism will have to be reevaluated.[26]

According to William Jones' mytho-geographical scheme outlined in the third anniversary lecture of February 2, 1786, the 'vast continent' of Asia has been inherited by 'five principal nations': the Indians, the Chinese, the Tartars, the Arabs, and the Persians. His stated intention is to study them all in every detail, so that a 'more perfect knowledge of them all' would be to the advantage of the European world.[27] He is also interested in knowing about the truth of their common origins, if any. He begins with the study of the Indians in the third lecture 'On the Hindus,' because, he says, "it is the country, which we now inhabit, and from which we may best survey the regions around us."[28] His own historical interest in India is decidedly partial for, he intends to keep the Muslim period out of his historical considerations of India. He says: "...in all these inquiries concerning the history of India, I shall confine my researches downwards to the Mohammedan conquests at the beginning of the eleventh century, but extend them upwards, as high as possible, to the earliest authentic records of the human species."[29]

Central to Jones' geographical-historical accounts are four or five dominant themes:

- The British who are now in command in the Indian territory (Bengal to begin with) and are now settlers on this land.
- Muslim rulers and their religion and culture present in the Indian territory are irrelevant for studying the history of India.
- India is the prized possession of the British, and its antiquity is directly linked to the antiquity of the Europeans.
- The Biblical (Old Testament, i.e., Mosaic) account of the history and geography of the peoples of the world can be attested by modern studies under the aegis of the Asiatic Society of Bengal that he had founded.
- The British have a God-given (Providential) role to guide the destiny of the Indian people.

Thomas R. Trautmann has noted that Jones' civilizational project owes itself largely to what the former calls the 'Mosaic ethnology'.[30] The Mosaic ethnology has its source in the idea of the Tree of nations mentioned in the Book of Genesis, and attributed to Moses. The tree-structure indicates relations of kinship among nations. According to Trautmann, "the Mosaic ethnology is a simple technology for determining the relations among peoples, conceived as branching lineages of the human family tree, as relations of far and near."[31] Significantly, Jones' modern historical studies are able to establish a more or less seamless mapping between the ancient Biblical accounts. In the 10th Anniversary lecture (February 1793) Jones is explicit and even ecstatic about his own discovery of the truth of the Mosaic ethnology and the role of Providence in aiding to establish the connection between modern Britain and the antiquity of India:

> ... all our historical researches have confirmed the *Mosaick* accounts of the primitive world; and our testimony on that subject ought to have the greater weight, because, if the result of our observations had been totally different, we should nevertheless have published them, not indeed with equal pleasure, but with equal confidence; for *Truth is mighty, and,* whatever be its consequences, *must always prevail*...[32]

And furthermore:

> In these *Indian* territories, which Providence has thrown into the arms of *Britain* for their protection and welfare, the religion, manners, and laws of the natives preclude even the idea of political freedom; but their histories may possibly suggest hints for their prosperity, while our country derives essential benefit from the diligence of a placid and submissive people, who multiply with such increase, even after the ravages of famine...[33]

Here again, Jones insists on the God-given responsibility that Britain has over the Indian region, and therefore its need to perpetuate the newly established colonial rule. The Mosaic ethnology is clearly articulated in Jone's 9th anniversary Discourse of February 23, 1792. As per this, the world is inhabited by the descendants of the sons of Noah, *Ham, Shem* and *Yafet*. After the great deluge, the Noah's family had initially settled in northern Iran. Then the expanding family of the descendants of *Yafet* spread over northern Europe and Asia. They were on the whole unlettered and far from being cultured. The descendants of *Ham,* invented the letter, were good in astrology, and produced an old mythology, and went on to settle in the regions of Misr (Egypt), Cush (Ethiopia), other parts of Africa and India. And, the descendants of *Shem,* settled in the region now known as the Middle East, and they consisted among others, of the Arabs, the Syrians and the Phoenicians. Jones' mythical ethnology will go on to state that the descendants of Abraham, would have come from all three families, and they are described as "bold adventurers of an ardent spirit and a roving disposition, who disdained subordination and wandered in separate clans," who began to cohere as a distinct group only about 1500 years before the beginning of the Christian era.[34]

It is also worth noting here that in the ninth anniversary discourse Jones makes a most unacceptable and disparaging reference to the prophet of the Muslims.[35]

The European civilizational narrative forcefully enunciated by Sir William Jones and which later emerged in a full-blown manner and with more intense political ramifications in the nineteenth has been submitted to an astute analysis in the work of Maurice Olender (1989/1992).[36] Historically, there has always been yearning to name the original language of mankind. In the European Christian religious context this was often spoken of as the language of paradise, where man was united with God, and the language was that in which God spoke to the first man, Adam. Augustine, claimed it was Hebrew, but then there were others who rejected this hypothesis, and some even proposed that the honour of being the original human language went to Syriac.

William Jones' declaration about Sanskrit, its 'exquisite refinement' and its possibly having come from a no longer extinct common source along with the European classical languages, Greek and Latin, upset the hitherto dominant position of Hebrew and related Semitic languages. His strong claims in this regard, as we know, led to the hypothesis regarding the Indo-European 'family' of languages, caused a seismic shift in understanding the racial composition of Europe and the rest of the world. In mid nineteenth century, after comparative and historical linguistics had been firmly established in Germany, F. Max Müller, who was by then Professor at Oxford University, had summed up the significance of this change thus:

> Thanks to the discovery of the ancient language of India, Sanskrit as it is called... and thanks to the discovery of the close kinship between this language and the idioms of the principal races of Europe, which was established by the genius of Schlegel, Humboldt, Bopp, and many others, a complete revolution has taken place in the method of studying the world's primitive history.[37]

The twists and turns in the conceptions of world history between 1750 and 1850 must be stated more specifically in terms of the fluctuating fortunes of Hebrew and Sanskrit, by then, the two main 'languages of paradise.'[38] As early as the 1750s the principal French Enlightenment philosopher Voltaire, was keen to detach the European civilization from its Biblical and Hebrew origins, and look for alternatives, possibly from 'the shores of the Ganges' in India. Along with the discovery of Vedic texts and the beginning of the colonial domination of the Indian subcontinent, there arose the talk of an 'Aryan' paradise in place of the Adamic Hebrew paradise. According to one critical reaction against the new European scientific orthodoxy, "(t)he Vedas became the sacred book of the religious origins of the race, the Aryan Bible."[39]

The European Enlightenment, it seems, brought race and civilization to the forefront, and relegated religion to the background, without of course, giving up all its genealogical narrative. The new history was claimed to be less religious and mythological and more 'scientific.' It was considered more scientific because it was based on language and race, which, unlike religion, could be objectively studied. In the process, the organic cultural connection that Europeans were thought to have with the other major Semitic religion, i.e. Judaism with its Hebrew texts, were sought to be abandoned. The Aryan-Hindu religion based in Sanskrit (along with the intellectually and artistically superior Greek civilization), which was thought to be older and spiritually superior to Judaism and Hebrew was now accorded the pride of place and identified as the foundation in relation to the European civilization.

If in Europe, Hebrew and Judaism underwent a civilizational demotion and something like a cultural expulsion, in the South Asian subcontinent, it was the Perso-Arabic languages and Islam which were subjected to a similar experience. Though William Jones had gone to India, initially to study and translate the Persian law as practised in India during the 18th century, he soon became acquainted with Sanskrit language, the Brahminical Hindu religion and its main system of laws, namely the Laws of Manu, which he went on to translate and publish. The civilizational act that Jones wrought in India was to divide a coexisting and contiguous world of the diverse Indian communities, particularly the Hindus and the Muslims. This was accompanied by a simultaneous elevation of Sanskrit and the culture associated with it, and connecting it with the European culture and civilization. The so-called scientific and modern notion of the 'Indo-European' as made possible by repressing on the one hand, the pre-existing religious connection between the European-Christian world and the Semitic-Jewish world, and on the other, the cultural-linguistic connection between the Sanskrit-Hindu world and the Perso-Arabic Islamic world.

The consequences of this civilizational paradigm-shift are rather well-known, and not difficult to relate. From the mid-19th century, there was a growing resentment among the Jews who began to sense that they were being treated as outsiders in Europe. The Zionist movement, calling for all Jews to return to their Promised Land of Israel, was intellectually and politically spearheaded by one of the then most progressive poets of Germany, namely, Moses Hess, who was a friend of Karl Marx, and a philosopher who acquainted Friedrich Engels with the idea of Socialism. Zionism became a more viable political movement for many Jews a few decades later, and particularly after the Dreyfus affair in France, under the leadership of the Austrian businessman, Theodor Herzl, leading to the founding of the Israeli nation in 1948.

Similarly, in South Asia, the Muslims began to forge a separate identity a decade after the anti-British Empire rebellion of 1857 in northern India. This movement became intense and acquired a clearly pan-Islamist character from the first decade of the 20th century. The intellectual and political leadership in this context came once again from a German-educated Socialist poet and philosopher from Lahore in today's Pakistan, Muhammad Iqbal. Iqbal, along with M.A. Jinnah, later became one of the pillars of the Islamist political party, Muslim League, which was instrumental in the formation of the Muslim-majority nation of Pakistan in August 1947. Iqbal is revered as the national poet, and his birthday is celebrated as a public holiday in Pakistan.

The story of the manner in which poets and philosophers

like Moses Hess and Muhammad Iqbal underwent conversions from their radical socialist political leanings to a strong orientation in religious and communitarian nationalism will have to be further researched. At the moment, it suffices for us to see how modern scholarship on languages and their histories have led to serious social and political repercussions at the world-historical level. And moreover, even at the level of any given people, it can be seen that colonialism has produced drastic effects on the knowledge, use and sharing of languages. This has been amply demonstrated in historian Bernard Cohn's account on the nature of the British colonial intervention at the level of languages and other discourses in the Indian context. Cohn has noted that:

> The years 1770 to 1785 may be looked upon as the formative period during which the British successfully began the programme of appropriating Indian languages to serve a crucial component in their construction of the system of rule. More and more British officials were learning the "classical" languages of India (Sanskrit, Persian, and Arabic) as well as many "vulgar" languages. More importantly, this was the period in which the British were beginning to produce an apparatus: grammars, dictionaries, treatises, class books, and translations about and from languages of India. ....(T)he production of these texts and others that followed them began the establishment of discursive formation, defined an epistemological space, created a discourse (Orientalism), and had the effect of converting Indian forms of knowledge into European objects. The subjects of these texts were first and foremost the Indian languages themselves, represented in European terms as grammars, dictionaries, and teaching aids in a project to make the acquisition of a working knowledge of the language available to those British who were to be part of the ruling groups in India.[40]

In his book, *Colonialism and its Forms of Knowledge—The British in India*, Bernard Cohn presents us with a rich empirical account of the inevitably repressive connection that existed between colonialism, culture, and languages, a pattern that can be seen to be repeated wherever modern forms of political domination, i.e., colonialism has existed. The philosophical underpinnings of the problem have been presented with a personal touch in a rare post-colonial text written by Derrida who insists on the inherent coloniality of all cultures, perhaps of culture itself, manifested and expressed in and through language:

> All culture is originally colonial.... Every culture institutes itself through the unilateral imposition of some "politics" of language. Mastery begins as we know, through the power of naming, of imposing and legitimating appellations. We know how that went with France in France itself, in revolutionary France as much as or more than, in monarchical France. This sovereign establishment may be open, legal, armed, or cunning, disguised under the alibis of "universal" humanism, and sometimes of the most generous hospitality. It always follows or precedes culture like its shadow.[41]

NOTES

1. An earlier version of this paper was presented as a talk at the Centre for the Study of Social Sciences, Kolkata, on June 20, 2012. Some of its contents were presented in my course on 'Language and Cultural Studies' at Jawaharlal Nehru University during the winter semester of 2012.
2. Foreword, in Olender, M., 2008, p. vii.
3. Quoted in Errington, J., 2008, p. 18.
4. Derrida, J., 1998, p. 1.
5. Anderson, 1991, pp. 44-5.
6. Ibid., p. 45.
7. Foucault, 1966/1970, p. 233.
8. Foucault refers to the publication in Petersburg, Russia, in 1787 the first volume of the *Camparitivum Totius Orbis* which "include references to 279 languages; 171 in Asia, 55 in Europe, 30 in Africa, 23 in America." This was possibly the largest comparative glossary of world's languages based on the notion of a basic vocabulary. (Ibid., p. 234).
9. Ibid., p. 234.
10. 'Inflection' is a grammatical mode where verbal morphology is based on the internal changes of the root. E.g., 'buy' '→ 'brought', or 'bring' → 'brought' as distinct from 'work' → 'worked'. The languages which have 'inflection' as their major mode of verbal morphology were traditionally referred to as 'inflectional languages' (e.g. Sanskrit, Greek and Latin), as distinct from the 'agglutinating' languages where grammatical elements are

added on the root (e.g. Turkish, Hebrew, Tamil), and the 'isolating' languages, where the roots and grammatical elements remain unconnected (e.g. Chinese).

11. Ibid., p. 235.
12. Said, E., 1979 edn., p. xii.
13. He had invited Lord Warren Hastings, himself a scholar, to preside over the Asiatic Society. On his declining, Jones became its first president.
14. *Sir William Jones, Discourses and Essays,* (ed.) M., Bagchee. New Delhi: People's Publishing House, 1984, p. 9.
15. Abraham Hyacinthe Anquetil-Duperron, a French scholar, had studied old Persian or Avesta, the language of the Zoroastrians (Parsis) in India. He also published *Recherches historiques et geographiques sur l'Inde* in 1776. Later, his Latin translation from the Persian of the Upanishads appeared in 1801-2. Twenty years before Jones' famous third anniversary discourse, a French Jesuit missionary, Gaston Cœurdoux (as attested in his letters of 1767) had noticed the connections between Sanskrit and European languages, Greek and Latin. He suggested that the existence of common words in these languages pointed to their 'common origin and their ancient fraternity.' Note that Cœurdoux and Anquetil-Duperron had religious motives for studying the Indian languages, whereas Jones' immediate and stated purpose was to translate and codify the Persian (Muslim) and Hindu laws.
16. Frederick Beiser says of Hamann: "It is difficult to exaggerate the many respects in which Hamann influenced the Sturm and Drang, and ultimately Romanticism itself. The metaphysical significance of art, the importance of the artist's personal vision, the irreducibility of cultural difference, the value of folk poetry, the social and historical dimension of rationality, and the significance of language for thought—all these themes were prevalent in, or characteristic of, the Sturm und Drang and Romanticism. But they were first adumbrated by Hamann, and then elaborated and promulgated by Herder, Goethe, and Jacobi." (Beiser, F.C., 1987. The Fate of Reason—German Philosophy from Kant to Fichte, Harvard University Press, p. 16)
17. See Olender, M., op cit., pp. 37-50. Olender devotes a full chapter to Herder.
18. Ibid., p. 33.
19. It is said Voltaire attacked Judaism in order to hit even harder at Christianity.

20. Olender, op cit., p. 42.
21. Ibid., p. 44.
22. Ibid., p. 43.
23. Ibid., p. 48.
24. Ibid., p. 49, endnote 28.
25. App, Urs, 2010.
26. App, Urs, 2009, p. 77.
27. Bagchee, M. (ed.) *Sir William Jones, Discourses and Essays*, op cit., p. 5.
28. Ibid.
29. Ibid.
30. Trautmann, Thomas, R., 2006, p. 10.
31. Ibid., p. 11.
32. Sir William Jones' 10th Anniversary Discourse (February 1793). Source: www.elohs.unifi.it/testi/700/jones/Jones_Discourse_10.html accessed on May 24, 2013.
33. Ibid.
34. See, *Sir William Jones, Discourses and Essays*, p. 91-2.
35. Ibid., p. 83.
36. Olender, M., op cit.
37. Quoted in Olender, M., op cit., p. 7.
38. Olender justifies the title and the contents of his book thus: "The sources on which this book is based invite us to consider Aryans and Semites as functional pair with a providential aspect, as elements of a theory of the origins... (op cit., p. 18) The dramatic story of the origin and development of civilization reads s follows: "Aryan and Semite: 'two twins' at the origin of civilization." [quoting Ernest Renan] Discovered in the "same cradle," they constitute a pair with unequal virtues. Separated in early childhood, Aryans and Semites follow singular destinies, are distinct in every way. In a divine drama whose theatre is universal history, Providence sees to it that each plays its proper role. The Aryans bring the West mastery over nature, exploitation of time and space, the invention of mythology, science, and art, but the Semites hold the secret of monotheism—at least that fateful day when Jesus comes into the world at Galilee. (Ibid., pp. 13-4)
39. Ibid., p. 9, Olender is here quoting J. Darmsteter.
40. In 'The Command of Language and the Language of Command', Chapter 2 of Cohn, B., 1997, pp. 20-21.
41. Derrida, J., 1998, p. 59.

Bibliography

Agamben, G., 1991. *Le langage et la mort.* (tr.) M. Raiola. Paris: Christian Bourgois.

Agamben, G., 1998. *Homo Sacer. Sovereign Power and Bare Life.* (tr.), D. Heller-Roazen. Stanford: Stanford University Press.

Anderson, B., 1991 edn. *Imagined Communities. Reflections on the Origin and Spread of Nationalism.* London: Verso.

App, U., 2009. 'William Jones' Ancient Theology' in *Sino-Platonic Papers* 191 (online edn.).

App, U., 2010. *The Birth of Orientalism.* Philadelphia: University of Pennsylvania Press.

Aravamudan, S., 2007, *Guru English. South Asian Religion in a Cosmopolitan Language.* New Delhi: Penguin.

Ariès, P., 1977. *L'Homme avant la mort.* Paris: Seuil.

Bagchee, M. (ed.) 1984. *Sir William Jones. Discourses and Essays.* New Delhi: People's Publishing House.

Bakhtin, M.M., 1981. *The Dialogic Imagination.* (ed.) M. Holquist, (tr.) C. Emerson and M. Holquist. Austin: University of Texas Press.

Barthes, R., 2000 edn. *Camera Lucida* (tr.) R. Howard. London: Vintage. Fr. Orig. published in 1980.

Beiser, F.C., 1987. *The Fate of Reason – German Philosophy from Kant to Fichte.* Cambridge, Mass.: Harvard University Press.

Benjamin, W., 1968 edn. *Illuminations. Essays and Reflections* (ed.) Hannah Aendt, (tr.) H. Zorn. New York: Schocken Books.

Benjamin, W., 1996. *Selected Writings, Vol. 1: 1913-1926.* (ed.) Bullock, M. And M.W. Jennings. Cambridge, Mass.: Belknap Press.

Benjamin, W., 1999. *Illuminations* (ed.) H. Arendt, (tr.) H. Zorn. London: Pimlico.

Benveniste, E., 1966. *Problèmes de linguistique générale.* Paris: Gallimard.

Bergson, H., 1962 edn. *Matter and Memory.* (tr.) Nancy M. Paul and W.

S. Palmer. London: George Allen and Unwin. Fr. Orig. published in 1908.

Bhartrhari, 1974. *The Vakyapadiya of Bhartrhari* (tr.) Iyer, K.A.S., Delhi : Motilal Banarasidass.

Bident, C., 1998. *Maurice Blanchot: Partenaire Invisible.* Champ Vallon: Seyssel.

Blanchot, M. 1982b. *The Madness of the Day.* (tr.) L. Davis. Barrytown: Staion Hill Press.

Blanchot, M., 2001. *Faux Pas.* (tr.) Charlotte Mandell. Stanford Stanford University Press Gallimard. Fr. Original: *Faux pas.* Paris: 1943.

Blanchot, M., 1949. *La part de feu.* Paris: Gallimard.

Blanchot, M., 1955. *L'espace littéraire.* Paris: Gallimard.

Blanchot, M., 1982a. *The Space of Literature.* (tr.) Ann Smock. Lincoln: The University of Nebraska Press. Fr. Orig. published in 1955.

Blanchot, M., 1988. *The Unawovable Community.* New York: The Station Hill Press.

Blanchot, M., 1992a. *The Infinite Conversation.* (tr.) Susan Hanson. Minneapolis University of Minnesota Press, Fr. original: *L'entretien infini*, Paris: Gallimard, 1969.

Blanchot, M., 1992b. *The Step Not Beyond* (tr.) L. Nelson. Albany: State University of New York Press, 1992.

Blanchot, M., 1994. *L'instant de ma mort.* Montpellier: Fata Morgana.

Blanchot, M., 1995. *The Space of Literature,* (tr.) Ann Smock. Lincoln, NE: University of Nebraska Press.

Blanchot, M., 1999. *Thomas the Obscure. (Station Hill Reader)* (tr.) R. Lamberton. Barrytown: Station Hill Press.

Bouriou, C., 2003. *Qu'est-ce que l'imagination?* Paris: J. Vrin.

Bruns, G.L., 1997. *Maurice Blanchot—The Refusal of Philosophy.* Baltimore: The John Hopkins University Press.

Buber, M., 1958 edn., *I and Thou.* (tr.) R.G. Smith. Edinburgh: T. & T. Clark.

Changeux, J.P., 1986. *The Neuronal Man – The Biology of Mind.* Oxford: Oxford University Press, 1986. Original French version, *L'Homme Neuronal*, Paris, Fayard, 1983.

Chatterjee, M., 1983. *Gandhi's Religious Thought.* Notre Dame, IN: University of Notre Dame Press.

Chesterton, G.K., 2008. *The Man Who Was Thursday.* London: Atlantic Books.

Chomsky, N. 1965. *Aspects of the Theory of Syntax.* Cambridge: MIT Press.

Cohen, T., (ed.) 1986. *Face to face with Levinas.* Albany: SUNY Press.

Cohn, B., 1997. *Colonisalism and its Forms of Knowledge. The British in*

India. New Delhi: Oxford University Press.

Couture, A., 2001. "From Vishnu's Deeds to Vishnu's Play, Or Observations on the Word Avatara as a Designation for the Manifestation of Vishnu," in *Journal of Indian Philosophy*, 29.

Damasio, A., 2003. *Looking for Spinoza—Joy, Sorrow and the Feeling Brain*. Orlando: Harcourt, 2003.

Deleuze, G. and F. Guattari, 1975. *Kafka – pour une littérature mineure*. Paris: Minuit. *Kafka—Towards a Minor Literature* (Eng. Tr.) Dana Polan: University of Minnesofa Press. 1986.

Deleuze, G. and F. Guattari, 1987. *A Thousand Plateaus. Capitalism and Schizophrenia* II, (tr.) B. Massumi, Minneapolis: The University of Minnesota Press.

Deleuze, G., 1977. "Literature and Life." *Critical Inquiry*, 23 (2), pp. 225-230 .

Deleuze, G., 1986 edn. *Cinema I: The Movement-Image*. (tr.) H. Tomlinson and B. Habberjam. London: Athlone. Fr. Orig. published 1983.

Derrida, J., 1976. *Of Grammatology* (tr.) G. Chakravorty-Spivak, Delhi: Motilal Banarasidass.

Derrida, J., 1977. 'De l'économie restreinte à l'économie générale. Un hegelienisme sans réserve'. In : *L'écriture et la différence*. Paris: Seuil. (369-407).

Derrida, J., 1978. "Structure, Sign and Play in the Discourse of the Human Sciences," Chapter 10 in *Writing and Difference* (tr.) Alan Bass. London: Routledge.

Derrida, J., 1981. *Positions*, (tr.) A. Bass. Chicago: Chicago University Press.

Derrida, J., 1982. *Margins of Philosophy* (tr.) A. Bass. Chicago: Chicago Universiy Press.

Derrida, J., 1985. "Roundtable on Translation" in *The Ear of the Other – Otobiography, Transference, Translation*, (tr.) P. Kamuf. New York: Schocken Books.

Derrida, J., 1996. 'Demeure. Fiction et témoignage.' In : *Passions de la littérature. Avec J. Derrida*, (ed.) M. Lisse. Paris: Galilée.

Derrida, J., 1998. *Monolingualism of the Other Or, The Prosthesis of Origin*. (tr.) P. Mensard. Stanfrod: Stanford University Press.

Derrida, J., 2001. *The Work of Mourning*. (Ed.) Pascale-Anne Brault and M. Naas. Chicago: Chicago University Press.

Derrida, J., 2005. *Sovereignties in Question—The Poetics of Paul Celan*. New York: Fordham University Press.

Derrida, J., 2005. *On Touching—Jean–Luc Nancy*. (tr.) C. Irizarry. Stanford: Stanford University Press.

Derrida, J., P. Lacoue-Labarthe, J.-L. Nancy, 2006. [Conversation] In:

"Penser avec J. Derrida" *Rue Descartes* 52 : 86-99.

Desai, M., 1973. *Day-to-Day with Gandhi*. Varanasi: Sarva Seva Sangh.

Desani, G. V., 1948. All About H. Hatter. London: Aldor.

Errington, J.J., 2008. *Linguistics in a Colonial World. A Story of Language, Meaning, and Power*. Oxford: Blackwell.

Foucault, M., 1970. *The Order of Things—An Archaeology of the Human Sciences*. (translation from the French of *Les mots et les choses*, 1966). London: Tavistock.

Foucault, M., 1976/1990. *A History of Sexuality—An Introduction*. (tr.) R. Hurley. Hammondsworth: Penguin.

Foucault, M., 1976. *La volonté de savoir* I. Paris: Gallimard.

Foucault, M., 1977. *Language, Counter-Memory, Practice*. Ithaca: Cornell University Press.

Foucault, M., 1994. *Dits et écrits I*, Paris : Gallimard.

Frege, G., 1994? "On Sense and Reference," in Harnish, R.M., (ed.) *Basic Topics in the Philosophy of Language*. New York: Harvester Wheatsheaf.

Gandhi, M.K., 1927-29. An *Autobiography OR The Story of My Experiments With Truth*, Translated from Gujarati by Mahadev Desai and Pyarelal. Ahmedabad: Navajivan Press.

Gandhi, M.K., 2010. *Hind Swaraj*. Delhi: Rajpal. Original English edition published in 1910.

Gandhi, M.K., 1957. *Leur civilisation et notre délivrance*, Introduction de Lanza del Vasto, 'Pensée Gandhiénne', Paris: Éditions Denoël.

Ghosh, Bishnupriya, 2004. *When Born Across – Literary Cosmopolitics in the Contemporary Indian Novel*, New Jersey: Rutgers University Press.

Greimas, A.-J., 1983. *Structural Semantics*. (tr.) D. McDowell, R. Schleifer and A. Velie. Lincoln: University of Nebraska Press.

Greimas, A.-J. and J. Courtés. 1979. *Sémiotique: Dictionnaire raisonné de la théorie du langage*. Paris: Hachette.

Guillaume, G., 1984. *Temps et Verbe. Théorie des aspects, des modes et des temps suivi de L'architectonique du temps dans les langues classiques*, Paris: Honoré Champion. (original 1929).

Hanklyn, N.B., 1997. *Hanklyn-Janklin or, A Stranger's Rumble-Tumble Guide to Some Words, Customs and Quiddities, Indian and Indo-British*. New Delhi: Banyan Books.

Harris, Roy, 2002. "Nagarjuna, Heraclitus and the Problem of Language," in H.S. Gill (ed.) *Signification in Language and Culture*. Shimla: IIAS (pp. 9-22). This article has also appeared in H.G. Davis and T.J. Taylor (eds.) *Rethinking Linguistics*. London: Routledge-Curzon.

Harris, R., 1981. *The Language Myth*. London: Duckworth.

Hegel, G.W.F., 1981. *Phenomenology of Spirit*. (tr.) A.V. Miller. Analysis and Foreword by J.N. Findlay. Oxford: Oxford University Press.

Heidegger, M., 1975. "The Origin of the Work of Art," in *Poetry, Language, Thought*. (tr.) Albert Hofstadter. New York :Harper & Row.

Heidegger, M., 1962. *Being and Time*. (tr.) J. Macquarie and E. Robinson. Oxford: Basil Blackwell.

Heidegger, M., 1962. *Being and Time*. (tr.) J. Macquarrie and E. Robinson. New York: Harper, 2008 edn.

Hill, L., 1997. *Blanchot—Extreme Contemporary*. London: Routlege.

Husserl, E., 1953. *Méditiations Cartésiennes—Introduction à la Phénoménologie*. (tr.) from German by G. Peiffer and E. Lavinas. Paris: J. Vrin.

Iyer, L., 2005. *Blanchot's Vigilance—Literature, Phenomenology and the Ethical*. New York: Palgrave Macmillan.

Jankélévitch, V., 1966. *La mort*. Paris: Flammarion.

John, B.K., 2007. *Entry From Backside Only—Hazaar Fundas of Indian-English*. Delhi: Penguin.

Jones, W., 10th Anniversary Discourse (February 1793). Source: www.elohs.unifi.it/testi/700/jones/Jones_Discourse_10.html accessed on 24 May 2013.

Kachru, B.B., 1992. World Englishes: approaches, issues and resources. *Language Teaching*, 25: 1-14. Cambridge University Press.

Kamwangamlu, N.M., 2003. "Globalization of English, and Language Maintenance and Shift in South Africa," in *International Journal of Sociology of Language* 164.

Kantorowicz, E.H., 1957/1977. *The King's Two Bodies. A Study in Medieval Political Theology*. Princeton: Princeton: University Press.

Kojève, A., 1980. *Introduction to the Lecture of Hegel. Lectures on the Phenomenology of Spirit*. Assembled by R. Queneau, ed. A. Bloom, (tr.) J. H. Nichols, Jr. Ithaca: Cornell University Press. .

Lacoue-Labarthe, P. and J.-L. Nancy, 1996. *Retreating the Political*. (ed.) S. Sparks. London: Routledge.

Leitner, G., 2004. *Australia's Many Voices*. Berlin: W.de Gruyter.

Levinas, E., 1993. *Dieu, la mort, et le temps*. Paris: Grasser & Fasquelle.

Levinas, E., 1961. *Totality and Infinity – An Essay on Exteriority*. (tr.) A. Lingis. Pittsburgh: Duquesne University Press.

Levinas, E., 1979. *Le temps et l'autre*. Montpellier: Fata Morgana.

Levinas, E., 1989. 'Reality and Its Shadow,' in *The Levinas Reader*. (tr.) A. Lingis. (ed.) S. Hand. Oxford: Blackwell.

Levinas, E., 1989. *The Levinas Reader*. (ed.) S. Hand. Oxford: Blackwell.

Levinas, E., 1992. *Otherwise than Being or Beyond Essence*. (tr.) A. Lingis. Dordrecht: Kluwer Academic.

Levinas, E., 2000. *God, Death and Time*. (tr.) B. Bergo. Stanford: Stanford University Press.

Lévi-Strauss, C., 1973. *Structural Anthropology* 2 (tr.) Monique Layton. Harmondsworth: Penguin.

Lévi-Strauss, C., 1978. *Tristes Tropiques*. (tr.) John and Doreen Weightman, Harmondsworth: Penguin.

Lévi-Strauss, Claude, *Structural Anthropology*. (tr.) C. Jacobson and B. G. Schoepf. New York: Anchor.

Lingis, A., 2000. "To Die with Others", in: *diacritic* 30.3: 106-113.

Malabou, C., 2004. *Que faire de notre cerveau?* Paris: Bayard. Eng.: *What Should We Do With Our Brain ?* (tr.) S. Rand. New York : Fordham University Press. 2008.

Malabou, C., 2005. *La plasticité au soir de l'écriture – Dialectique, Destruction, Déconstruction*. Paris: Leo Scheer.

Maniglier, P., 2008. *La vie énigmatique des signes*. Paris: Léo Scheer.

Maniglier, P., 2011. "*Processing Cultures:* "Structuralism" in the History of Artificial Intelligence," in: S. Franchi and F. Bianchini (ed.), *The Search for a Theory of Cognition – Early Mechanisms and New Ideas*. Amsterdam: Rodopi.

Manjali, F. 2004. "Roy Harris and Integrational Linguistics," in *International Journal of Dravidian Linguistics*, Vol. 33, No. 1.

Manjali, F. 2008. *Language, Discourse and Culture. Contemporary Philosophical Perspectives*. New Delhi: Anthem Press.

Manjali, F., 1991. *Nuclear Semantics – Towards a Theory of Relational Meaning*. New Delhi: Bahri.

Manjali, F., 2001. *Literature and Infinity*. Shimla: Indian Institute of Advanced Study.

Matras, Y. and P .Bakker, 2003. *The Mixed Language Debate—Theoretical and Empirical Advances*. Berlin: Mouton.

Mazière, F., and S. Auroux, 2006. 'Introduction: Hyperlangue, modèles de grammatisation, reduction et autonomisation des langues.' In : *Histoire Épistémologie Langage* XXVII, Fasc. 2 : Special issue on 'Hyperlangues et fabriques des langues.'

Mead, M., 1964. *Anthropology—A Human Science*. New Delhi: East-West Press.

Milner, J.-C., 2002. *Le périple structural—Figures et paradigme*. Paris : Seuil.

Mondzain, M. J., 2007. *Homo spectator*. Paris: Bayard.

Mondzain, M. J., 2003. *L'Image, peut-elle tuer?* Paris: Bayard.

Mukherjee, M., 2005. *Twice-born Fiction.* (rev. 2nd edition). New Delhi: Oxford University Press.

Mukundan, M., 1992. *Mayyazhipuzhayude Theerangalil.* Kottayam: D. C. Books. (Eng. Tr.) G. Krishnankutty, *On the Banks of the Mayyazhi.* Chennai: East West Books, 1999. (Fr. tr.) Sophie Bastide-Foltz. *Sur les rives du fleuve Mahé.* Paris: Actes Sud, 2002.

Nancy, J.-L. 2008a. "The Name *God* in Blanchot" in *Dis-Enclosure – The Deconstruction of Christianity.* (tr.) M. Smith. New York: Fordham University Press.

Nancy, J.-L. 1997. *The Gravity of Thought,* (tr.) F. Raffoul and G. Recco. Atlantic Highlands: Humanities Press.

Nancy, J.-L., 1986. *La communauté désoeuvré.* Paris: Christian Bourgois. Eng., *The Inoperative Community.* Minneapolis: University of Minnesota Press. 1991.

Nancy, J.-L., 1993. *The Birth to Presence.* (tr.) B. Holmes et al. Stanford : Stanford University Press.

Nancy, J.-L., 1997. *The Sense of the World,* (trans.) J.S. Librett. Minneapolis: Minnesota University Press.

Nancy, J.-L., 2003. *Noli me tangere.* Paris: Bayard.

Nancy, J.-L., 2005a. 'Le témoin du négative,' préface in : *Le Spectre juif de Hegel* by Joseph Cohen. Paris: Galilée.

Nancy, J.-L., 2005b. *The Ground of the Image.* (tr.) J. Fort. New York: Fordham University Press: Orig. Fr. publication: *Au fond des Images.* Paris: Galilée, 2003.

Nancy, J.-L., 2008. *Corpus.* (tr.) Richard A. Rand. New York: Fordham University Press.

Neogy, A.K., 1997. *Decolonization of French India—Liberation Movement and Indo-French Relations 1947-1954.* Pondicherry: Institut Français de Pondicherry.

Olender, M., 2008. *The Languages of Paradise. Race, Religion and Philology in the Nineteenth Century.* (tr.) A. Goldhammer. Cambridge, MA: Harvard University Press.

Pandit, P.B., 1970. Review of F.R. Palmer (ed.) *Selected Papers of J.R. Firth 1952-59.* London: Longman. *Journal of Linguistics* Vol. 6, No. 2.

Peperzak, A.T., S. Critchley, R. Bernasconi, eds. 1996. *Emmanuel Levinas: Basic Philosophical Writings.* Bloomington: Indiana University Press.

Petit, P., 1993. *The Common Mind: An Essay in Psychology, Society and Politics.* Oxford: Oxford University Press.

Petitot, J. 1985. *Morphogénèse du sens.* Paris: PUF. 2004. *Morphogenesis of Meaning.* (tr.) F. Manjali. Berne: Peter Lang.

Petitot. J., 2004. *Morphologie et Esthétique*; Paris: Maisonneuve et Larose.

Plato, *Phædo*. 1950. In: *Dialogues of Plato*, New York: Simon & Schuster.

Prayer, M., 2009. "The Vatican, Church and Mahatma Gandhi's India, 1920-1948," *Social Scientist*. Vol. 37, Nos. 1-2.

Propp, V., 1968. *Morphology of the Folktale*. (tr.) Lawrence Scott. Austin: University of Texas Press.

Raja Rao, 1939/1967. *Kanthapura*. New Delhi: New Directions.

Rancière, J., 2007. *The Future of the Image*. (tr.) G. Elliott. London: Verso. Fr. Orig. published in 2003.

Ricœur, P., "Metaphor and the Semantics of Discourse," in Gill, H.S. and B. Pottier (eds.), *Ideas, Words and Things*. Delhi: Orient Longman.

Rolland, R., 2000. *Mahatma Gandhi. The Man Who Became One with the Universal Being*. New Delhi: Srishti.

Rushdie, S., 1980. *Midnight's Children*. London: Vintage.

Rushdie, S., 2008. *The Enchantress of Florence*. London: Jonathan Cape.

Said, E., 1979. *Orientalism*. New York: Vintage.

Sartre, J.P., 1986 edn. *L'imaginaire*. Paris : Gallimard. Orig. edn. 1940.

Saussure, F. de, 1967. *Cours de linguistique générale*. Publié par C. Bailly et A. Séchehaye. Édition critiqué par T. de Mauro. Paris: Payot (here referred to as *Cours*); Saussure, F. de, 1983. *Course in General Linguistics*. (here referred to as *CGL 1*) (tr.) Roy Harris. Paris: Duckworth; Saussure, F. de, 1969. *Course in General Linguistics* (here referred to as *CGL 2*). (tr.) Wade Baskin. New York: Philosophical Library.

Saussure, F. de, 2002. *Écrits de linguistique générale*. (ed.) S. Bouquet et R. Engler. Paris: Gallimard.

Simondon, G., 2009. "The Position of the Problem of Ontogenesis." *Parrhesia* 7 (online: *www.parrhesiajournal.org*): (4-16).

Stiegler, B. and J. Derrida. 2002 edn. *Echographies of Television – Filmed Interviews*. (tr.) J. Bajorek. London: Polity. Fr. Original published in 1996.

Strauss, J., 2000 a. 'The State of Death'. *diacritics* 30.3: 3-11.

Strauss, J., 2000 b. 'After Death'. *diacritics* 30.3: 90-104.

Tiercelin, C., 2003. Description of a University course on 'Image' on the Internet. (Internet site, http://www.lemonde.fr/savoirs-et-connaissances/article/2004/06/30/claudine-tiercelin-le-concept-d-image_371085_3328.html) Accessed on 17-3-05.

Trautmann, T.R., 2006. *Languages and Nations. The Dravidian Proof in Colonial Madras*. New Delhi: Yoda Press.

Vasto, L. del., 1971. *Return to the Source*. (tr.) Jean Sidwick. London: Rider & Co.

Volsoshinov, V.N., *Marxism and the Philosophy of Language*. (tr.) L. Matijka and New York: Seminar Press.

Watts, P., 1998. *Allegories of the Purge – How Literature Responded to the Post-War Trials of Writers and Intellectuals in France*. Stanford: Stanford University Press.

Wittgenstein , L. 1958. *Philosophical Investigations*. (tr.) G.E.M. Anscombe. Oxford: B. Blackwell

Wittgenstein, L., 1974. *Tractatus Logico-Philosophicus*, (tr.) D.F. Pears and B.F. McGuiness. London: RKP.

Wolfe, A.S., 1990. *The Suicidal Narratives in Modern Japan*. Princeton: Princeton University Press.

Yeshe, T., 1983. *Life, Death and After-Death*. Boston: Wisdom.

Yule, H. and A.C. Burnell, 1996. *Hobson-Jobson: The Anglo-Indian Dictionary*. Ware: Wordsworth.